Confessions of a
DOMINATRIX

My Secret BDSM Life
BY KAZ B

Chapter 1: Exploring Femdom

2007

I cracked the whip down onto the pasty white flesh of the slave that knelt before me. He whimpered – a mixture of agony and ecstasy. I sauntered around him slowly, biding my time. The high heels of my black PVC boots thudded loudly on the laminate flooring, and my PVC skirt and corset rustled with every movement.

What to do next? I thought and wavered briefly. He glanced up at me and I snapped, "Bow your head, slave. Do not look up unless I address you – do you understand?"

"Ye—ye—yes, mistress," he stuttered, and bowed his head, his body trembling.

The truth is, I'd only practised domination on a boyfriend, and while I had read up on the subject extensively, I hadn't put my skills to practice on a stranger. Being new to the arts of dominating men, well I was completely bluffing it. Fake it till you make it, they say, and that is exactly what I was doing! My mind raced and my brain sought hard for the right words and actions. Now and again, my movements didn't quite resonate with my words, and there was a slight tremor in my hand.

Fortunately, he seemed to be none the wiser, which boosted me slightly and gave me a little confidence.

In the beginning, I hated it when the subs met my eyes. I felt that if they could see my eyes, they would see beyond them into my soul, and they would then know that I was winging it! It seems a distant memory now, as I rely heavily on eye contact to make my point and exert my power over them.

He started to look up again and so I ordered him to bend over my knee. "Didn't I tell you not to look at me without permission, slave! As punishment, I will administer a hard spanking until your bottom is red raw," I threatened.

He complied, lowering his body across my knee so that he hung across my lap, his body limp. After years of spanking bottoms, your hands toughen up. You learn how to cup them to lessen the impact on your palms, but of course back then, my hands were softer than a bowlful of jelly and after a series of hard spanks on his backside, sharp stinging pains traversed through my palms. I began trailing my fingernails across his cheeks and talking to him in a soft voice, warning that another spanking would ensue shortly. The slave moaned and absolutely loved it. He seemed to have no idea that I was allowing my poor sore palms chance to recover. In time, I learned that many of my slaves loved the variation of soft, tender strokes across the rump, between hard whacks on the buttocks. It's a technique that I still use. For the spankee, it's an exquisite blend of pain and pleasure, and what's more, they never know where they stand when you flip between sweet seductress and evil taskmaster. Adjusting my mood as if I'm pressing a light switch is something that installs fear into them and amuses me greatly.

As I slapped, pinched and stroked his buttocks, he was making all the right noises. I had learned to listen to the sounds they uttered, the rate of their breathing and to pay close attention to their body language. Over time, I discovered that these cues would give me far more clues about the slave's desires and fears than anything else. Initially, I found first-timers often struggled to vocalise their fetishes, and so I would introduce any new activity gently, watching and listening to their responses and slowly building up the intensity. It's a good method to practise with any new slave and a warmup is essential to get the most out of them. If you go straight into fetish play at the intense end, you often won't get the best out of your slave. I prefer to coax them in gently, tease and then when they are least expecting it, turn up the intensity so that it hits them like a bolt from the blue! By this point they are slipping deeply into subspace and are happy to carry on!

Anyway, back to the slave in question! I was silently applauding myself, when I stood up to fetch a leather whip, and in the process, I tripped over my pile of wooden paddles on the floor … *Well done*, I scolded myself internally. *That's exactly what a sexy, mysterious and domineering woman would do – fall over her own paddles and look like an idiot!*

For a moment, a sense of overwhelming panic threatened to surge through me. My adrenaline was racing around my body and my insides seemed to burn. *God, I can't do this! Sexy dommes don't trip over their own paddles and end up in a flap, what the hell am I doing?* A vision of Catwoman struck me, one of the all-time sexiest villainesses, Poison Ivy, Drusilla the vampire from *Buffy the Vampire Slayer*. The vision soothed me, and I decided to channel my inner villainess. I loved a hero or heroine, but often loved their evil counterparts too, and so I looked to them for inspiration, slinking around the room and breathing vicious threats in a soft, throaty purr.

"Look what you made me do, imbecile," I adlibbed.

"Sorry, mistress," the slave replied, his chubby cheeks wobbling, his eyes fixed firmly on the floor.

I'd gotten away with it. He didn't laugh or move and seemed to genuinely believe that he had been at fault. I giggled, sat myself back on the purple velvet futon and ordered the slave to suck my toes. He obliged eagerly and I thought to myself, *I could get used to this!*

Chapter 2: Training Men

When you are a dominatrix, everyone wants to know how you got into it, if you enjoy it, if people really like getting hit or taken with a strap-on. I've heard it all: "You seem too nice to be a dominatrix!" or "But you are so tiny!"

People are always surprised when they learn what I do. That's the main emotion I'm greeted with, not so much judgement or disgust, but sheer bewilderment! Then come the endless questions that every domme hates to hear, "So how much do you earn?" "How many slaves do you see a day?" "Do you have sex with them?"

I always answer, "Enough to pay my bills and taxes," "It varies," and "No, I never have sex with slaves."

I always find this line of questioning odd. If someone was a plumber, a rocket scientist or accountant, you wouldn't start questioning them about their earnings or sex life, so why is being a domme any different? I've never once asked my plumber if they've had a jolly good rogering recently!

The other thing that seems to baffle people is the fact that many of my clients desire pain and punishment. "… and they *pay* for that?" they implore, their eyes wide in abject disbelief.

Most vanilla (non-kinky) people don't understand that BDSM (bondage and sadomasochism) isn't about sex, it's about consensual power exchange, and so they always assume that you must be sleeping with your clients. They struggle to understand why anyone would pay to be whipped, tied up, suspended from a ceiling or rigged up to an electric power pack that sends volts through their nipples and genitals.

It's also a myth that you need to be a six-foot Amazonian

to be a dominatrix. I'm four foot ten, and on a good month I'm seven stone ten and on a bad month I'm eight stone five. My weight swings between the two and I wear size eight to ten dresses. By average standards, I'm much at the petite end of the scale. This has in fact made me a lot more popular than I ever could have imagined. There are so many men out there that want to be dominated by someone diminutive in stature. It's ironic, as my size was something that always bothered me in the past. In commercial business, with my petite figure and babyish face, I struggled to be taken seriously. Then when I modelled, I didn't always meet the height requirement for some of the more exciting jobs. Even acting parts, I'd often get a second audition and then I'd get, "We were looking for someone a bit taller!" *Goddammit, just pop a Yellow Pages book under my feet,* I'd think.

It was a bit like queuing up to go on an insanely fierce roller-coaster ride, then just as you are able to step into the cart, some-one pulls out a tape measure, measures from your toes to your head and says, "Forget it, short arse. Go grow a few more inches!" This did happen once. I was queuing up for what I thought was a ghost train type ride at Thorpe Park. When I reached the height requirement, the thirteen-year-old in our group and myself were pulled to one side and told we didn't quite measure up. I was somewhat confused as to how I could be too short for a ghost train. I took the kid to one side, and we waited for the rest of the gang who were all at least over five foot. When they returned, they were a deathly pallor. It turned out that the ride hadn't been a ghost train at all. It was a horrible, high-speed death trap that soared miles into the air before crashing down again, and so it had been a lucky escape for me and the kid. That's the thing with being a short arse – it's swings and roundabouts really! Mostly because you can't get onto the real rides, but also because sometimes it gets you out of something spectacularly awful.

Returning to the topic of auditions. If I didn't get the part, I used to leave feeling dejected. If it was my skills or style, these would have been things I could have worked on, studied and improved, but being told it was my height just felt like dipping out on the genetics lottery! It's funny, as I never planned to go into BDSM, it found me! So, it seems bizarre that my height is now something that's seen as a bonus. I regularly have men who are six foot seven and built like rugby players kneel before me and obey my every command. Femdom is not about size, it's about confidence and it's about being able to get into someone's mind. Any woman can slip into saucy lingerie and excite a man's nether region, but it takes a different kind of skill to get inside his head and arouse his mind. Perhaps along the way, some of what I say might resonate with you and you'll learn how to get inside a guy's mind, and not just excite his penis, but touch his emotions and make him crave you. That's the thing with men. At first, they fall for how you look, but if you learn what makes them tick, and how to get inside their minds, they will fall for you more deeply. That's why loyal slaves will come back time and time again. It's not *just* to get their fetish fix. It's because they love the way you make them feel, and in that you find yourself a loyal and obedient servant. I'm speaking in terms of Femdom-style scenarios specifically as I cannot say my personal relationships have been particularly successful, but this is more to do with the poor judgement I have exercised in the past rather than anything else.

You, however, can even use some of my training techniques on your husband, boyfriend or lover if they are interested in learning how to be a more submissive partner. All kinds of men will respond to these 'training' methods if they are eager to learn. Humans are much like dogs in that sense and Pavlovian conditioning can be used to train your human pet to be loyal and obedient. Allow me to explain.

Pavlov was a Russian physiologist who predicted that dogs would begin to salivate when food was placed in front of them. He soon realised that the dogs would salivate when they heard approaching footsteps at mealtimes, when his assistant brought the dogs food. He understood that certain triggers would act as stimuli for the dogs and that they could learn to associate specific things with food.

You might be wondering how this applies to training a man. Well, a dog is always hungry for food and can be taught to associate performing a trick with being given food or a doggy biscuit. In much the same way, a man can be trained that good behaviour will be rewarded with a treat. In the early phases of his training, the slave may perform a 'trick' or display good behaviour and will subsequently receive a treat. Bad behaviour should be punished, of course, not with a punishment he enjoys, but rather something that makes him uncomfortable. So, if he is into being spanked, this would not be a suitable punishment for bad behaviour. Instead, one could choose something that would trigger shame or disappointment in him; for example, depending on the individual, it could be making him wear a pair of women's underwear or a chastity cage, or even forbidding him to speak or to look you in the eye.

It's necessary to use both disciplines and in many men, the hope of a reward is much stronger than the fear of punishment. So, you can phase out the rewards in the long term so that they become less frequent, but they should never become obsolete. The hope of a reward – such as a flash of your cleavage, the privilege of kissing your legs or even lavishing him with praise and attention – will have a far more positive effect on your subject in the long term and keep him loyal.

Training a man is simple when you know how. This style will not suit every relationship and let's not forget that every domme/sub or D/S relationship is not the same. It's important to remember that all D/S relationships should be based on mutual respect, and you should always consider your play partner's welfare.

Chapter 3: Wiltshire Life

So, you might be wondering how I became a dominatrix, what my backstory is. Do I come from a long line of Mafiosi? Am I a man-hating feminist that loathes mankind? Am I a sadist? These are all genuine questions people have asked, well maybe not the first one!

I grew up in the ordinary town of Swindon in a working-class family.

As far back as I can remember, my imagination was active, and I often saw things that terrified me. In hospital aged two, I saw a dancing skeleton on the windowsill outside the hospital. I climbed out of my cot to investigate, tumbled and then darkness surrounded me. This is my earliest memory. As an adult I asked my mum if it could have been people playing around outside, but she insisted I was in a ward in a floor high up.

Aged five, I woke in the early hours of the morning and saw a translucent, white-coloured grim reaper standing by my body. I pulled the covers over my head, praying they would keep me safe. The cover trick seemed to work. Another night I was convinced there was a huge bear on the landing and screamed. Everyone ran at once to my door; lights were switched on and suggestions were offered that the bear was in fact a big pile of washing. After that, I was given a night light as I couldn't sleep in the dark, fearful of what might be lurking in the shadows waiting for me.

Perhaps this imagination spurred on my dream to be an author and inspired by Enid Blyton, I was an avid reader from the age of six and immersed myself in a world of fantasy. By the age of ten, I was reading my dad's horror and thriller novels – Stephen King, Dean Koontz, James Herbert and Shaun Hutson, whose work was particularly graphic. I was addicted! My dad allowed me to watch horror movies – *Night of the Living Dead, The Day of the Triffids, House,* you name it, I'd seen it. It's because of this that I'm still unable to sleep without the light on; fear of some horrific bogeyman in the wardrobe troubles me. *Poltergeist* was particularly disturbing. In the film, there is a scene where a little girl looks under the bed and she is dragged under by a child's toy which is under demonic possession. The thought of something reaching out from under the bed has stayed with me. Now, I have a bed that touches the floor, as I can't abide a bed with a gap underneath. My mind summons up visions of a gnarled old hand reaching out to grab me, the skin rotten and decayed, but its grip relentless. As it pulls me under, I come face to face with something hideous, its merciless eyes reaching into my soul and threatening to suck the essence from me, but anyway, that's enough about my last date!

The obvious advantages of reading adult literature as a child meant that in many ways I matured more quickly. I could slip in and out of worlds that other children my age didn't have access to. Of course, this resulted in me being a bit of a loner, but if I had a book, I didn't really care for the company of other children that much. I was a bit of an oddball and when someone suggested I go and play with the other children, I always wondered why. Other children were loud and annoying. I would much rather paint, read or escape into a world of fantasy with my daydreams. Those books gave me a thirst for knowledge, and a desire to find my place in the world and make my own imprint on it.

By the age of nine or ten, I realised I wasn't destined for a normal career. I wanted to travel, write books and explore the world, but I couldn't have guessed in a million years that I would be wielding a whip and shooting and directing fetish movies! I think ten-year-old me would have found such a notion hilarious, and probably a little bit gross. I would have ridiculed the notion of working alongside humans instead of animals.

I suppose it may be relevant that around that age, I happened to chance across some Black Lace books (saucy adult novels) in the top of the spare room wardrobe. I was a real bookworm and read anything and everything, and there were no set rules I was told to adhere to. My reading level was more advanced than other children in my year and I was told by my teachers that I could have free choice over what to read in both the school and public library. I simply assumed 'adulthood', dove into the saucy novel and learned about the birds and the bees in a different way to my peers!

The more I learned, the more different I was from my class-mates. They didn't understand my humour or references about films and books. The fact I always had a book in front of my face didn't help much either. I was a misfit. Being so isolated from the other children, I struggled to understand them. To me they seemed loud, obnoxious and thuggish, and I arrogantly thought to myself that my peers would all end up on the dole or on benefits (although this mostly turned out to be true).

I was being severely bullied at the time and my karmic fanta-sies of justice kept me going! There were various restrictions on me as a child and I wasn't allowed to cross the road or play with the 'rough children'. I was called 'snob' and even 'slut', which is a ridiculous accusation for any child, let alone a particularly bookish one! Soon the bullying went from psychological to physical too. Being so tiny in stature, I was easy prey for cowards who were too scared to pick on someone their own size. By the age of eleven, I was about three foot six and weighed about five stone, and my peers towered over me. Despite the terrifying time which I expe-rienced in the schoolyard, I've learned to let go of the past hurts; if one day I see any of my tormenters on their way into town to get their dole cheque, I'll be sure to smile and wave.

I've always been a sucker for justice. When I was a child, I would write poems about animal welfare and letters of complaint to companies that tested on animals. I was also a member of the charity Animate (now the Humane Society) and my neighbour Ellie and I sat on the street, in a paddling pool filled with beans, to raise money for animals (anyone for sploshing?).

In many ways, I was mature when it came to ethics and human and animal rights, but in other ways I was so childlike. I still loved to play with Barbie dolls and collected little toys called 'Puppy in My Pocket'. The Barbie dolls would live complex and diverse lives. They were also polyamorous. It's almost as if my subconscious mind understood concepts that my conditioned conscious mind couldn't. I would role play with the dolls and do voices for them. They would crush on Ken or another of the dolls and plot how to seduce them. I didn't really have many friends to talk to, so I suppose it was my way of exploring relationships and sex in a safe environment.

Several years later, I reached the age of fifteen, got a serious boyfriend and the Barbie dolls were forgotten about for many years. I suppose my first forays into domination were with my first real boyfriend. Let's call him Matt.

Matt was in the year above me at school and I met him on a trip to Wales with youth club. He had his hair shaved quite close in a number 2 style and I thought he was the bee's knees.

The youth club trip was an activity week learning how to build fires, and we did abseiling and canoeing, and ate marshmallows by the campfire. I remember coming down the stairs and Matt was playing "Trouble" by Shampoo. I later went and bought the record and played it non-stop.

After the trip, peering out of my tutor room and catching glimpses of Matt would be my excitement for the week. I'd go ridiculously giddy and feel all fluffy for about ten ridiculous minutes. These 'sightings' of Matt went on for a while and the highlight of my week would be youth club on a Thursday, as I would casually wander across to the tuck shop and try to watch him playing football, while attempting to maintain a look of disinterest. It wasn't that I was an astute game player at the age of fifteen, I was just shy and was convinced I'd pass out with shock if he spoke to me. Eventually, my friends got bored of my longing looks and going on about Matt, and so they did the humiliating thing of going up to him and saying, "Our friend likes you." I nearly had a full-on panic attack and stars started to dance around my eyes. I ran and hid behind the coats in the cloak room.

Eventually, it was time to go home, and I had to come out from the safety of the coat rack. To my horror, I bumped into Matt, who turned red, looked at his trainers and said, "So, do you want to go out with me or something then?" I studied his trainers too and mumbled, "OK then."

He said he would pick me up and walk me to school the next day, and that was that. He knocked on the door the next day and we bonded over our shared love of animals and music. It turned out we had a lot in common and he'd make me mix tapes of his favourite band Blur with a little love note inside, and we'd hang out, go for walks and laugh at the hit TV show *Friends*.

Teenagers are frisky little buggers, and we would snog non-stop in the beginning. We'd been together a while when I lost my virginity to him and was surprised at how uninspiring it was. Compared to how thrilling all that kissing had been! All the books I had read had led me to believe that sex would be a magical moment, my heart would do a merry dance, my nethers would sing and a cacophony of explosions and fireworks would rain down around me. It was nothing like this. After a brief stinging sensation, he awkwardly humped me for a couple of minutes and then it was over. I was deeply in love with him at the time, so the disappointment didn't linger, but I had more of a sense of, *Oh, is that it?*

As the years went on, I turned to my glossy magazines for help. *Cosmo* warned that "The Spark May Disappear" and ever fearful of my devoted boyfriend growing tired of me, I looked for ways to spice things up! I had never had somebody who was so utterly devoted to me (except for my dogs and cats) so losing him wasn't an option I was happy to consider at that point.

I learned that handcuffs were a popular way to add a fun element in the bedroom. My first pair were from Ann Summers and were just two bits of fluff with a chain in the middle.

We had a giggle testing them out, but I felt that something

that could restrain you might be more exciting than easily break-able fluff. The next week I bought a metal pair of handcuffs with a lock and key, and we experimented with cuffing each other to the bed and subjecting each other to teasing. Matt was a quick learner and I read out loud some of the tips from *Cosmo* magazine to him. "Try teasing the underside of the shaft with a cupped hand, while pinching a nipple and giving him a sexy knowing stare ..." OK, I'm ad-libbing, I can't remember exactly what a magazine article from over twenty years ago said, but you get the idea! I could probably teach *Cosmo* a thing or two now!

Another time we covered each other in cream and banana slices and ate them from each other's bodies. That one wasn't for me so much; if I'm hungry, I just want to eat and don't want an interruption. If I'm in the mood for sauciness, I'm not interested in food! I don't mind smearing it all over someone, but it's unlikely that I'll suddenly get a case of the munchies or want to bang them while swimming around in custard. I'd much rather stay dry and be throwing pies at someone else! If you are a huge sploshing fan and I've just killed your fantasy, well, sorry about that old chum!

Matt and I tried 'public sex' in a deserted field where no one ever ventured. We played around with light spanking, and even made a home movie, which we deleted immediately afterwards for fear of our parents finding out! We were sixteen by this point and both living at home.

So, those were my first explorations into the real world of sex. Back then, I didn't even realise that there was a name for it, I just referred to it as 'spicing things up', but at the age of sixteen I had experimented with various kinky practices!

To answer the initial question, I am neither a sadist nor a man-hater. I see life as an opportunity to learn and enjoy richly diverse experiences. Men come to be taught how to be more submissive and sometimes part of that is punishment. Over the years, I've been on all sides of the coin, but having naughty boys kneel at my feet and hang on my every word is by far my favourite thing, and why wouldn't it be? I have a great relationship with my slaves;

they are respectful, thoughtful and have treated me far better than 80% of my exes ever did. Submissive men are often talkers outside of the playroom too. They don't hold everything in, and I have learned a lot about men from them. Part of my path to becoming empowered was down to my subs, a fact I will never forget.

Chapter 4: Imaginary Friends and Early Influences

If you've made it this far in my book and stuck with me, then I feel comfortable enough to reveal a little about my childhood. It's a subject I sometimes feel a little cagey about. I hate talking about it in person and seeing the pity in someone's eyes. I've made it this far through life, so I think I've done well! When I hear the words "Poor you," I regret to say it makes me feel a little defensive, as I don't want to be viewed as a victim, so I promptly change the subject.

Let's go back to my grand arrival as I slid into existence, wailing! My mother and I nearly died when she went into labour with me. She regales me with stories about what a problem baby I was and how I nearly killed her. Apparently, I was a breech birth and every time the nurses turned me around in her stomach, I turned myself back around and apparently nearly killed us both. I can just imagine myself inside the womb as a tiny baby, whining, "It's too early. Just give me five more minutes. Where's the snooze button?"

I was several weeks overdue – always late to the table – and born weighing five pounds, allergic to milk and with chronic asthma at the time. I suppose asthma was bound to be chronic when the adults around me were puffing twenty to forty cigarettes a day. Food was a struggle to keep down and I would have recurrent asthma attacks. The hospital was practically my second home as I suffered from asthma and sickness. Illnesses struck me; there was chickenpox, German measles and scarlet fever, which made my skin peel off in sheets. The infection affected my feet and my nethers, leaving me crying in agony. The silver lining in this has been a robust immune system as an adult. What doesn't kill you …

Despite all of this, I was an explorer and enjoyed climbing! Whether my challenge was to be a sideboard or a dining room table and my reward an overripe tomato or a forkful of leftover mashed swede, there was no holding me back. I was the pint-sized equivalent of Edmund Hillary, one of the first men to climb Mount Everest! It was great practise as there were a lot of years afterwards when it felt like I was struggling up a mountain!

When I think back to my childhood years, I never think of them as my carefree days. Of course, I have many fond memories and can recall our childhood dog Solo, a Cavalier King Charles Spaniel. I would curl up in her dog bed with her, sharing digestive biscuits while listening to children's stories on cassette. My favourite audio tape was *Gobbolino the Witch's Cat*. It was a story about a little cat that wanted a loving home but always ended up alone. I used to wish that Gobbolino was my friend and even though it was only make-believe, I always felt a little bit sad after each story.

When I was around three years of age, my favourite time of the week was when *Fame* came on the TV. My sisters would run excitedly to the living room and the theme tune would start up. They would sing along and dance to the soundtrack, and I'd do my best to join in. I loved being with my sisters and it's such a happy memory for me. Often, we would sing to Boy George songs, and they would plait my hair like his and put ribbons in it. This was the only time I was extroverted around my sisters and their friends. I was shy around people I didn't know well and not keen to lower my barriers and let anyone in.

Sometimes the girls would have their friends round and didn't want to have their style cramped by having their kid sister around, so I would hide under one of their beds so I could listen into the conversation. I could never help myself though and would eventually start singing or saying silly things from under the bed. Once they set a tape recorder to record themselves singing.

It wasn't until they played it back and heard me imitating the television show *The Young Ones*, that they realised I was under the bed! They played back the tape later and there was me imitating the character Neil, played by Nigel Planer, and saying, "Heavy, maan!" Like I said, I was a strange kid!

My sisters and I were often played off against each other by my father and we were never set a healthy example of how to love and treat others, but somehow, we found our way.

My middle sister Clarissa often says she feels she was awful to me as a kid, but I really don't think she was any worse than any siblings are in their teens! Both my sisters would come home with presents for me on birthdays. They always made a bit of a fuss over birthdays, whereas my parents might remember to wish me happy birthday at some point in the afternoon and begrudgingly give me a tenner. Or, in my dad's case, promise a tenner that never materialised. Once, my sisters presented me with not one, but TWO Barbie Twirling dolls and I was disappointed when my mum created a fuss and said that one of them would have to go back to the store, because I couldn't have two dolls the same.

Melania was sort of like the mummy sister who made my food and dressed me.

Clarissa was the fun sister. She would create little adventures and build me dens made of sheets. We'd have picnics in the garden and eat that awful sort of pizza that was popular in the Eighties. It didn't have much flavour and was also soggy in the middle because we grilled everything then instead of using the oven, as it was too expensive to run! Still, as a kid, I thought it was great! I remember watching movies like *The Breakfast Club*, eating economy choc ices on a summer's day and running from the tortoise in case he nipped our toes! Often, I would do things to wind my sister Clarissa up and amuse myself. One time, I hid in a chest of clothes in the corner of her room for an hour, just so I could jump out and shout boo and make her jump. It had the intended effect and so perhaps we both had our little quirks!

***

By the time I was four, my older sister Melania had left home and Clarissa was thrown out by my mum at the tender age of sixteen. It's quite a traumatic story and something that never needed to take place. Mother had stacked up all the dinner plates precariously on a metal shelf over the stove. Clarissa approached to ask what was for dinner and one of the plates slid down and smashed. You would have thought she'd pulled the pin on a grenade if you witnessed what happened next. My mother shouted, "You've ruined your father's dinner!" and there was screaming and shouting as poor Clarissa was shoved out of the side door and locked out in the middle of winter, with no coat or shoes.

I'd thought it a game initially, but as my sister called desperately through the letter box and my mother screamed at her, I felt powerless. It's only as an adult that I can truly understand the horror and feeling of abandonment my teenage sister must have felt at being shoved out in the freezing cold on a winter's day. As adults, my sister and I only have pets, not children, and we simply couldn't imagine subjecting them to this. Even the thought of them being scared and cold breaks my heart! Imagine that feeling of not knowing where to go or what to do. Your parents are supposed to protect you, so if they don't, what the hell do you do?

If I continued on to write, "And she never came back again," you probably wouldn't blame her. However, fortunately sometimes people change and move on from these things. We have all matured and moved on. You have to break the generational curse at some point.

The funny thing is, items still often fly out of cupboards at my mum's house or a glass jar will shoot out of the fridge. Mum blames it on supernatural occurrences and says she is sure we have a ghost. I say that I think the cupboards are too full. Maybe she's right. What do the laws of physics know!

Life changed when both my sisters were gone from the house and I will shortly explain the psychological changes that took place in myself, but first some fonder memories.

Aged five, I went into hospital for having a lazy eye; in fact, my eye still wanders when I'm feeling tired and I lost some vision in it, but I would have lost my vision completely in one eye if it had not been corrected. That part isn't a fond memory, but there were some perks at the time! I recall going down to surgery and the doctors having to try and inject me several times in the hand as my hands were too small to find a vein. Afterwards, I sat in my hospital bed and waited for my mother's return. When she reappeared, I called, "Where were you? They stabbed me in the hand three times!" Mum thought this hilarious that I said they had stabbed me instead of saying injected. I was infuriated. I was then handed a Barbie doll I'd coveted for months and all the 'stabbings' were forgotten in an instant. She was beautiful and wore a red velvet bodice with gossamer sleeves and a matching gown. OK, so it was all made from polyester, but in my mind the doll was a magical fairy tale princess, and everything was OK in my world at that moment.

One afternoon, a man came around the ward telling jokes to cheer up sick children. He kept saying "What's your name, Carrot?" and I told him he was stupid. He asked if I would like a song on hospital radio and I requested Michael Jackson's "Thriller". They never played it and I thought why bother asking me then.

My first experience of a suitor attempting to dominate me was at the tender age of five. I was in the infants and a boy called Richard asked me to be his girlfriend and I said yes. We'd grown up together when we were toddlers and he had lived next door. His family moved when I was young, but he still attended the same school as me.

At playtime, we would trade, and I would give him sticky buds for pieces of rock and stone with crystal in them. We discovered that we could collect sticky buds by rolling down the bank and the little buds would attach themselves to our clothing. We would cross our arms and hurtle down the hill at high speed, and this fun game carried on until a teacher decided it was far too dangerous and forbid it. I was gutted and missed the thrill of a good roll down the steep bank.

With bank rolling now out of the question, other sources of entertainment were sought. The next playtime, Richard decided he wanted to kiss me. We had these little tunnels to play in on the playground and once I was inside, he got his mates to sit either side and said I could not leave until I kissed him. I refused out of principle, having been given an ultimatum. Eventually, the bell rang to signal the end of playtime, he went off in a huff and we all ran off to our classes. That was my first break-up and we didn't trade sticky buds again.

***

Our family holidays were usually to the Butlin's in Bognor Regis and later to Lanzarote, where we met singers Brian and Michael, who played in a local bar every night. They thought it was sweet that my mum always danced with me. My nans came along and often looked after me some of the time, which was brilliant. We'd play all sorts of games such as 'Bird Beast'. This consisted of writing a list of places, people or animals, picking a letter, then you would have to think of a type of bird, beast, plant or other suggestion starting with that letter. We made our own entertainment. We'd have a wonderful time and then once they went to bed, my parents would slag them off behind their backs and moan about how much food they'd eaten.

Dad would occasionally take me off to buy a Mivvi ice cream; I'll come to the reason why he had to shortly, but let's not ruin the fantasy just yet. Let me indulge myself, and you the reader, a little longer. A Mivvi was a vanilla-flavoured ice cream on a stick, in a red strawberry coating. I thought they were ace! My dad would then give me a coin to play the arcade games. Space Invaders and Pac-Man were always my favourites and kept me quiet, and the machines were always conveniently located inside a pub.

I think back to balmy summer nights and Tuesday evening

walks to the library with Dad, where I would fill my arms with books to lose myself in. On the way back, we'd stop at the Working Men's Club and Dad would have a few pints and I'd have a coke and sometimes a packet of Worcester Wheat Crunchies. Sometimes we'd stop at Nanny B's, where she had a well-stocked bar. Nan's house always felt like a furnace, and she sat almost on top of the fire. She would always sit on the edge of her seat so as not to disturb Spotty, a ratty old terrier. The poor dog was full of tangles and his tongue stuck out the side of his mouth.

Despite his tiny size and lack of teeth, I feared Spotty, as he was a feisty little devil and would go for you. He would probably only have gummed you to death, but he was full of spirit. Perhaps he'd have been a bit better-natured if he had been taken to the vet's occasionally, but he was loved at least, even if a bit neglected when it came to brushing and bathing.

Sometimes, I would stay with my nan, and she would take me to jumble sales and I would hear her mutter, "What a load of rubbish." I'd then embarrass her later when I copied her words a little too loudly. She would buy me Lardy cake to eat, then we'd visit Uncle Eric. I'd have to sit on his kitchen table so his dog Rinty couldn't attack me, but I didn't mind as he always gave me a cherry Bakewell tart to eat with a cup of tea. Afterwards, we'd go home and watch *Baywatch*. Nan would let me stay up, then we'd watch TV in bed. We'd always go to town in the morning and buy bags of chocolates and eat them in bed. During these periods I stayed with my nan, I was always a bit chubby, as everything we did revolved around shopping or eating.

Nan was kind to me but probably lacked boundaries a little, as she would sit there and regale me with stories of all the men she had been out with and the affairs she'd had when she was a youngster. She would tell me about a fellow who had been a train conductor and she used to sneak on the train with him for a smooch in return for a box of chocolate. I suppose in a way I was her confidante. I just sat and listened without judgement, as I didn't know any different. She never said it was a secret, but I somehow knew to keep it to myself.

I adored my grandad, Walter. Everyone said he was a grumpy old man and my sisters had feared him, but he had a great sense of humour, and I was close with him. I didn't see him as much as I would have liked to, but he would encourage me to write stories and would make me laugh. I remember coming back from the airport with my mum and dad when I was little; I think we had been to Spain with my nan and were dropping her home. I was desperate to use the loo and becoming quite distressed. I needed to use the loo and the reply was, "Ooooh, I don't know, you'd better check with Grandad when we get there." It was said as if Grandad was an ogre. Grandad greeted me with warmth and enthusiasm and had no issue with me dashing to the loo. He could be sarcastic and had an acidic tongue, but I never saw that moody side to him that others did. I suspect I take after my late grandad in many ways and perhaps that's why we got on. He was also quite funny without knowing it, and if someone rang him, he would say, "Flaming Jesus Christ on crutches! If ever I feel a bit lonely, I'll go and have a sit on the toilet and no doubt the blimming phone will ring!"

***

I loved to collect Barbie and Sindy dolls, Trolls with brightly coloured hair, and loved reading *The Beano* and *The Dandy*. I would fall in love with any stray cat that came my way and would spend my pocket money on buying cat food to give them nice meals. I also had a strange fascination with memorising things. I had a nature book and memorised every single butterfly in it. I'd ask my dad to test me, and he'd ask me the names of two, covering up the names and just revealing the pictures, then he'd say, "That's enough. Why don't you go play in the garden?" Later on, he'd look out the back door and say, "What are you doing, Kora?" And I'd say, "Talking to the ants."

I entertained myself for hours studying insects and animals, and after reading Blyton's *The Magic Faraway Tree*, I was convinced a seed I'd planted would grow into a giant tree, its branches stretching into the sky and leading to wonderful, magical lands. I was gutted when my mum dug it up and said it was ruining her flowerbed, convinced she had stolen away my chance to meet Silky, Moon-Face and the Angry Pixie. *The Secret Garden* had a big influence on me and convinced me that gardens were places of escape and fantasy. Digging for treasure with my next-door neighbours was an enjoyable pastime too, until we were admonished for ruining Mum's pansies.

Looking back at some of my memories, it's like looking into the minds of two different children. I suppose in my mind I have separated my memories and self into Version A and Version B. Version A is the me that feels invincible and able to achieve anything. She is positive, nurturing and full of love. Version B feels tired, overwhelmed and a little afraid of the world. She can also be a coffee-guzzling, antisocial bitch. I'm never exactly sure which version of myself is going to wake up and who will win the battle for prime position. I'm certainly not schizophrenic as both versions are me, but they feel like yin and yang, so there is the trip down memory lane that I like to remember, and then there is *the truth*. I'm unsure whether these split versions are down to my elders rewriting history so many times over the years and informing us what idyllic childhoods we had, or whether my brain detaches itself from reality at times as a form of self-preservation.

In fact, I think both statements are true. For one, I remember my dad telling me about taking me for a Mivvi far more times than it actually happened! My mother's narrative of our upbringing conjures up visions of a cross between *The Darling Buds of May* and *The Waltons*, when in reality it was more of a cross between *Kes*, *Shameless* and *Steptoe and Son*, and that's still being generous with the truth. My dad flipped between charismatic and emotionally abusive and was often out of work. This made my mum's life difficult, as she was the breadwinner and working hard to keep a roof over everyone's head. I'm sure she would rather forget when times were hard.

The truth is, I've tried to push much of it to the back of my mind too. The problem with doing that is when you repress thoughts and emotions, a sudden jolt means that they can come crashing back down around you. On one hand, I was a child who loved animals, was obsessed with make-believe and had notions of happily ever after. Most of these memories involve me being away from home or with my head stuck firmly in a book. On the flip side, I was lonely, felt unloved and suffered from severe bullying at school.

If I look back now, *really* look, I see things differently. I remember Solo – our Cavalier King Charles Spaniel and my best friend. She was balding and in poor health, but she was the sweetest girl. The dog was treated unkindly and as a nuisance – Dad would aim a kick towards her bottom and say, "Out the way, bastard dog." It wasn't hard but enough to make her run and not a nice thing to do to any animal. Perhaps that's why I felt such a bond with her. Solo would follow me around eager to exchange cuddles for biscuits! That dog loved me, and she was probably my first love.

We also had a little tortoise called Frederic who I'd have a chat with and feed dandelions too.

Of course, I absolutely idolised my dad as a child. I think I was eight or nine years old when the disillusionment set in. There were too many broken promises, too many hypocrisies, too many mood swings. Still, I'll always think back with fond memories, and remember his love of music, playing the harmonica and blasting out music on the stereo – The Beatles, The Kinks and The Shadows. When he was in a good mood, he could be hilarious too. I remember when my next-door neighbour and I were playing in the back garden, he put all the teddy bears by the windowsill and put on a puppet show, using different voices for each of the stuffed toys. You can't put a price on memories like that, even if they are a little rare on the ground.

Often, I felt like my mum didn't want me around when I was a child. Mum suffered badly from postnatal depression when I was born. She had no choice but to return to work six weeks after I was born – after nearly dying in childbirth – and had to provide for a new baby, two teenage kids, a husband and my nan. She was struggling to cope and went through periods of suffering from alopecia where her hair fell out. Life was too much for her back then; she had no support.

I was a curious child and always asking questions. I had a lot of energy and wanted to learn. I would ask what I thought was a simple question and she would lose her rag. "She's doing my head in. Get her away from me, get her out of my sight!" my mother would shout at my dad. Hence the reason for my father having to take me off my mother's hands sometimes.

I never knew what I had done wrong and would run into my dad's arms. My dad loved playing the hero in this scenario and would take me off on an adventure, in the vicinity of a good pub, and would tell me that my mother was stressed and didn't mean it. I didn't understand what I had done wrong as I only wanted her attention. I think I was an extra unwanted burden; she always said that she had never planned to have another child and that I must have been an immaculate conception. My father maintained that this was nonsense.

Later, I maintained that she must have been pissed on the evening of the big event. I'm sure we've all had nights like that! How could you possibly forget the conception of your fabulous youngest child? Well, I suppose a few snifters of Bacardi and coke might help.

***

In families like mine, where there are three or so siblings, there is usually a hierarchy. There is the *Golden Child*, which in our case was Melania. This might sound like a coveted position to be in, but it's not without its own disadvantages. The *Golden Child* often ends up parenting the parent and has so many pressures placed upon them. They are often mini-Cinderellas who from a tender age must act as cleaners, cooks and emotional props for their parents. The downside for the *Golden Child* role is that there is potential for them to become narcissists. On the opposite side of the spectrum (which thankfully my sister is), they often mature at a younger age and usually end up making excellent parents. My sister Melania did, and has several amazing children, who are all now grown up.

Clarissa was the unfortunate *Scapegoat*. The child who is always blamed for anything that goes wrong in the family. The *Scapegoat* is often the child that speaks out against injustice and calls the parents out for their poor behaviour. They then become the one that is punished the most, whether physically, emotionally or psychologically. Clarissa had always been my dad's favourite but when I came along, she was forced to take a back seat. Any teenage girl would feel put out.

As number three, I witnessed all this take place from an early age. I became the classic *Lost Child*. The *Lost Child* has seen what happens if they dare speak out, protest or get in the way, and so they start to withdraw into a world of fantasy. I do suspect, however, that I was born this way, and that my upbringing simply exacerbated my strange ways a little. By the age of four I knew that being myself was something that could get me in trouble, so I created a character called 'Suzie'. If Suzie spoke, I couldn't possibly get in trouble for it, because it wasn't me! I'd spend ages changing my clothes and dressing up as Suzie, and would call to my parents, "Have you seen Kora?" Then I'd change back to my normal clothes and would ask if anyone had seen Suzie. It was an elaborate and trouble-free way of entertaining myself and it made my parents laugh too.

During lockdown, when families were all meeting up online to do Zoom calls, myself and my three sisters celebrated my mum's birthday via Zoom. We decided upon fancy dress, and I chose to bring back Suzie as my costume character. She was dressed in an eccentric manner with floating scarves and quirky mannerisms, and kept stealing my drink when I was out of the room!

Another character I created as a kid was called 'Girlsworld'.

She was the head of a doll which you could put make-up on, popular in the Eighties. I created a voice for her and whenever my sisters went past the door, Girlsworld would call, "You bitz!" (I wasn't able to pronounce 'bitch' yet.) "You are horrible, go away!"

This was my escapism, and soon the family would all put on her voice, which was a strange warbling sound. Girlsworld occasionally returns; she is a family joke that has not been forgotten.

***

Of course, the childhood roles can often shift and at times when I wasn't able to retreat into my shell, I unwillingly fell into the role of either *Golden Child* or *Scapegoat*. Each parent would criticise the other and ask me to take sides, and I didn't want to invoke the wrath of either! Apparently, my sisters had experienced this too, so they'd had a good thirteen years of practising it! Later, my mum would get stuck into the rum and coke and disparage my father and inform me of all his indiscretions. She'd then slur, "The problem with you, Kora, is that you run with the hounds and hunt with the wolves!" I didn't fully understand where the reference came from, but I thought she was calling me a traitor.

On a Saturday night, we'd all go to the Working Men's Club and Mum and Dad would knock the drinks back. Then we'd go home about half eleven. Dad would blare music out from the living room and pass out on the sofa. I'd be propped up at the breakfast bar with Mum and she'd tell me all her financial worries as she slurred into her glass and scrubbed at an imaginary speck on the counter, while ignoring a whole roomful of other dirt.

Eventually, I'd put myself to bed and she would then decide to prod my sleeping father, shrieking, "Fred! Fred, you're drunk. GO.TO. BED. FRED. You ass'ole!" That was a pretty standard Friday and Saturday night in our house. Sometimes she'd come into my room and try to talk to me, but I didn't like the smell of rum and I'd shout at her to get out and we'd argue.

Just to be clear, I am close to my mum and also adored my

dad. I think they both had undiagnosed depression and didn't know how to cope with life. There was no Internet back then, no parental guidelines, no support for working mothers. They just had to muddle their way through life and get on with it. They were in poverty for most of my childhood and alcohol on the weekend was an escape for them. I can understand as an adult as I have been through times when I have turned to the bottle. When I think of how lost they both must have felt, I feel terrible sympathy for them, and I feel sad for the three little girls that grew up in a household that was often dysfunctional.

When I found out my friends next door had a set time for a bath and bed, and were told when to do their homework, I was so envious. Children need stability and boundaries. Us girls had neither of those things. I struggled to understand and make sense of the world around me, and often things just didn't feel real.

I experienced a lot of death from an early age. First my beloved Solo. I went to school one day when I was five years old and when I arrived home, she was gone. Mum said she had to be put down because she was ill. I was distraught because I hadn't had chance to say goodbye to her that morning, as we'd left in a rush. I would miss sharing her bed and crunching biscuits together, and her sweet, loving face.

My lovely cousin Warren died a couple of years later. He was a sweet-natured boy and like a brother to me. He would play with me in the garden and push me on the swing. My aunt and uncle (his parents) were extremely dysfunctional. His father was a severe alcoholic and his mum suffered from mental illness. The children were badly neglected and there were padlocks on all the food cupboards, so they had an awful life. Warren got into sniffing gas in a glass and ended up collapsing and being rushed to hospital. When he awoke, he was told that his heart had been badly affected and that if he ever did it again, he would die. A short time after, he was having an argument with his brother Adam about using the bathroom when he fell down the stairs. We'll never know if he had been sniffing gas in a glass again or if his heart had just been weakened too much by the previous abuse, but he never woke up again. Our dear, sweet Warren was gone.

Sad, I clutched my pink Popple teddy to my chest. At the time, Popples were the cool new trend. They were stuffed animals which you could roll up into a ball, and I carried mine with me everywhere. Soon this small stuffed toy was to save my life.

A condolence party was thrown, and my parents took me over to my uncle Craig's house. Everyone stood around talking in a few subdued tones and my aunt was sobbing hysterically. It was a sombre affair and some of the adults were already drunk.

In the corner was a table full of stodgy sausage rolls and some stale-looking crisps that no one touched. My grandad always said you had to be careful not to drop one of my auntie's sausage rolls on your foot as they would break your toe.

My uncle had just bought a big Doberman dog. The dog approached me and latched onto my pink Popple with its mighty jaws. I loved dogs and didn't see the animal as a threat. Gently, I tried to take the toy back. Everything happened in a blur next as I was dragged around the room, the ceiling whizzing by as the dog latched onto my arm and mauled me, shaking me like the stuffed toy.

The dog was trying to get a better grip on me, aiming for my neck, but it still held the Popple toy in its mouth, which prevented him from latching onto my throat. Adrenaline must have surged through my body as I felt no pain to start with, only bewilderment. There was shouting, screaming, my mum's voice screaming, "Get that bastard off of her."

My dad was kicking the dog in the balls at full pelt to try and get it to let go, but the dog didn't want to lose its juicy human prize. I must have been like a lovely, lean little steak to him. It was pandemonium, yet during the attack I didn't feel afraid, just confused at what was happening. Time passed like as if on the hands of a faulty clock spinning around, and at some point one of the men present prized the animal's jaws open wide and I was released. His hand was slashed open but him, my dad and Popple saved my life. Not today, Mr Reaper. My guardian angel must have been by my side.

Once free, the fear set in as my adrenaline levels dropped. I must have been in shock. I wanted to leave immediately as I was terrified the dog might come back, even though it had been shut in another room. An ambulance was called and my wounds examined. I had a deep slash in my right upper arm which poured with blood, and some more superficial cuts and bruising. Someone said it was fortunate the dog hadn't grabbed me by the neck. Luckily, Popple remained intact too and still lives with me to this day, even though she looks old and tatty now.

I was rushed to hospital and tended to. I am allergic to the tetanus jab and so had various foul medicines in its place, much to my disgust.

This all happened on the weekend and by Sunday, I was out in my neighbours' back garden playing doctors and nurses as my friends pretended to dress my arm and asked me questions about the dog attack. I took it in my stride and lapped up the attention, declaring it was no big deal.

There were talks about the dog being put down and I cried and said I didn't want him to die, that I was sure he was sorry. My uncle was upset at this news and it's alleged that in a drunken stupor he said, "I wish it had bitten her fucking head off." I'm not sure why my mum told me that, but I never spoke to my uncle again. It's a shame, he adored me when I was small but he was an alcoholic and in no way functional.

Terrible dreams and night terrors plagued me for years. There were the classic anxiety dreams – teeth falling out, being lost, a monster chasing me but me not being able run, deep floods and water rising around the house – but there was one that stands out and which was particularly disturbing. I was walking with my mum and she turned into a frog. We were suddenly in our bathroom, and she leaped onto our green bathroom tiles, where she blended in and then vanished, becoming part of the pattern on the wall. Calling for her in distress, there was no reply – she'd vanished. Waking up in a sweat, I struggled to shift the sense of unease. Going to sleep was something I dreaded.

Soon after, our dear tortoise Frederic died. He had been brought into the cool spare room for winter to hibernate, as it was a harsh winter. One day I wandered in to see Frederic's neck poked out all the way, a bead of blood on his little nose. He was gone. Mum said someone must have turned the heating on and he'd woken up and had no food or water. I tortured myself wondering if it had been me that had turned the radiator on. I couldn't recall. Mum said it must have been Nan, but I still felt terrible, like a family member had died. Well, he was like family and I missed that little chap. No more would I see him plodding happily round the garden, chewing dandelions and enjoying the sunshine.

My wonderful grandad, who had always had time for me and a funny joke to tell, was the next to pass over. Grandad suffered a heart attack and was up in hospital. My mum, dad and I were going up to the hospital to see him one Sunday. I hadn't seen him for ages and was excited at the prospect. My parents then became angry with me for some reason. I can't remember the exact cause, I think it was not doing what I was supposed to quick enough, and as punishment Dad said I wasn't allowed to go with them, I had to stay at home alone. I cried my heart out.

A few days later, Grandad was released from hospital and told by the doctors not to drink. The next day, he was found dead in his bed by my nan. There were cans of beer littering the kitchen table, and I'd not been able to see him before he died because my dad had decided I should be punished for not performing to a high-enough standard.

My dad went to visit Grandad in the Chapel of Rest before the funeral. I wasn't allowed to go. I decided that when I was an adult, I would do the same when the time came, and no one could stop me. It was bizarre, because my parents said it would be too distressing to see my grandad in the Chapel of Rest, but my dad had no problem revealing how sickened he felt when they heard them dragging Grandad down the stairs in a body bag and he heard his head hitting every stair. For one, how did he know it was his head? It could have been his feet. Two, why would you tell a ten-year-old child that?

Anyway, Dad said he walked into the pub after he had visited the Chapel of Rest and Grandad's favourite song "A Whiter Shade of Pale" was playing. This I believe. I was witness to many strange happenings in my parents' house as a kid and over the years I have seen so much synchronicity and I realise there is much to this universe that we may never understand. Music has always been a guiding force in our family, the right song coming on the radio at the right time, and the right words telling you just what you needed to hear. Everything around us is energy and sometimes you can just tap into that.

My dear nan was distraught by the death of my grandad. They had both annoyed each other and had affairs, but she was lost without him. I spent most weekends with my nan for a while afterwards. It was nice for me to get away from the chaos and have some stability, and it was good for Nan to have some company while she was grieving. I would have thought my dad would have visited her a bit more, but I was offered like the consolation prize, not that Nan ever seemed disappointed.

Waking up in Nan's twin bedroom with the sunlight streaming through the window as her clock played the classical piece "Turkish March" by Mozart was like soup for the soul.

Nan was always up before me. Breakfast would usually be tapioca or rice pudding. Lunch would probably be cakes. Nan wasn't much of a cook, but she knew how to make a tasty dessert! We'd head off to some jumble sales and would eat more chocolate in bed later that night. During the week, I would come home from school and once my friends went in, I would just sit in my room reading. At the weekends my diet was appalling! I really started to pile on the pounds!

Nan never spoke down to me and wasn't condescending. She could be a bit funny at times, as old people can be, but she was mostly kind. She talked to me like I was an adult, which I loved.

I quite enjoyed her illicit stories about the past, and the fact she trusted me. I've always had that effect on people though; strangers in the street just open up to me and tell me their life stories. I think they can sense a certain energy about me and know their secrets will only be met with non-judgement and empathy. As an adult, I look back and I'm glad my nan felt she could share her secrets with me back then. I didn't really know her that well later on when I was as an adult (she never wanted visitors in her old age). I would call up and ask to go round and she would say she didn't want any visitors today because she was watching something on the telly. She was certainly a character and if there is an afterlife, I can just picture her now, sat on the edge of her armchair, her elbows on her knees, the dog sprawled out comfortably behind her taking up 90% of the chair. She'd have the fire on full, and the TV blaring out at maximum volume in her lounge, which would be filled with dolls, knickknacks and children's toys. You'd say, "Are you all right, Nan?" She'd say, "Just a minute, I'm watching this programme!"

I would love to be able to sit and chat with my grandparents now. I'd probably have a few hair-raising stories to exchange with my nan now! I wonder what she would make of my career choice. I think she would say, "Good on you! Wish I could have done that!"

I also felt close to my Nanny W. I didn't see as much of her, as she lived further away, but she would sit for hours with me when we did meet up, sew gorgeous little dresses for me and take me out. She's in her nineties now and lives far away, but I do my best to visit her a few times every year. I do wish she lived closer.

Aged eleven, I liked a boy called Nicky who was my friend Sharon's brother. He was in the year below me, but I thought he was cool with his shaved head. We all used to hang out at the park and listen to music and chat. One day when we were at the park with Pepsi the dog, Sharon and Angela. Tracey and Angela went off to chat to someone. Nicky saw this as his big moment and swooped in to kiss me. It was all going well, and I was eager to try a kiss, but then at the last minute with his face half an inch from mine, I panicked and pulled away. It all felt a bit too serious.

Nicky then got angry at having been rejected and stormed off. I'm not sure what he said to his sister, but she came over and threatened to beat me up. Then Angela took Pepsi and ran off. My heart was in my mouth. Sharon chased me and I ran, then Angela reappeared and taunted me that I couldn't love my dog that much, as I'd ran from Sharon instead of looking for Pepsi. I was so upset, as I felt that she was right. Running home with Pepsi, I was in tears. Feeling dramatic, I played "It Must Have Been Love" by Roxette.

My parents spoke with their parents and a couple of days later, Angela showed up at my door with apologies and a box of Matchmakers. She looked subdued, and her apology seemed genuine.

"I accept your apology, but I don't want the Matchmakers, thank you."

I just couldn't get past the fact she had ran off with my dog. She proffered the chocolates again and I rejected her gift and said goodbye.

"Who was that?" my dad asked.

I filled him in on what had taken place.

"I feel a bit sorry for her. She'll probably go home with those chocolates now and get in trouble for still having them. Her parents will think she didn't offer them to you." He chuckled.

He was right, but the trust had been broken. I was extremely stubborn and if someone hurt me, they were dead to me. Forgiveness is such a powerful thing, but I had not yet learned this.

It hadn't helped that Nicky did not seem to regret the incident at all. At school, he shouted that I was frigid, and his mates shadowed me, calling me frigid and other crass variations. My face burned with shame, but I was glad now I hadn't kissed him.

I later had my first kiss with a female friend. We were having a sleepover and she said we should practise for when we got boyfriends. I went along with it. It wasn't really a kiss; it was a weird motion of clashing our teeth together. It was horrible and she was a bossy girl. She then lay on top of me naked. Disgust mingled with panic, and it all got a bit too much and I ran off downstairs, much to her annoyance. I was around thirteen and just wasn't ready for snogging. I wasn't attracted to girls either.

I wanted my first proper kiss to be with someone special and so I waited. In my schoolgirl fantasies, I imagined it might be someone like Damon Albarn from Blur or Jarvis Cocker from Pulp. Well, a girl can dream, can't she?

Chapter 5: Bullied

When I discovered books, it was a wonderful outlet for me. Declaring I was bored would risk inviting wrath from my dad and being criticised for having no initiative or imagination. I learned to stay out the way and a good book would turn my humdrum existence into a magical world. Even if my parents had hit the rum and were battling it out downstairs, I'd escape into Middle-earth, a secret garden or to a land of evil wizards and magical fairies that would save the day. When I was absorbed in those books, they felt more real to me than real life. I would read about princesses that were rewarded for being kind and young children that were saved from horrible monsters and demons. I prayed that if I was good enough, that perhaps a miracle might happen, and I would be saved from the monsters. I had a lot to learn! I sometimes wonder though, if I hadn't so desperately needed that outlet back then and dedicated so many hours to being a bookworm, would I still be me? Would I have ever written a single story? Everything that has happened over the last four decades has made me who I am. Would I want that taken away? I don't think so.

I think the fact I stayed out of the way also meant that I escaped some of the treatment Clarissa received. She tells me she felt like she was completely unwanted as a child. She always got given the tatty, ripped clothes and dreadful mullet haircuts. Food in the house was scarce even though Dad's alcohol bar was usually stocked, and he'd chain smoke all day long. My dad would often finish up the last of the crisps or bread after a few drinks and the girls would get punished for it.

There's twelve and thirteen years between me and my sisters, and the Childline adverts had started by the time I was a child.

I remember my mother once smacking my backside and me retorting that I would call Childline. I was threatened and told I'd get a thick ear or get my ears 'boxed' if I was cheeky to her again, but it never happened. I remember my father smacking me on one occasion and I didn't speak to him for a week. I remember him trying to make amends and offering me all kinds of sweets, and I repeatedly uttered, "No thanks, no thanks," in as cold a voice as I could muster.

In fact, it wasn't so much the whack on the bottom that ignited my utter disdain and resulted in my father toppling from his pedestal. It was the savage comments he inflicted on me one day as I sat soaking up the sun in my swimsuit. He was in a foul mood and decided to announce that I used to be such a pretty little girl, and now I was fat and spotty! That caused me to retort, "Huh! Look at yourself!" That is the comment that got me the slapped arse. There was no way I was accepting sweets off him after the fat comment, and it influenced me for many years. I do remember forcing an apology out of him years later after he'd had a few drinks. He said he couldn't remember it and seemed genuinely embarrassed.

So, at home, I suppose it was more like psychological warfare for me and physical punishments were rare, unless you include not being allowed to be physically active in case it made a noise, hence my puppy fat. If I made too much noise skipping or moving around, Dad would holler up the stairs angrily to keep the noise down. I'm surprised he could hear over the thunder of his television set or the stereo belting out hits at full volume. His favourite saying at the time was, "Do as I say, not as I do."

Unfortunately, at school I didn't get off so lightly.

My first experience of bullying was aged five; I was tiny for my age, and I struggled to walk far. That first day was when I gave up dummies, having generally had one if not two in my mouth. My family used to call me Kazzy Two Dums. To start with, I enjoyed school, and loved art, story time and climbing trees until it was banned. Graham was a big, fat kid who liked to pick on little girls smaller than him and he chased me home from school before I was even allowed to leave the premises on my own. It started off an asthma attack and I gasped for breath, my chest feeling like a boa constrictor had wrapped itself around my ribs, constricting them. Mum went down the school and his nan turned up on our doorstep ranting and raving. He later went to prison and his nan said it was my mum's fault for reporting him in the infants. Go figure.

At the age of ten, I was still only just over three-foot-tall and an easy target for bullies. Most of my problems started when a woman called Lana who lived across the road started telling stories about me. Lana was a woman into her mid-thirties who let her children run riot. Her kids were always in the street effing and jeffing, sometimes naked in the middle of winter. Her youngest, Tracey, a three-year-old, would lie on her back naked kicking their front door repeatedly and screaming. Sometimes she would scream insults across the road, such as "*Fucking snob*," for no reason.

My friend Ella and I had once fed one of her cats, Cammy. The cat was pregnant and shut outside most of the time and followed us round mewling pitifully. We took pity on the poor thing and made sure it was well cared for. We would spend whatever little pocket money we had on tins of cat food to make sure the cat was well nourished. Later, the cat gave birth and Lana's husband let me adopt one of the kittens, a gorgeous tabby we named 'Pebbles'.

At some point, Lana started a rumour that I poisoned her cat and various horrible other stories. She considered our family snobs because my parents had bought their house and didn't live in a council flat, presumably, or perhaps it was because my mother gave her the cold shoulder when she made conversation in the street. I wasn't allowed to play with her children and was forbidden from even crossing the road, and so the bullying began in my local area.

My school was full of idiots and horrible bullies, and that was just the teachers!

The kids were even worse. There was classroom disruption, verbal bullying, pushes, shoves and slaps. Eventually, the silly rumours were forgotten, but by this point I'd been identified as an easy target due to my small stature and so the bullying escalated. The bullying would take place at school and between there and home, and so I didn't feel as if anywhere was safe apart from my bedroom. In class, drawing pins would be put on my chair. In the changing rooms before gym, the mean girls would surround me and poke fun at my figure or height. I was punched in the face by one boy who gave me a black eye, while a girl called Lyns would often pull my hair or push me over. Lyns repulsed me and I tried to steer clear. She was scruffy and unwashed, with a mullet-style haircut, and on more than one occasion I saw lice crawling through her hair.

I had a few friends, but they were too terrified to intervene. Even the teachers were no help. One day in class, I sat in my chair, straight onto a drawing pin. Letting out a yelp, I was reprimanded by the teacher. I tried to protest that I'd sat on a drawing pin, but the teacher made me go and stand outside as punishment for making a noise. That was often the way at Hreod Parkway. It was a rough school and many of the teachers couldn't handle the pupils. They would simply put their heads in sand and deny there was a problem. It was impossible to hide the level of damage to my body, property and well-being from my mother, and she had words with the school on various occasions.

The bullying got to a point where every day I'd arrive home with new bruises, hair missing, items stolen or mud over my uniform or bag. I'd either be in fits of tears or just looking shell-shocked. My Cavalier King Charles Spaniel would always run to me, and I'd bury my face into her fur, sobbing into her coat as she comforted me. My animals were my world. There was Pepsi, who was like my little shadow, following me around and sleeping by my side; Poppy, a tri-colour King Charles, who was a little more aloof but slept at my feet; and Pebbles, my tabby cat who took position on my head at night. In bed with my three pets, I felt content; they were the best friends a girl could have ever had, and they helped me get through so many tough times. It was something that I really needed at that time.

One day, I was chased home from school again and arrived wheezing and having another asthma attack. My mother was furious with the school. "Enough is enough," she snapped, and stormed off down to the school to have it out with them. The headmaster hid in his office and pretended to be out in a meeting, his secretary covering for him. Not to be perturbed by this, my mother stated, "Fine. I'll sit here all day and wait if I have to."

Eventually, the headmaster crept out of his office and spoke with my mother. He denied that the school had a problem with bullying and inferred that she was lying, or that it wasn't happening on school property. My mother sat there and drew a map and pinpointed all the locations across the school where the bullying was taking place. The headmaster was speechless and began blustering, unsure of what to say. Boris would have been proud! I'm not sure exactly what took place after this, but the bullying died down for a couple of weeks and a couple of the girls involved were excluded from school for a couple of days.

I don't have many fond memories of school unfortunately. I used to live for my English and Physics lessons each week, which were run by my two favourite teachers – Mr Barlow, and I fail to remember the other teacher's name, but he was a marvellous fellow, with a white beard and a bald head, who talked excitedly when he spoke about Physics.

Mr Barlow didn't take any nonsense in his class, and he had a brilliant sense of humour. If anyone acted out, he'd humiliate them in a funny way, which made them realise that they'd better not step out of place. One day, a boy called Mark was fooling around, so Mr Barlow began acting like a chimp and climbing onto the chair, mimicking the boy. Then he mimed picking fleas out of his hair and eating them. The class roared with laughter and the boy slipped back into his seat, quiet for the rest of the lesson. He knew that these kids played up because they wanted attention, but when they were made to feel silly, that stopped them seeking attention. Of course, these unorthodox methods would not be permitted nowadays and would be considered bullying or not PC. That's why there are so many little thugs running riot! I really applaud teachers like him who knew how to command the children's respect and get the best out of the studious ones. Controversial opinion alert!

Mr Barlow really encouraged my writing and insisted I pursue it. One day, I'd written a short story about a girl who was stranded on a desert island and trying to survive. He read it out to the class. The whole class sat in silence, leaning forward in their seats until the end. Mr Barlow pulled me up in front of the class and my face went red and I allowed my hair to drop forward to cover my face. I was so used to being bullied and humiliated that I assumed that something dreadful was to follow. Then Mr Barlow told everyone to applaud. As the class clapped, I peeked up shyly through my hair. I could see the looks of approval on their faces and part of me loved that, but another part of me felt deeply embarrassed at having everyone looking at me. I just wanted to crawl into a corner and not be seen.

When I think about it, the story I'd written was a metaphor for how I was feeling at the time – isolated, alone, struggling to survive and looking for help. It helped me cope with many of the emotions I was struggling with, and so writing for escapism became a way of life for me.

In some ways, it's easier to write this book than something fictional, as the narrative comes from my memory. On the other hand, it's troubling to drag up some of those old feelings, but with that comes clarity and closure. In a way, I am opening my soul to you, the reader. You may feel some of what I say resonates with you on some level, or I may manage to offend you somehow. You may enjoy my writing, or you may hate it, I may revolt you, but I am OK with that and accept that not everyone will be able to understand my choices. If someone reads this and can relate to it or enjoys it, then that's all that matters. I am not trying to please the masses, but simply tell my story and hope that it reaches someone's heart and reassures them that we are all a bit screwed up. Some people just hide it better. I should know.

***

I'd like to say that with Mr Barlow's encouragement, life was simple, but that wouldn't be the truth and that is not how life works. A couple of things happened that brought everything to a head when I was fourteen. I was walking home from school with my friend Rachel one sunny afternoon when I felt someone grab my hair from behind. A foot kicked into my ankle and in a second, I was on the floor wondering what the hell had happened. The foot made impact with my legs, then my ribs, then my head. My head was spinning but I was aware of a sea of faces which had circled around us. Voices were shouting, "Fight, fight, fight!"

"Kill her!" someone yelled.

My friend Rachel had covered her face with her hands in horror, her shoulders hunched, not knowing what to do. I have no idea how long this went on for; in one way it felt like minutes, and in another way, it felt like an age.

Confused, I looked up at the perpetrator for a moment and could see it was a girl called Michelle that I'd never even spoken to before. As I saw her foot flying towards me again, I tried to cover my head with my hands, but it was no use. The foot kept coming, and the sound of her shoe reverberating against my head was dizzying and filled me with nausea.

"Cry, you bitch, cry!" I heard her scream.

The chanting had grown to a lull now and some of the children had started to back away a little, realising the severity of what was taking place.

"Cry, I said! I won't stop kicking you until you cry!"

I was too much in shock to cry, I was dumbfounded, I was bamboozled. A part of me realised I had to cry though. My survival instinct crept in, and the tears came. I have no idea how long this took place for, it's all a blur, but I heard shouts, and then the bully and the circle of children scarpered. I felt hands pulling me up from the ground and I stood dazed, looking at my mother, who was running towards me with her face like thunder. My friend Rachel and a girl called Joanna had run to my house to fetch my mum, God bless them.

"You little bastards!" she shouted. I think it was lucky for the bully that she ran, as in that state of distress my mother would probably have lumped her one and would have been in a whole lot of trouble. My family may have been a bit dysfunctional over the years, but we certainly do our best to protect each other.

After the event, I was in complete shock, and I didn't realise the severity of the situation. I had become so used to being a punching bag that it was just another school day, but a bit worse than normal. I sat bewildered while the girls bustled round and made cups of tea, and I heard my mother talking on the phone in dramatic tones. It seemed to me that everyone was making such a fuss. I was thankful that some of the other girls had helped but was a little suspicious and wondered why they were being nice to me.

Soon, a policewoman arrived and told me I had to write a statement. I said I didn't want to get anyone into trouble, and she looked at me sternly and said, "I don't think you realise how serious this is." The truth was, I didn't. It was what I had become accustomed to.

The policewoman took photos of my injuries next. I had clumps of hair missing and blood blisters at my hairline. I was covered in bruises and had a swelling on the head. I was taken to hospital and advised not to sleep as I may have concussion.

In the following weeks, Michelle the perpetrator was charged with ABH and ordered to pay me £60, in monthly instalments of £10 per month. I gave some of the money to the animal charity Animate and spent the rest on books. It was important to me that the money was spent on things of spiritual value rather than frivolous items, as I needed to feel that some good had come from the ordeal.

The kids at my school weren't afraid of being excluded, in fact they welcomed it, but one thing they were all scared of was the police, and so the bullying mostly stopped at that point. I still spent my days looking over my shoulder, waiting for someone to attack. Most of the bullies looked through me now, as if I was invisible. Then there were a couple of kids who decided I was an absolute hero and would ask me over and over to tell them about the story. I became close to a boy called Roy. We hadn't been friends before but bonded in Drama classes and I would hang out with him, and he and Clara would slag off the bullies. Years later, he came out. I wasn't surprised at all; I was just waiting for him to tell me. Most boys of fourteen aren't that naturally hilarious and fun to hang out with!

I also formed good friendships with Shirley and Ann Marie, who were in my year. We became the misfits and didn't care if we were popular or not. We'd sometimes go to the chippy at lunchtime to get away from school and we'd usually make excuses to skip P.E. and head back to mine.

P.E. was my idea of hell because I would have to play sport with some of the bitchy girls. I was quite good at hockey and remember one girl saying to me, "If you get the ball off me again, I'll give you a smacking with my stick." I'd ask my mum if she minded me writing a letter on her behalf to say I couldn't do P.E. She understood my reasons and agreed, she was good like that, so I'd write a letter excusing myself with whatever excuse I could come up with that week – usually about me having a bad ankle or knee. I knew not to be overly dramatic and get caught out. If the teacher was onto me, she certainly turned a blind eye. I think they realised that they had failed to curtail the bullying problems at the school.

I was only attacked once ever again. I was walking over the bridge to get to my class on the north side when I saw Lyns coming the other way. My stomach dropped and I did my best to look in the opposite direction and keep walking.

She grabbed my coat and pulled it over my head so that I

couldn't see, and then tried to push me over. Remembering the last incident where I had been kicked in the head, I panicked and refused to allow myself to be pushed to the floor. With the coat covering my eyes, I flailed my arms in all directions, then I felt my hand meet solidly with something and heard a piercing scream. There was the sound of feet running and getting my wits about me, I pulled the coat off my face to see Lynsey running off into the distance. *Now I'm in trouble*, I thought, and spent the whole day waiting to be called to the headmaster's office. They'd probably say no wonder I had problems if this was how I behaved. I'd gotten used to having the blame passed onto me by the teachers, being gaslighted and being the school's scapegoat. Nothing happened that day and so I arrived home, expecting the school to have called my parents, but again nothing had occurred. It was only during registration the next morning that the incident was noted. My tutor Miss O called me up to her desk. "Karen, is it true you punched Lyns Hershall?"

"Yes, Miss," I admitted, terrified of what was to take place next.

"Good!" she said with a smile. "Now, go sit down."

I took my seat, a warmth filling my insides. Finally, a teacher who understood. When you feel alone and as if the world and its dog is against you, a little understanding or a few kind words can go such a long way, and in those few words, she had acknowledged the problems I had faced and given me validation instead of punishing me. I had struggled to trust adults, but now knew that I had a few on my side. I even had a few of the pupils commend me on finally standing up for myself. They looked at me with a new appreciation, but it was too late to buy my friendship with words, as I no longer trusted anyone.

After the Lyns incident, no one dared to touch me again. For one, no one else had seen the incident, so they just assumed I'd snapped and punched her in the face, and I wasn't about to correct them.

With the bullying now over, I was able to focus on my lessons. As a result, I started to do well in other subjects. I wasn't great at Maths or Woodwork, but I was moved up into the top set in French and started to get As in English Language and Literature and French, and Bs in Physics and History.

Shortly afterwards, I had met Matt. I'd had a crush on him for ages and just seeing him walk into the same building would make me feel happy all day. Before we got together, I was worried that he would laugh at me. I kept thinking of the last time I'd had a crush on a boy at school called Gary and it got back to me that he would, "Rather chew a brick."

The first time I brought Matt home after school to meet my pets, Mum was retraining as a hairdresser and was out till late, so the house was quite messy. I was a little bit embarrassed and kept apologising about the mess. Then Pepsi got so excited at an extra person to give her fuss that she peed all over the floor. I was absolutely mortified, but Matt didn't bat an eyelid.

Soon, he was walking me to school and home again every day. I was safe now. I was known as the girl who 'hit the bully back', I had a cool boyfriend who was older than me, and I even had some highlights put in my hair, courtesy of my mum, who was training for her NVQs. I finally felt as if the pressure cooker had been turned down a little, and when I sat my exams that year, I came out with a few As, some Bs, Cs and Ds in Maths and Home Economics (Home Ec was cookery. Ironically, I can whizz up some pretty awesome dishes in the kitchen these days, which are far removed from the brick-like rice pudding and fruit salads our Home Ec teacher had us make).

One day in Physics, Kelly – one of the cool girls – came up to me and said, "I heard you got an A in French. Are you proud of yourself?"

"Erm, no," I said, afraid to admit that I was rather pleased I'd done that well.

"Well, I am proud of you, Kora, well done."

I had never expected to get approval from one of the cool girls, and for a moment, I revelled in the acknowledgement and the fact that she had even noticed me. Then I wiped such daft notions from my head. None of them had been there during my tough times, so it shouldn't matter a damn what their opinions of me were now. I gave her a polite thank you and then went back to my papers on the desk. I had learned to push people away before they rejected me, and this would be a habit that would span a great deal of my life.

Chapter 6: Heartbreak and New Beginnings in Cyprus

After school, I studied English at college. Home life was difficult; my parents' relationship was fraught with drama, hostility and there was constant rowing that I would be dragged into. Saturday nights were often the worst. By this point, Dad was a functional alcoholic, and his moods would shift rapidly. He could be the life and soul of the party and have you in fits of laughter, or he could have you in tears when all you'd done is walk into the room when he was in a mood.

On a Sunday morning, I'd go into the kitchen, and it would be like wading through Brecon Beacons on a foggy morning. My dad smoked about sixty cigarettes a day and I just couldn't bear the smell. I'd go in the lounge next, and my mum would be sat in a dark room with all the curtains shut. If the door was open for longer than a second, she'd yell, "Shut that bastard door! You are letting all the cold air in!" None of this was new, but I hadn't known anything different as a child. Now I was older, I could see I was in an unhealthy environment.

Spending as much time away from the house as possible, I took a weekend job working in retail and an evening job cleaning office blocks. I was constantly on the go and started to feel permanently exhausted. I never had the time to concentrate on my studies and as a result I left college with D-grade A Levels and an ONC in Video Production. Funnily enough, I remember when I chose Video Production, my mother said to me, "How is that ever going to be useful?" It's come in extremely handy, as it happens. Nowadays, I edit videos for my fetish clip stores every day! Perhaps it was my intuition or perhaps it was a coincidence, but I'm glad I took those classes. Isn't it peculiar when you look back at life and you start to see all the dots connecting and the pieces of the jigsaw fitting together? Perhaps some things really do happen for a reason, but I struggle to accept why some of the great cruelties in the world might be necessary. There's never any need for children and animals to starve and be hurt, or for any human to suffer either.

I can't deny that I wasn't disappointed with my grades, but I decided to become a travel agent. I took a trainee position at Co-op Travelcare and began to study everything I could about all the different tour operators and holiday destinations. I gained various qualifications; I can't even remember if they were BTECs or ONCs now. At first, I loved the thrill of learning about different countries and sending people off to exotic climes. Then my supervisor Sarah sent someone off to Cuba instead of the Maldives. Back then, when initiating a booking, you had to enter the three-letter airport code into the system. Sarah had looked up the code in a massive book that looked like hieroglyphics and managed to enter the wrong code. She should have entered 'HAQ' Hanimaadhoo International Airport. Instead, she entered 'HAV', Havana Airport in Cuba. This is something that simply wouldn't happen nowadays, but back then it seemed to slip past everyone at every stage of development. The paperwork which followed didn't list the destination, just the airport code, and no one was any the wiser until the agency received a frantic call from two customers enraged to find themselves in Cuba for their honeymoon!

Sarah partly blamed me, as I'd overseen her work, but as a new trainee I wasn't held accountable for the error. Not that I didn't feel bad about it, but the system was flawed, and I could see this. I don't know if my suggestions to improve communication and list the destination were ever taken on. I'm sure they don't make that mistake nowadays though, I'm sure everything is checked thoroughly! Our manager in the Co-op was often taking sick days or swanning off to Cancún, so it was stressful running a travel agency with just a supervisor and a trainee. Tension between Sarah and the manager Ken thickened, and the work atmosphere was extremely uncomfortable. Shortly afterwards, Ken went on indefinite sick leave with mental health problems. Sarah then followed suit and claimed the stress was too much. That left little old me, sixteen years old and alone in a travel agency running the show, and all for £60 per week. Part of me enjoyed the challenge, but I was also resentful that I was being used. I wrote a letter to the company explaining that I was running the office alone and asked them to kindly consider a small pay raise considering the circumstances. My request was denied, and I was livid.

My relationship with Matt was up and down. He was quite immature for his age, as was I in some ways. I remember one time he wanted my mum to shave his head with a zero grade. She phoned his mum to check, who said no. He ran upstairs crying and shouting how unfair it was.

He was my first relationship and I loved him dearly, but then Matt cheated on me and all my respect for him went out of the window. After that, I didn't think twice about snogging a cute guy in a club. I was childish and self-sabotaging. I thought if I did that, if and when he cheated on me again it wouldn't matter as much.

Then something terrible happened that shattered my heart into pieces.

Leaving the office one freezing cold evening, I shivered at the bus stop. At the time, Swindon buses ran on their own schedule and not according to the timetable. Instead of a bus every twenty minutes, you could be waiting up to an hour before getting on an overcrowded bus, and then you would be swung from side to side manically until you reached your destination. A sense of dread curled in my insides and when I finally got home, I was cold to the bones. Pepsi greeted me with a wagging backside and jumped up at me, clawing my legs. "Ow, Pepsi, in a minute, I've had a shit day," I moaned at her.

Poppy, my other King Charles, looked up and went back to

sleep again. Pebbles, my tabby cat, jumped onto the worktop and made a purring sound. I tipped a can of meat into her dish, switched on the kettle, and threw a jacket potato in the micro-wave, then I heard a strange noise. I turned sharply to see Pepsi lose control of her bladder and collapse to the floor. A piercing scream reached my ears and I realised it was coming from me. I ran to her side and gathered her up. I could see she was in big trouble. The life was fading from her fast. Without thinking, I opened her mouth and blew into it, and pressed rapidly on her chest, to no avail. I could feel tears streaming down my cheeks and a sense of blinding panic threatening to overwhelm me. In a flash, I ran to the phone. "Mum, quick, come home. Pepsi has collapsed, we need to get her to the vets."

She said she would get there as fast as she could and I sat holding Pepsi, urging her to survive. Mum arrived and we jumped straight in the car. The vet's surgery was a distance from our house, and I was most likely clutching Pepsi's corpse by this point, but I was in complete denial and refused to believe that she wouldn't make it. When the vet confirmed that she was gone and had suffered from water on the lung, I broke down. I whispered into Pepsi's ear that I would always love her and miss her so much. My mum was present and has always been a bit deaf, so was saying, "What's that? What are you saying?" To this she was met with a glare.

The next few days I spent in limbo. I was a shadow of myself; everything reminded me of Pepsi, and I kept putting my hand out to my side to stroke her, except she wasn't there. My little shadow was gone for good. It was a tough few months and I don't know how I made it through. I had grown apart from my school friends and felt alone, which was my own doing, if I'm honest. I had put too much focus onto my boyfriend Matt for one, and when I did go out with my friends, I would drink too much and become a pain in the backside.

I was completely lost for weeks and didn't know how I would ever feel happy again without my little Pepsi. Then I had a revelation. There was nothing keeping me here anymore. I wasn't particularly close to my family at that time (now we are so close) and I was a troubled soul. Over the years, we have grown together, but at the time it wasn't that way. I had no *real* friends and I had employers that were taking the piss out of me. While I did care deeply for my boyfriend Matt, I could see we were different and wanted different things out of life, and so began our on/off relationship. We must have broken up and got back together more times than Ross and Rachel from *Friends*!

I applied for a couple of jobs overseas as a holiday representative. An offer came up for a job in Cyprus and I jumped at the chance. I went for an interview and was offered a position as an overseas rep. We had a week's training course down in Eastbourne and this consisted of team jollies and creating a cabaret show where we would sing, act and dance. When the resident gay guy asked me to do his make-up for the show because he liked the way I did mine, I was thrilled.

Less than three months later, I was living in a house on the beach in Paphos and hosting welcome meetings, airport runs and guiding boat trips and excursions. I also had the wonderful opportunity to visit Egypt and the pyramids while I was there. It was a trip that we would be expected to sell to our guests. It was awe-inspiring, but certainly not glamorous like the holiday shows make out. There were dead bodies covered in shroud at the side of the River Nile as many families could not afford to bury their dead. That was devastating. There were also children as young as three trying to sell heads of flowers. I had never seen such poverty and counted myself lucky. Aside from the heart-wrenching sadness of how some of the people had to live, it was an amazing experience and great to learn about a culture different to my own. We visited the tomb of Giza and the museum where they hold some of Egypt's most ancient artefacts. Of course, the Brits stole a lot of the treasures and display them here in the British Museum in London, but that's another story.

The trip was over all too soon and it was back to work. At first,

I struggled with all the admin. I had never been taught organisational skills and I struggled to discipline myself.

Some weeks were great, and others were terrible depending on who your guests were. Sometimes you couldn't wait for them to fly home and occasionally you would get guests that would literally come on holiday just to complain and get some compensation. Health and safety protocols were strict in the hotels. If a fly so much as sneezed in the direction of the pool, you would have to fill out a report form. When you are eighteen years old and a holiday rep, you sometimes must remind yourself that you are not actually on holiday and have a job to do. In the early days, there was a lot of last-minute panics when I realised, I had forgotten to deliver welcome packs to my hotels and I would run around like a mad thing, flying across to my hotels on my moped and delivering everything. Sometimes I would have to pop the packs under the guests' doors before the welcome meeting the next morning.

Planning was not my strength. Mostly, I had just turned up and would wing it, but I was a little out of my depth now and I found it difficult to start with. I might start some days with an early morning airport run, meeting guests and taking them to their hotels by coach. In the afternoon, I would guide some of the excursions and entertain guests that had booked onto glass-bottom boat excursions or a Mezze dinner in the evening. In between I would greet and host welcome meetings and fill out copious amounts of paperwork.

My first ever welcome meeting was terrifying. I had about fifteen guests seated, waiting to hear my spiel. I handed out shots of the local liqueur, which I later discovered would get most of the guests onside. When I said it was my first day, they soon warmed to me. I think I stopped saying it was my first day about ten welcome meetings in! I started to grow a little bit of confidence and eventually after muddling my way through, I fell into a steady routine.

It felt strange mixing with people my own age. All I seemed to have in common with them was drinking, so that's what we did at first.

I made great friends with the kids' club rep Sharla, and we would have such a giggle. I'd hop on my moped over to her hotel and we'd get chatting. Then she'd panic and say, "My kids! Where have my kids gone?" Then she'd dash off. She'd always find them two minutes later but would have an absolute meltdown in between.

There were always dramas among the reps. They were always sleeping with everyone else and having arguments and I had my share of dramas too.

I fell out with my flatmate Cally, a loud, man-eating Mancunian that was a little self-obsessed. Within a couple of months, she'd met a Cypriot fella, moved him into our flat and he was always stealing my food. I later took on a little tabby kitten called Missy and Cally decided she hated the poor thing as it was quite clingy and tried to climb her leg a couple of times. When she reported me for having a kitten in the flat, I couldn't believe the cheek. My response was that she had her boyfriend living in our flat 24/7 who didn't contribute, but I wasn't allowed a kitten! My supervisor Beth said, "Oh yeah, I knew about her fella, but I was waiting for you to say something!" Cally and I ended up not speaking and did our best to avoid one another. Well, to be factual, she slammed around a lot, and I ignored her.

Later, I fell out with my friend Sharla. During an off phase with Matt, I'd had a fling with her cousin, not realising he was due to be married. If I'd have known, I wouldn't have touched him with a barge pole. Some things are just off limits, and I could see why she was so angry. While falling out with Cally was no loss to me, I was distraught at losing Sharla. I vowed to myself never to make the same mistake again and I only dated Greek men for a while. As far as I was concerned, you don't shit on your own doorstep and getting involved with colleagues or guests was not an option. I live by the same principles today.

This all hit me hard, but I bounced back from it. Eventually, I came out of my shell a little and started to open up to others. I gravitated towards the older reps. Helena, my supervisor Susanna and a gay guy called Dave were wonderfully chilled people with a good energy about them. I hadn't got on with my supervisor at first, but we eventually became firm friends when I started to take my job more seriously.

I'd often hang around with Helena and Dave and we'd eat in the hotels or hop on a moped and explore the island. Another time we found a deserted lake and went swimming in the hilltops of Cyprus. The rest of the reps always went skinny dipping, but I always kept my thong on, not wanting to flash my moo-moo. I have since become a lot more relaxed about my body, although I'm not sure skinny dipping is for me.

During my off periods with Matt, I would date and had various crazy adventures, although nothing *particularly* kinky springs to mind. I do remember a certain guest (not one of mine fortunately). I remember during our staff training sessions we were told that it was a conflict of interest to sleep with our guests, but we could sleep with guests who had travelled with other tour operators! The first question we were told to ask potential flings was, "Which company are you holidaying with?"

I took a shine to a lad who we'll call Tom. He had travelled with a rival firm and asked me to show him around and so I took him to a few nightspots. After a few cocktail pitchers, we were in high spirits and in the mood for adventure. I took him to a nearby hotel and slipped around the back to the pool. I knew how to get into all the hotels, and it wasn't one that I worked in, so it wouldn't matter too much if we got caught, I reasoned. So, we stripped down to our undies and dove into the pool, giggling and making out against a backdrop of stars, in the cool rippling water.

Despite it being a warm evening, we soon got chilly and decided to venture into the hotel and find our way out. We stumbled across the banqueting room and thought it would be the perfect place to continue our make out session for a while. Just as things were starting to get exciting, we heard a noise and dove under the tablecloth of a nearby table! The sound of a trolley containing cutlery and utensils clanked and rattled, and we realised that a member of staff was setting up for the next day. We put our palms over our mouths to stifle our giggles and soon, as we heard them exit the room, we made a break for it! We ran down the corridor at full pelt, exited the hotel and ran out onto the street gasping, and broke down into fits of giggles. Tom was great fun, but soon he was due to fly home and that was the end of that. There was no point saying we'd keep in touch; we both knew it wouldn't happen. I wonder if he remembers that crazy holiday rep that took him under her wing and on an adventure?

Another particularly weird night happened after a friend's wedding. I hadn't wanted to go but felt it was impolite to say so and felt pressured into it. I ended up sitting next to a friend of a friend, I think he might have been called Chris, or something. Chris was cute, intelligent and, more importantly, hilarious! I had been apprehensive about this event, but he kept me entertained with jokes and mickey-taking and when he invited me out for drinks afterwards, I agreed. We hit a couple of bars on the strip, then decided to get a taxi to Rainbows, the local club. Rainbows played some great tracks but was full of sleazy men waiting to prey on young girls. They would always stand at the end of the dance floor watching the girls in the same way a lizard watches a fly. Chris and I decided to leave and sat on the kerb just down from the strip chatting and waiting for a taxi to appear.

Sometime later, a couple in a red Porsche pulled up. Behind the wheel was a short, stocky Greek man with waves of curling hair. He was in his mid-to-late forties and his partner was slim, with a pointy face and long, dark hair.

"Jump in, we give you lift," the man beamed.

"No thanks, we're all right, thanks," we replied politely.

"Ah, where you go?"

"Just down the Lighthouse Beach."

"Ah, is only short way. I take you."

In Cyprus, it was quite common for drivers to stop at bus stops and offer lifts to tourists for an extra few quid, so we thought nothing of it but still declined.

Then the woman leaned over to us, smiling charmingly. "Let us take you, it's no trouble," she purred.

A back-and-forth conversation between the four of us continued for around ten minutes, then relenting, Chris and I looked at each other and naively agreed.

Once we were in the car and zooming down the road, the Greek started to talk at high speed.

"What's your name?" he asked.

"Chris."

"Ah, Chris, I am Christos, we are the same! I live here thirty years. Before, my father he live here, before him my grandfather. I build my house myself, with my own hands. I show you my house."

"Errr, no we couldn't possibly impose," I interrupted.

"It's no problem. I like to show you my house. We go now, then I take you home."

The woman didn't speak again and Christos rattled on about various things in a strong Greek accent. I started to feel a rising sense of unease. I knew we had made a mistake and looking at Chris, I could see he felt the same way. Eventually, we reached a small town called Polis and drove up a big hill. We were led into the house and all I could think was how strange it was that the lady wasn't making any conversation.

"You like my house?" Christos asked.

"Very nice," we nodded, not wanting to upset him.

"I give you tour!"

We made all the right noises as he showed us around the house, commenting on how lovely the tiles were and we were relieved when it was over.

"OK, I make you drinks, now, you come with me," he pointed at Chris.

The silence was deafening, trying to make small talk with … I think it was Millana, who only answered "Yes" or "No" to my questions. I was trying to figure out her accent and she told me she was Russian.

When Chris appeared again, relief flooded me until I noticed he was ghostly white, with panic written all over his face. He sidled up to me, making as if he was whispering romantically in my ear, "She's a hooker and he just suggested we swap! WE need to get out of here," he blurted.

"Whaaat? Are you serious?" I looked into his eyes, hoping he would say it was a joke, but I knew from the look on his face that he was deadly serious. My heart started to pound in my chest, and I had visions of the two of us being tied up and used as sex slaves, before being bludgeoned to death and thrown off a fishing boat into the Med!

"We have to leave," I whispered.

"Shall we just tell him?" Chris asked.

"No. He's mental, he won't let us go. We'll have to escape!"

"OK, you go first, and I'll distract him, then I'll catch up with you."

"No!" I snapped. "We go together, it's not safe for one of us to stay. I saw a window in the toilet, go, go, go."

I grabbed his hand and practically ran towards the ground-floor toilet, closing and locking the door behind us. There we fiddled with the clasps on the window. They were stiff and it obviously hadn't been opened for a while. My heart was pounding in my chest at ninety to the dozen and I suspected that Cristos would come crashing through the toilet door with an axe at any moment like something from *The Shining*, yelling, "Heeeeere's Cristos!" But we managed to force the window open and clumsily climb out. Once outside, we didn't pause to look back, we just ran and ran. We didn't stop to see if he was following, we didn't take a rest, we just ran until our legs could take no more and our lungs gave up. Eventually, when we felt a safe distance away, we slowed to a walk and realised we were in the middle of nowhere. Polis was twenty-two miles from the Lighthouse Beach in Paphos, home to my cozy villa, and we had a long walk ahead of us. Dreaming of a nice cup of tea and my bed kept me going! We were just glad to be safe, though having realised what a foolish mistake we had made in our naivety. Fortunately, it wasn't cold, and we had plenty to chat about along the way.

When we reached Paphos, it was morning and the sky had a soft golden glow. It felt like an omen, as if we had been assisted in our safe passage. We were starving, thirsty, tired, but so happy to be alive!

"McDonald's?" Chris asked, pointing to a sign.

I was just about to say, "I don't eat McDonald's," when I paused and then replied, "Actually, that sounds amazing!" I've eaten it about three more times since in twenty-one years. It's something that only ever happens in dire circumstances, so if you ever see me eating a McDonald's, you'll know that something has gone seriously wrong!

Looking back, I can't even recall Chris's face now, but I do remember the thrill I felt escaping the jaws of death. Perhaps I'd just used up one of my nine lives.

Another time, I remember waking up still tipsy from the night before with no purse or phone. I was in such a panic and so angry with myself for getting drunk on cocktails. Luckily, I knew all the bus drivers and one of them allowed me to hop on in the direction of my apartment on the beach free of charge. I had the world's fastest shower and headed off to my hotels to meet my guests.

I was called into the Limassol office later. A guest had complained that I had smelled of alcohol. When it occurred that I had nearly jeopardised my job, I was distraught and couldn't apologise enough. I think my superiors could see how genuinely regretful I was and agreed to keep me on. Looking back, they probably needed me. I had some of the top performance sales for selling trips and mini-cruises to Egypt to my guests, and it would have been difficult to replace an experienced rep so late into the season.

A few days later, I managed to get my phone back via a friend of a friend. A woman then phoned me up checking to see if I was OK. She then said, "And any time you feel like you want to have a sleep under my jeep, you are welcome!" I was mortified. Not knowing what to say, I uttered a pathetic, "OK, thanks."

It was outrageous behaviour on my part, but I was good with the guests, listened to them and did everything within my power to help when there were issues with the hotel.

I remember two couples who made my life hell for a couple of days. It was peak season and Sunworld had double-booked and put them in a lower star hotel. They screamed at me until I was in tears. I went to the loos, washed my face and composed myself. I then explained the situation to the hotel staff and sweet-talked them into giving the guests some free drinks, which made them soften towards me slightly. I sympathised with them, spent hours on the phone trying to fix the issue but couldn't move them for a few days.

Then I decided to change tack and ask them what had drawn them to Cyprus. They said they were thinking of doing a glass bottom boat cruise. That was my opportunity to fix the problem. I regaled them with stories of my trip to Egypt and all the ancient wonders, the pyramids, the artefacts and how relaxing the cruise itself had been. In reality, us reps had been given a tiny cabin with no window, but I envisaged how the guests' experience would be, with glorious views of the Aegean coast and the Med and described it as "an unforgettable adventure and one for the bucket list"! They were sold!

The next morning, they were off on their trip to Egypt. When they returned three days later and were placed in the original hotel they had booked, I went to visit them. They were in much better spirits and couldn't say enough good things about their trip. They also praised me for all my help, apologised profusely for their earlier treatment of me and insisted they would give me glowing feedback upon their return to England. I was just glad that it had all been resolved. Often guests say that and then forget, but they sent wonderful feedback and I felt that I had somewhat redeemed myself after my earlier teenage discretions that involved a bus to Coral Bay!

Another time, I had a female guest complain that her child wouldn't eat the food and didn't like "foreign muck".

You are in bloody Cyprus, I thought. But you can't say that to a guest. An episode of *Fawlty Towers* sprang to mind when Basil Fawlty encounters a similar situation and starts ranting. *What would he like then? Thomas the Tank Engine spaghetti?* Thinking of humorous things helped keep me going when dealing with difficult guests.

This was a tricky one. I tried to discuss this diplomatically with the hotel staff, omitting certain things she had said, but they seemed a little offended. I explained that he was only a little boy and had not eaten anything different before. Eventually, they agreed to make him some simple meals that he would be happy to eat. A lot of reps would have probably said, "Sorry, the menu is the menu," but I liked to fix problems and make sure my guests enjoyed their holiday.

I started to take a lot of satisfaction in doing a good job, but it wasn't always a bed of roses. I remember one day I had an elderly couple staying in one of my hotels and the wife's husband died of old age while they were staying there. I recall thinking she was so brave, as she didn't cry, but I realise now she was probably in shock. I kept feeling like I was welling up and had to compose myself and be strong for her. I got another rep to cover for me and spent the afternoon with her, chatting and arranging her flight back to the UK. She was such a kind lady and tried to tip me, but I refused, insisting it was my job and any decent human would do the same. Things like that are sad, but I was able to make those awful circumstances a little less stressful for her.

Another time, I had taken my guests by coach to a Mezzo restaurant. A mezze is a spectacular feast. It begins with small courses such as a beautifully baked tomato, then followed by strips of delicious halloumi, vine leaves stuffed with fragrant rice and later succulent cuts of meat and locally caught fish. We would also be encouraged to keep the guest glasses filled, as this guaranteed they would return jolly and in good spirits. After the meal, the restaurant owner Spiros would do a Cypriot dance to the sound of "Zorba's Dance" from *Zorba the Greek* and skip around in fake fire. One fella had probably had a few too many ouzos and jumped into the fire to prove it was fake. I saw Spiros's face drop and he walked off upset. It looked like the guest was about to ruin the evening for everyone. I encouraged everyone to jump up and dance with me and soon the incident was forgotten and even the tipsy guest was forgiven by all.

As I got more confident in my job, my sales got even better. I would also tell the guests where the best restaurants were, what to avoid and where to drink – definitely not wherever I was planning to go!

I went from being an awkward teenager who did stupid things to a rep that got on with most of my guests like a house on fire. I would often be on my moped in the town, and I'd hear a guest shout, "Oh look, there's Kora! Hello, Kora, come and say hello if you are in the hotel later."

Chapter 7: It Didn't Feel Like it Oughta in Menorca

I was asked to stay on in Paphos until November. Given I had nearly faced the sack six months earlier, it was an absolute honour to help with the closing down of the resort.

I spent my nineteenth birthday over there and was thrilled when the other reps threw me a surprise birthday party with cake. I was so touched! Birthdays hadn't particularly been a big deal in our family in those days, although there had been a fuss for my eighteenth. It had been a tough year for me after losing Pepsi and I was still suffering from PTSD and trauma from the bullying at school.

One of my dad's friends ran a limo hire company and so he gave my parents a particularly good deal on a limo for the evening of my eighteenth birthday. I dressed in a long black gown and crimped my hair, and I felt like a princess as Matt, my family and I entered the limo. Looking back at the photos now, I cringe. With my blue eyeshadow, I look like some kind of Eighties reject. However, some of those who had caused problems for me witnessed the event and it put me on a real high, not just because I was going out in a limo, but because my family had pulled out all the stops to make my eighteenth special and put a smile on my face. Jock, who owned the limo company, turned up himself, popping on his chauffeur cap and opening the door for me like a gentleman. It was a lovely touch and brings a tear to my eye to remember it. He was a lovely old boy and, unfortunately, he passed on long ago. I will always remember him fondly.

But back to Cyprus – it was November 1999 and still blissfully warm. The sun was a gentle glow that warmed the skin without the fierce heat of the summer. I didn't want to go home, but winter work is short on the ground and the ski jobs tend to go to experienced reps. I worked in the travel shop in Thomas Cook, Wiltshire for the winter.

My colleagues were lovely, and I enjoyed learning about the world. Being a travel agent in a town that is non-too-affluent can be a touch frustrating, as the customers who walked through the door had high expectations and little-to-no budgets. A typical request would be Big Barry and Bertha from Penhill (a rough area in Swindon) who would wander in and say, "We wanna book a 'oliday."

Regardless of who walked through the door and however rude they were, I would be courteous and helpful, and try to find them something, so I would say, "Well, what are your specifications, sir?"

"My speci-what, love?"

"I mean, what is it you would like? Self-catering, half-board, etc.? Are you looking at Spain or Greece …?"

"Right. What it is, love, we want a fortnight in the Maldives, all-inclusive, for two adults and three little 'uns."

"Fantastic, and what budget range am I looking in?"

"About £300, love."

"Oh, I see. Well, I might be able to do you a week's self-catering in Alicante."

At first, I would wonder if it was a wind-up, but they were always completely serious.

About two in twenty customers booked, which was a bit of an anticlimax after my sales records in Cyprus. However, I'm sure I learned the art of patience from my time as a rep and travel agent!

The best customers were those in their twilight years. They would tend to book a Kuoni holiday (exotic and exclusive travel brand) and would create wonderful, tailor-made trips taking in all the sights of the Far East and far-flung corners of the planet. It made me long for another trip myself. I've never enjoyed wintertime and I tend to feel over-tired when deprived of sunlight.

As a travel agent, I was entitled to a generous discount on a holiday and so Matt suggested we go on holiday. There was one holiday in my budget, which was Tunisia, I think it was £200 for a week for two people with my discount and Matt treated me. I nearly fell out of my chair when he offered to pay. I hadn't forgotten Korma-gate, I'll explain this in the next chapter.

Unfortunately, it rained most of the week and it's the sort of place where there is nothing to do if the weather isn't good. We were on half board and didn't have much spending money, so we ended up sat in the hotel room most of the time, going insane with boredom. When we did go out, the jokes from the locals were always the same. They would shout at Matt, "I'll give you twenty camels for your wife!"

I think I laughed, the first thirty times.

More than ever, I wanted to get away for the summer, and so I decided to work as a holiday rep for another season. This time I was sent to Menorca, and it was nothing like I had anticipated. Too much expectation can often lead to disappointment.

Quickly, I made good friends with two reps called Jodie and Amanda, and we got on like a house on fire, which was great for me as I was out of my comfort zone again. We got chatting and joking one eve and they just took me under their wings. Jodie was great fun and talented. She had a beautiful singing voice and would perform amazing backflips during a *Flashdance* routine. She was upbeat and the sort of person you immediately feel good around. Amanda was a real sweetheart too. She was stunning, a softer-looking version of Pamela Anderson with a gentle nature. I felt lucky to have made two good friends so quickly.

In the first month, I was placed in a region, and I started a friendship with the receptionist in one of my hotels. She would teach me Spanish, and I would help her with her English. I was starting to fit in.

Unfortunately, my supervisor Claire took an instant dislike to me. I'd had a hair disaster before I'd flown out a couple of months prior. I'd put some black streaks in my hair and my mother had insisted on taking over and helping me rinse them out, but she had accidentally let the streaks fall against the rest of the hair and it turned half of my blonde hair a weird blueish black!! Claire made my life a misery over this and anything else she could think of. She also moved me to a Spanish town area in a tower block, away from my new friends.

In Claire's eyes, I could do nothing right. When I taught the other reps a dance routine and song from the previous year in Paphos, she scowled at me and said the reps could perform the routine but not me as my dancing wasn't up to scratch. I'm certain this was an unfair assessment as although I'm not the best dancer in the world, I'd performed the dance once a week for nine months the previous year in the rep's cabaret! Then my mum, nan and sisters flew over to see me, and she wouldn't even allow me an afternoon off to spend time with them, even though all my work was up to date and the resort was dead. Claire was a bully and enjoyed pushing people around and hurting them. I hid my true feelings as I didn't want her to know she was affecting me, but I felt miserable and lonely. She had done her best to isolate me from the people I'd bonded with, wouldn't allow me to see family and would speak to me in a condescending manner.

I shared the flat in the townhouse with a woman called Jada who looked like the love child of Neil from *The Young Ones* and Wednesday Addams from the animated version of *The Addams Family*. Her personality was less attractive. It was clear she was pinning her hopes on a supervisory role for the next season and seemed to feel the easiest way to achieve that was by throwing her weight around. During the first couple of days in the new resort, she would fire questions at me.

"Have you spoken to all of your guests?"

"They don't arrive for another two days. My hotels are empty, Jada."

"Have you done your health and safety checks?"

"Yes."

"Properly?"

"Yes."

"Hmmm, well you should come in with me early anyway in the morning and look round your hotels."

Jada also had this unfortunate habit of screwing her mouth up like a bulldog chewing a wasp marinated in lemon juice when she was annoyed, which was most of the time. Her mouth often resembled a cat's bottom hole, all puckered up. These secret thoughts both amused me and kept me sane. I'd often wonder what she would have said if she could have read my thoughts. She'd probably have had steam blow out of her ears!

I also struggled with some of the excursions we were supposed to sell. In Cyprus, I had done well selling blue lagoon boat trips and cruises to Egypt and Israel. However, the excursions on offer at the time in Menorca were sorely lacking. As a group of us reps boarded the coach to go on one of our excursions that we would be selling, a smug Claire told us, "This will be one of your biggest sellers!"

We sat on the coach anticipating something extraordinary, then sat baffled as we pulled up to a boggy patch of ground. We exited the coach and stood around a stagnant duck pond while our speaker told us it was one of the highlights of Menorca. I thought, *If this is one of Menorca's highlights, I'm not keen to see the worse bits!* I kept expecting Jeremy Beadle to jump out at any moment and laugh, "We had you going there for a minute, didn't we?" No such thing happened, and we were indeed expected to sell a trip to a stinky pool of water dressed up as 'The Wonder of Menorca!'

Hoping things might get better when my first guests finally arrived, I was excited to meet them in the hope I might meet some normal human beings, and they were sweet. There was an elderly couple in their seventies, another couple in their sixties and a family with a lady in a wheelchair with osteoporosis. They had all been to Menorca year after year and didn't want for much. They didn't need or want anything from me and so I was at a loose end. When my shift was due to end, Claire called me at the hotel. "How many trips have you sold?" she demanded.

"Well, none, you see …"

"That's not good enough!"

"My two elderly couples said they have seen it all before and the other family has a lady in a wheelchair with osteoporosis. They said they don't want to risk her going on an unnecessary coach trip."

"You will stay in your hotel until you have sold some trips!" she snapped down the phone.

It didn't make a difference, no one was going to buy a trip. I just ended up staying in the hotel for longer that evening, reading a book and occasionally making small talk with anyone who walked past me.

It was my sister who made me see sense in the end.

"Why the hell are you bending over backwards for some piece of work who wouldn't even let you have an afternoon off to see your family, who flew all the way from England to see you? Tell her to stick it!"

I decided that my sister was right. Not being able to see my family took the biscuit, as the resort wasn't busy. I tried speaking with Claire, but she'd shut me down and dismiss me. After much deliberation, I realised that this wasn't going to work out. I applied as an entertainer in one of the hotels and wrote a letter of resignation which I handed to Claire.

She turned her back to me and read the letter. Even from behind I could see her trying to conceal her anger. Her hands were twitching, her breath became more ragged, and her shoulders hunched. Eventually, she put the letter down and said, "Come and see me tomorrow."

The next day, I was back in her office expecting her to hand over my passport and say I had to work a month's notice. What came out of her mouth absolutely stunned me.

"I am not prepared to accept your notice," she trilled, her eyes narrowing. "Perhaps you haven't quite settled in yet and are finding the work schedule a struggle, but in time you will learn our way of doing things. We are not like Cyprus here and deal with things differently, but you'll get up to speed. I know you can become a better rep."

I was utterly gobsmacked! Not only had she refused my resignation, but she had also delivered a scathing put-down and attempted to turn it all back on me. Normally I was a meek little thing, but there was only so much I was prepared to take. I felt a fire in my belly and a surge of energy. I looked into her eyes, smiled and said, "See you tomorrow."

With that, I turned and left the office.

Back at the townhouse that night, I was seething. It was a poky little house in a high-rise block, old and worn with little light in the rooms. There were long black curtains which hung from the window, tattered and dirty, and when you opened them thick clouds of dust would billow out of them. The windows were smeared and filthy, and the town below looked grim, a grey landscape with the occasional tobacco store or scruffy side-street café on a busy road.

There were no nearby shops, and I was completely isolated from civilisation. There wasn't even anywhere to get food from, and I was hungry most of the time. Just remembering it twenty-one years on gives me the creeps and a feeling of dread in the pit of my stomach.

I felt as if I was being held hostage. I was being bullied by my boss, wasn't allowed to see my family and my passport was being kept from me. Plus, I had no way to call or contact my family. In Cyprus, you could pay to use the hotel phones to stay in contact with family. If it was a brief call, they would often let you off and not charge you.

I was kept from seeing or socialising with other people, apart from the few elderly guests in my hotel. Claire wanted me as her little slave, and I couldn't help but think of Stephen King's novel *Misery*. In the book, an author has a car crash in the snow and is injured, then Annie Wilkes, who turns out to be a big fan, finds him in the snow and saves him from death's door. At first, he is thankful, but then Annie does everything in her power to gaslight the author and keep him there. She tells him the snow is too deep, and the power is all out, so he can't make a phone call. When he finds out that she is lying, she smashes his feet in. Feet aside, I was down a rabbit hole in the land of *Misery* with my very own Annie!

In the book, the author Paul Sheldon must use all of his wits to escape, and I wondered how an author would escape this predicament.

By George, that's it! I thought. *I shall pen a strongly worded letter that she cannot fight.* I was small in stature and shy, but the pen was my sword. When I enter battle with my mighty pen, I fight to the death, and none shall pass!

I can't remember the exact words I wrote, but they were along the lines of this:

Dear Claire,

I recently delivered my notice of resignation letter to yourself, due to many ongoing issues that we've been unable to reach an agreement on. In our meeting yesterday, you stated you will not accept my resignation and are keeping hold of my passport. I am not sure if you are familiar with employment law, but it states that once notice is given, it cannot be refused by an employer. Upon giving you my notice, it is reasonable that I should serve a notice period, but it is not reasonable to detain me against my will. My family are extremely distressed at these recent events and are talking about going to the British Embassy and the English tabloids and telling them I'm being held hostage. Of course, I've told them that I'm sure this is all a silly misunderstanding and that we can come to a reasonable agreement.

One small concern that I should raise, my British passport is my personal property and if you have no valid reason for detaining it, then I kindly ask you to return it to me.

Yours sincerely,

Kora

I dropped it into her pigeonhole and crossed my fingers, my eyes flicking towards the heavens.

The next day, Claire had one of her lackeys order me to go to her office. Sensing something had changed, I entered, wary. She wouldn't look at me and her movements were forced and hurried. She was clearly holding down a whole lot of rage. She asked me to sit down and practically threw my passport at me across the desk. Her eyes fixed on a point in the distance, she snapped, "I will arrange for your notice to begin from today. You will need to complete four weeks' notice to allow us to replace you."

I could have argued that my notice started the day before, but I could see no reason to split hairs.

Only then did she look at me through slanted eyes, the corners of her mouth tight in a grimace.

"Thank you, Claire, for everything you've taught me," I smiled, picking up the passport. Then I skipped happily out of the room and closed the door softly.

The pen really is mightier than the sword, I thought to myself.

Chapter 8: A Proposal and Too Many Toilet Breaks

A couple of weeks before I was due to leave the island, Matt flew out and proposed to me. We were sat on the terrace of a pizza restaurant on a balmy summer evening when he popped out a platinum gold ring, with a cute, tiny stone at its centre. He dropped to one knee and asked me to marry him, and I flung my arms around him and agreed.

I think I had planted the seed in his head, which was foolish. I did love him, but I was only nineteen and I naively thought I was ready. In hindsight, it was all immature. I didn't even know what my plan was when I flew back to England, and we had no plans to move in together. Matt was lovely, but when it came to money, he was tighter than a ferret's bottom. Every penny of his money went on nights out with the lads.

On one of my previous birthdays, he had offered to take me out and celebrate, and he'd taken me to a local curry house, ordered one Korma and one boiled rice all to the sum of £5, then said I wouldn't eat that much and poured most of it onto his own plate. He had a well-paid job, but he was extremely frugal. For birthdays or Christmases, he would spend about £3 on a little teddy bear for me from Treats, or sometimes he'd make a mix tape instead. There were few occasions when he took me out, although his parents took me to a Chinese buffet once or twice and insisted on paying for me. They were a kind and lovely couple and I felt awkward when they insisted on paying. Matt would always go up to the buffet about four times and heap his plate with a mountain of food, sweet and sour pork balls bouncing off his plate behind him. I'm surprised the restaurant owners didn't ban us for cutting into their profits.

I was glad to get home to England initially. It was nice to spend some time with Matt, catch up with everyone and see Poppy and Pebbles, oh and the family!

My enthusiasm for being back in Swindon wore off quickly! Being back and finding temporary work was an anticlimax. I signed up with a recruitment agency and temped for a while – office work, waitressing, anything that came up. I spent about three weeks at Thames Water saying, "Good afternoon, would you like to be put through to billing or leakages?"

Little did I know that less than ten years later, I would be causing 'leakages' myself when talking naughty to men on the phone, who paid £1.99 per minute for the privilege.

The work I did at Thames Water was brainless work and frustrated me. What really pushed me to quit though was when a supervisor told me that I had taken too many toilet breaks that day. We had to clock in and out every time we visited the loo and she had tallied up my timings and deduced that ten minutes per day was over the allocated time allowed for urination. To be fair, I had been drinking a lot more water as an excuse to leave that godforsaken hell hole for a few extra minutes, but I felt that I was being treated like a robot. I just wasn't suited to that kind of role, so it was for the best when I handed in my notice, and a week later I was free from the tyranny of scheduling my bladder appointments!

There were few opportunities in Swindon for a person to progress and when talking of my frustrations to my good friend Ella, she suggested I go to university. I had always assumed university was for rich kids, but she told me you could get a student loan to cover your university fees. I reasoned I could also get part-time work too to help me manage, so I applied to three different universities to study Media Writing and was delighted to gain a place at Southampton Institute. Now my crazy adventures were about to start!

Chapter 9:
Hedonism in Hampshire

2000

We arrived at my halls of residence in Southampton and after a walk around, I waved my tearful goodbyes to my sister, brother-in-law and Matt, who had helped me with my things. Part of me was sad to see them leave, but a bigger part of me was excited to start the academic year. We were scheduled to meet downstairs later that evening and the plan was to head down to one of the local bars. I was a complete nervous wreck. Socialising was not my strong point. If someone approached me, I could manage, but the thought of starting a conversation with a stranger brought back all my fears of rejection. The bullying at school had deeply affected me and I struggled to assert myself.

I walked down to the halls entrance and a crowd was starting to gather. Students were laughing and joking, and many had seemed to make acquaintances already. The sound of groups of people laughing was triggering and took me back to my schooldays when the laughter was aimed at me. I twisted my fingers awkwardly, a sick feeling swirling round my stomach. My arms and legs took on the consistency of jelly and for a moment I thought about darting back to the safety of my private room and hiding out.

This is ridiculous! I admonished myself. *You hosted welcome meetings for up to fifty people in Cyprus, you can do this.*

I suppose the difference was I felt useful to the guests, I was giving them information, whereas being in a sea of students was unfamiliar to me. I gnawed at my fingernails, and my legs were like dead weights. Then I was struck by a possible worse fate – the thought of spending the next three years being a loner and not having any friends. I had to break the mould and act.

The two girls stood next to me were sticking together for comfort, as their body language matched mine, their arms huddled close to their bodies. They watched everyone else instead of talking and seemed as apprehensive as I felt. I pondered – everything I thought of saying sounded stupid – but I blurted out, "I hope they haven't forgotten us; do you think we'll still be here at midnight?"

They turned and laughed with me, not at me fortunately. "Oh, I do hope not," they chuckled.

I'd gotten away with it; they hadn't sneered at me, or worse, turned away as if I was a speck of dust.

"Me too," I joked, "I don't fancy sleeping out here tonight."

It was a lame joke and none of this came naturally to me, but it broke the ice and we got chatting. When it was time to leave, we all walked together and ordered a drink in the bar. After a couple of drinks, my anxieties would all start to flow away, and I found myself chatting to people more easily. More people came up to me to chat and I ended up heading to another bar with a big group of students. This was so different to my life in Swindon; people were so open and friendly. I didn't feel ostracised or unwelcome. Moving into my halls of residence, I made more friends; there was Smoky – who became one of my best male friends for many years – Kaylie, Jemma, Sara and Loulou. Most of them were from middle-class backgrounds and quite serious most of the time, apart from Smoky who was a real joker and had me in fits of laughter.

One evening, I was sat in the shared kitchen eating carrots as I was convinced my size six figure was humungous, when a tall, black guy with a contagious grin called Andre popped in with a bunch of flyers. He was promoting for a club night called 'Derelict' and asked me if I liked hard house and trance. Well, that was the start of a beautiful friendship. I did end up going to the club on many occasions and became a regular on the clubbing scene. Twenty years later, Andre and I are closer than ever, and he is one of the smartest, funniest people I have ever met. It's funny how the roads in life fork off in different directions and intertwine.

At uni, I was never short of someone to hang out with or make merry with, and my confidence grew. Don't get me wrong, often inside I still experienced that horrible swirling sickness, but I now had the strength to fight it and argue with the voices that told me I wasn't good enough. I had spent my whole life thinking that I wasn't interesting and that my opinions were not valid, but I was starting to see those thoughts were simply the product of low self-esteem and my childhood.

I loved my uni course and spent a lot of time in the library; I just loved the quietness and being surrounded by books. Don't get me wrong, I enjoyed a good night out and copious amounts of cheap student alcohol, but if I ever just wanted some me-time, the library would be where I headed off to. I loved the look of it, all those book-lined shelves on so many fascinating topics, the smell of the bound leathers and a feeling of stability and safety. If there had been a zombie apocalypse between 2000 and 2003, I would probably have holed myself up in the library, and my weapons of choice would have been books. Either that or I would have headed to the refectory, where they made a mean blueberry muffin!

In the campus library, no one called me a geek, a swot or a goody-goody; they just looked up and smiled, and I would smile back. I read up on all sorts of subjects, everything from psychology and philosophy, through to subcultures, history, society and club cultures. It opened my mind like a blossoming flower, and it was wonderful to realise that there were so many non-judgmental people out there. People that didn't think that life started and ended with an office job and having 2.4 children. People that encouraged your dreams and didn't try to belittle them. A couple of months into my course, I realised that I'd already got my money's worth. It had helped me realise that the world was a different place to the one I'd envisioned as a lonely sixteen-year-old.

We were actively encouraged to join some student societies to give us a broader experience of different industries. I had always had an avid interest in radio, and so I joined the student radio station, Star AM. I went to regular student radio meetings and hosted two shows per week. One was a playlist show where I would play the latest charts and then I'd do my own dance show on a Friday night. This was fun but after a while I needed a little more excitement and I decided to do something no one else was doing at the station. I invited various up-and-coming DJs to play on my show. They were happy to get the airtime and I enjoyed helping to create something people enjoyed. I'd run competitions for free mix CDs and students would often pop notes under the door saying they loved the 'banging tunes' my DJs and I played on my show. A warm swell filled my heart; people were expressing gratitude and pleasure at something I made happen, which was a good feeling. This is an example of the more positive side of my people-pleasing tendencies.

I'd met a lot of the DJs through the clubbing scene and some of the message boards I used. This was pre-Facebook and Twitter, and so young people tended to use niche forums such as music or film sites.

***

The first time I tried Ecstasy was mind-blowing. All my friends had done it already, but I wanted to know what I was taking first before I dabbled. I headed back into the library and found some books on drug culture. I even had to be a geek about getting wrecked! In the library, I found various texts that referred to Ecstasy. Many academics at the time were saying that it was relatively harmless and that it could help sufferers of PTSD. I wondered if it could help me.

A week later, I decided to take the plunge and after a long

debate with my good friend Loulou, we agreed it would be best if I started with a quarter of a tab to see how it affected me. I swallowed a bit of the pill and looked at my friends, who were already high. They all had that sweet, dreamy stare on their faces, the soft smile of the *Mona Lisa* and a contentedness about them. If Ecstasy had a symbol of its own, it would be two stickmen hugging. While you are under its influence, you are overwhelmed by warm feelings of affection radiating out towards the world and everyone in it. After a while, my vision slightly altered. You know on a hot day when you look at an air vent and you can see the heatwaves? It was a little like that. The atmosphere thickened and I felt connected with everyone in the room. Smiling at my friend Lou, I said, "You're the best."

She laughed and said, "You are all loved up on Ecstasy, babe, I love you too! I knew you'd like it!"

Like it, I bloody loved it! For years, I had carried a heavy heart, gripped by a terror that something was about to go wrong, and I had an inexplicable distrust of people. The Ecstasy in my system washed all of that away and I felt a deep contentment and a sense of being alive. All at once, I felt as if I was being cuddled by a fluffy cloud and bathed in a ray of sunshine. I was the joyous heartbeat at the centre of a conscious, living universe. My heart soared and my body moved in harmony with the music, sounds that tapped into my soul and reached new heights of consciousness I had never known before. It was as if the music spoke to me, taking me on a beautiful journey with peaks and dips with the sweetest melodies.

Suddenly, everything made sense. Everything was connected and I wasn't an outsider, I was part of the thrum, a cog in a giant mechanism that moved along harmoniously. I was stunned by the notions and thoughts that slid into my mind, stories of the universe. It seemed that every possibility would be played out to infinity in the universe and even its darkest times would be followed by a glorious resolution. I saw hope and love in everything, love at the core of every action and outcome, and love as our planet's saviour.

A short time later, I was totally mashed and, in my opinion, throwing some killer moves on the dance floor! I liked to imagine myself as an ethereal, golden-haired pixie on the dance floor, shining radiantly, my eyes wide in revelation. I suspect I better resembled a glassy-eyed fruit loop, contorting my face into ridiculous expressions and jumping around like I had an earwig up my trouser leg. However, nobody judged; we were all there for the same reason, to connect and escape our troubles for an evening. Taking Ecstasy was the pharmaceutical equivalent of going to your happy place, checking your brain in for a spa mini-break or popping your past traumas into the local sanctuary for twenty-four hours. I went home with the other ¾ of the pill in my pocket. Just that ¼ was enough to get me really bamboozled. I suppose I was what you might call a lightweight.

A group of us started to go clubbing every few weeks. We would hit a club, dance our little socks off and then go back to an after party. The after parties were a mixed bunch. There would always be some insecure wise guy at the centre telling stories and making jokes. He would be snorting lines, hollering, and saying something along the lines of, "Everybody look at me."

A couple of potheads to the side would titter nervously from time to time, though they appeared to have no idea what was going on. One of them would always be a real philosopher and know how to obtain world peace and would preach to his circle. His disciples would nod along in awe. This character took many shapes, but he often went for the traditional Jesus look, with long hair, and carried a guitar. If anyone offered a counter theory, his stock response would be, "I'm not here for war, man, I'm here to spread the love."

There would usually be a guy in the room going, "I'm mental, me! Give me a dare!" He would end up doing something like eating dog food, snorting a crushed-up Ecstasy pill or some other high jinks that would have a group of lads laughing and egging him on. At the time, a lot of these characters probably came across as mere attention seekers. In hindsight, I think (like myself) they were lost children. They were looking to have their needs validated and to escape their past traumas. They were self-medicating and seeking out the people they thought would give them the love they desired.

Even when things got silly, it was mostly harmless fun and there was never any violence or people partaking in physically dangerous activities. Pill-heads tend to revert to a child-like state when under the influence. Everything becomes shiny and new again and it's hard for even the most Machiavellian character to be an arsehole when on E, although there were a couple of people who gave it their best shot!

Mixing between groups was an education in itself. I loved the excitement of hearing different conversations and mindsets, and bonding with different people.

After the after party, there would be the comedown party. As the effects of Ecstasy wear off, the effects of the comedown amplify. Depending on your state of mind, circumstances and the company you keep, this can vary between a sleepy, floaty vibe to a feeling of impending doom. Therefore, ravers would often hang out together afterwards and feel soothed by the presence of like-minded spirits. At the time, I was more acquainted with the former, fluffy vibe and enjoyed these hangouts. We'd watch movies, listen to music and chat until we all fell asleep cuddling a cushion in someone's hall of residence.

I dabbled with other types of herb and chemicals too while at uni but drew the line at hard drugs. I was a risk-taker, but not reckless. Pot did absolutely nothing for me. Attending a couple of pot parties, I sat there scratching my head and wondering what the thrill was in smoking a bong and 'pull a whitey' (feeling extremely sick and out of it). The feeling of having my brain scrambled was extremely unpleasant and I detached myself from the reefer crowd. It just seemed like an immense waste of time for me.

One particularly memorable event took place in my second year when I lived in a student house share with my then-boyfriend

Len and various friends. Liam, a guy in our friendship circle, brought some mushrooms down from Yorkshire and was giving them out. I had recently read that the taste alone could make you want to vomit and that the best way to prepare them was to boil them up with red wine, and delicately sip the noxious liquid. My suggestion was met with much enthusiasm and soon British-grown psychoactive mushrooms were floating around in a pan of cheap red wine, which was barely palatable to start with. I insisted that the offending liquid was put into a blender to create a smooth texture – we were students, not savages!

The brew was poured into glasses while there were puns thrown around about being a fun-guy, or there not being mush-room! Groans followed. We all sipped our drink expectantly, looking around at each other and waiting for something to happen. There were many statements uttered, such as, "I don't feel anything yet?" "I don't think it's working." "Are these mushrooms duds?"

The high from mushrooms came on slowly to start with. The first thing I noticed as I said "I'm not feeling anything yet" was the bizarre sound of my own voice. It sounded squeakier, like a cartoon character's voice. A burst of giggles emitted from my throat. All my friends and acquaintances were smiling and laughing too and seemed to be acting differently. A shadow seemed to move in the corner of my eye and the colour and light in the room shifted subtly. I felt playful, like an enchanted being in a magical world. Cracking jokes, I danced around, although I can't remember what I said. For all I know, it could have been, "Put a pickle on the radio." Everyone giggled. They could have been laughing at my hilarious joke, or more likely a dancing hallucination of Popeye the Sailor Man getting stoned on a pipe of spinach!

My hearing adjusted and an incoming high frequency rang through my ears, then the colour shifts became more pronounced and the world was suddenly in technicolour. I often wonder if the makers of *The Wizard of Oz* were inspired by hallucinogenics, as the dramatic shift in colours was akin to Dorothy travelling from Kansas to Oz.

They weren't like the mushrooms you get in Amsterdam that have people projectile vomiting up the walls and spiralling into an intense trip. These were fluffy and fun and included an elevated mood and beautiful psychedelic visuals. I'm sure every trip is different, but for me, there were dancing flowers with smiley faces on them, giggling lips, geometric patterns, sprinkles of light and dancing cartoon characters. There were also beautifully choreo-graphed dancing lights and words in the air that looked like they had come out of a 1960s-themed cartoon, with big puffy orange words like 'FUNKY' and 'WOW' which span around 360 degrees vertically and horizontally and increased and decreased in size. My brain was certainly working at a high capacity, although if you would have asked me what I thought about hot political issues at the time, I would have no doubt spouted some sort of nonsense about hugging everybody.

My brainwave patterns changed once more, and my thoughts took another shift. I was seeing symbolism in everything. It's like the universe was telling me that everything had a purpose, that every event, action and living creature was filled with meaning. I felt as if I could tap into the energy and secrets at the core of the universe itself. I visualised the Earth and felt its sadness and its love simultaneously. At this stage of my trip, the Earth seemed to take on the role of mother to all its inhabitants and seemingly radiated a message that us children must learn to live more harmoniously, but Earth would still love us.

I felt a stronger connection to nature, as if everything was how it was meant to be, and I pondered how us humans are so privileged to live on such a beautiful planet and felt deeply sorry for how we pillage Earth. During this trip, I decided I would put more effort into treating the planet kindlier. My feelings of compassion for Earth and everything on it intensified. I had the feeling that I was supposed to ingest the mushrooms on this day so they could impart their wisdom to me. I felt the message I was to learn was to spread kindness, and light everyone's path with sunshine. It was stuff I already knew subconsciously perhaps, but

I now felt it on such a deep level, it was almost as if it engraved its symbolic coding onto the blueprint of my mind.

Of course, when people take any kind of drug, they might not have a pleasant trip. The experience depends on so many factors and caution should be exercised. In fact, I'd go as far as to say don't do drugs at all! Yes, I know that's hypocritical, as I've done them myself, but I feel that drugs are more contaminated these days, that there are less trustworthy people distributing them; the world is a somewhat darker place and mental illness is a lot more prevalent. Drugs have the power to tip someone completely over the edge if they are in the wrong frame of mind. A sickening event took place when I was in Ibiza in 2000. A group of us were walking back from a club giggling and laughing, only to see the area full of police. Some clubber had taken a dive off the balcony and word on the street was that he had passed away. Drugs can make you lose your inhibitions or fears, and make you act impulsively. For some people that may not be a noticeable difference if you have a strong sense of self or a lot of self-control, but it can cause some to act recklessly. There are thousands of people that take clubbing drugs, then go home and pop a film on. At the other end of the scale, there's the minority that jump off balconies or take their own lives. It's impossible to know if the drug is likely to trigger a mental health condition, so it is always a gamble.

My dear reader, you may choose to disregard my advice, and if you do, then please at least research what you are doing first, and make sure you are with good people who love you.

When someone has a bad trip, they may feel as if they have gone to hell and back ... or if they are unlucky, just hell with no return. I am in no way endorsing drugs. They can be extremely mind-altering, and I reiterate they should never be taken by anyone that suffers from mental health issues.

I didn't make my decision to try hallucinogenic substances lightly. I had read a great deal of literature and academic journals about the effects and consequences of ingesting psychoactive drugs and made a calculated decision. Many scientists at the time were starting to realise that some hallucinogenics which contained Psilocybin could have a positive effect on the mind, and there were various studies that showed that they could assist in healing past traumas. Well, I didn't have a scientist to hand, but I certainly had some past traumas.

Even though I'd read many self-help books that helped me on the surface, I felt as if a lot of my issues were impossible to heal. I felt like I was climbing a mountain with no top, and self-medicating seemed like a viable option at the time. Overall, my mushroom experience left me feeling as if something had shifted inside me; the hard rock that weighed me down began to lift away a little. This probably wouldn't work for a lot of people, and you shouldn't try this at home if you have never taken a hallucinogenic, but it is worth reading some of the more up-to-date studies about this if you suffer from PTSD or trauma. I believe nowadays you can even discuss such things with your GP and ask to get involved with case studies or attend specialist clinics. The other day, I read an article about a clinic in Bristol that does this. There are also shamanic healers on the Internet who have studied for years in healing and work with psychoactives. Back when I was a troubled young person, anxiety and trauma were almost a taboo topic. Now there is a lot more support for people going through troubled times. The media didn't help either and demonised drugs and those that used them recreationally.

I remember back in the Nineties, the media used to love to lead with headlines such as "Teen Smokes Pot and Attacks Grandmother" or "Cannabis – the gateway drug". Cannabis, however, is not a gateway drug. *Trauma* is a gateway drug. Low self-esteem is a gateway drug. Feeling worthless is a gateway drug. Young people who are struggling mentally often look for a way to escape their own critical inner thoughts and feelings of impending doom, and self-medicating can feel like an answer to these issues. I was one of the lucky ones because I was on a university course I loved and had some good people around me, but I can see how it's possible for others to fall deep down the rabbit hole if they don't have an anchor to the real world.

To me, trauma felt like a buried rock that threatened to bubble back up if I was feeling particularly stressed out. Sometimes I might party, but other times I would play babysitter to my raver friends, make cups of tea and give a reassuring hug if they didn't seem to be having a good time. On other occasions, I would go to bed with a good book, or a good friend! I always sought balance. This was my way of ensuring I didn't lose control and fall down the rabbit hole.

Chapter 10: Clubs and a Naughty Mermaid

Derelict was a club night in Southampton where hard trance and hard house DJs played, such as Andy Farley, Ed Real, Lisa Lashes and more besides. The first time I went with my friend Fleur, and I was blown away by the excitement of it all. She advised I wear hot pants, as it would get quite hot on the dance floor. I opted for short, white-hot pants and a matching halter-neck top, which was a great call under the Ultraviolet (UV) lights, and I managed to pick them up for a great price. Saving money is always at the front of your mind as a student.

At the front of the room, the DJ was going hell for leather on the decks and blasting out tunes to a crowd of students, who were reaching for the sky and dancing their little pants off. The room was bathed in UV light and streamers hung from the ceiling. To the side of the room, there was a stand where a lady clad in fluorescent clothing painted patterns in UV paint on some of the revellers' faces. Many of the crowd had made or customised their own outfits, consisting of fluffy materials in bright neon yellows, pinks and greens, metallic designs, bikini tops, little rara skirts, fluffy booties, combat trousers and Cyberdog tops. It was as if a rainbow had spilled down from above and been absorbed by the revellers below. More enchanting were their radiant faces, eyes wide with blissful expressions. Later, at say 4 a.m. in the morning on one of these nights, you would see some rather disturbing, contorted faces when too many drugs had been taken and the revellers looked rather messed up! A stark contrast from the fresh, radiant skin, glowing eyes, white teeth and contagious smiles you saw at 9 p.m.

Clubbing, I felt confident. I had always struggled to fit in, but now I was part of something. I was part of the clubbing community. It's a bit sad that I felt I needed to belong to a group rather than being happy doing my own thing, but it was all part of the learning curve.

It was at Derelict I met Len the promoter. Initially, he struck me as quite funny and extroverted. I was single again by this point as the distance between me and Matt was proving too problematic for us, and I hadn't seriously dated anyone since. I can't even remember how we broke up. I think we just stopped contacting each other.

Len always chatted to me at the club. He wasn't much to look at with his fine, limp hair, skinny body and large hooked nose, but there was something about him that appealed to me … my low self-esteem perhaps. When I spent time with him, I was always entertained. We often ended back at the same parties and one night a group of us all ended up back at his place, talking into the small hours. Four of us fell asleep on his bed and when I awoke, he'd entwined his feet with mine. As I left, we were talking about food, and I said I liked making curries. He cheekily joked, "I'll be round tomorrow night for one then," and I quipped, "OK, it's your funeral."

The following night, he came round and tried my home-made Chicken Madras, and lived to tell the tale. Then he invited me on a 'proper date' Saturday night.

He pulled out all the stops for our date, took me to an Italian restaurant and then got us a room for the evening in his aunty's hotel. Looking back, it was extremely presumptuous of him to assume I would share a room with him, but at the time I was besotted and didn't have the faintest clue about the rules of dating. No one had ever seemed this fascinated by me, and I was love-bombed into a fast relationship. Len regaled me with witty stories about his family and Sicilian connections, while we sank a couple of bottles of wine and dined on some delicious Italian food. I was extremely squiffy by the time we headed back to the hotel, and we engaged in some highly charged sex.

We became a couple pretty much straight away and I often stayed over at his if I didn't have early lectures the next day. At the time, everyone around me was hooking up and so I didn't even question if it seemed a little fast. I just assumed that's what people did.

He introduced me to his mother Lila quite quickly and from then on insisted I accompany him to all his meetings with his mother, which was met with my protests, but I always ended up giving in. I'm sure it was a form of triangulation designed to both antagonise his mother, and to throw me to the lions simultane-ously. She was a terrifying woman with blow-dried, golden-brown hair, and had the voice of a sixty-cigarettes-a-day smoker. In front of Len, she was all sweetness and light, "Oh darling, darling, you must have some champagne, you must!" Whenever Len wasn't in earshot, she would make digs and say things such as, "It's not that I don't like you, darling, but I would love to have my little boy to myself sometimes!" Her little boy was twenty-six and a mature student compared to the rest of us, but the way she spoke about him was as if he was her precious little angel that could do no wrong.

Len suspected that in the past his mother was a lady who 'entertained clients'. To what degree she entertained them I do not know or care, but I could see she could be charming when she chose to switch it on. Len's father, a Sicilian man, had left many years before, and Len would have me believe that he was part of the Sicilian mafia, although I think that was certainly fantasy on his part. Perhaps I am mistaken, but I have always been of the impression that mafioso, the original gangsters, tended to be family orientated. Either way, much of the story didn't seem to ring true and was based on empty words with no substance.

If Lila was at times self-absorbed and self-serving, Len was at the upper end of the Narcissism spectrum. He could be having a joke with you one minute, then from nowhere would fly into a rage and spit cruel, vicious words. Later, I learned that he would manufacture these arguments as an excuse to storm off and do what he wanted, leaving me bewildered and wondering what the hell had just happened.

I was rather fond of Len's aunty, who was a kind lady and always good to me. Their family friend Linda was also sweet. At Len's family dinner, I had been summoned by the she-devil herself to attend a meal in a local restaurant one evening, and not wanting to create a conflict, I went along with it. Linda watched as Lila made disparaging remarks towards me and I sat there willing the earth to swallow me up. Every word felt like a slap in the face, and I cringed inwardly, fidgeting in my chair. My legs tingled with the urge to run, and I resisted, not wanting to cause a scene. Linda must have seen my discomfort, as she turned and whispered into my ear, "Don't worry, she's just jealous of you."

Before, I had tried to justify Lila's cruel words by thinking I was imagining their intent or overreacting. Linda's reassurances validated my thoughts and I started to realise that this family was not just dysfunctional, they were not like most people. There was something almost reptilian about their need to control and damage others. When it came to affairs of the heart, I was a slow learner. It took me a while to extricate myself from the savage grip of Len and his motley crew.

It was a hellish journey, but in such a remarkable way. Imagine a rollercoaster, where at the top of every peak there are sparkles, fireworks and magic, then in the dips there are monsters, extreme darkness and demonic entities. That was our relationship, and I never knew if we would be on a peak or in a dip. We could rise and fall several times in one day. I knew it wasn't normal, but I just didn't realise how toxic it was. Although Len was far worse, the relationship wasn't that dissimilar to that of my parents and how my dad would treat my mother.

As a promoter, Len could get us VIP entry into clubs all over the country. I was working for Derelict now as their media manager. This role involved me sending the club listings to magazines such as *Mixmag*, promoting the event, writing pieces for some of the local student magazines and papers, and planning forthcoming events. It was a bonus if I ever got paid. The once or twice he threw a tenner my way, he made sure he got it back by using up my phone credit or insisting I buy him food or fags. When we went out, Len introduced me as his P.A., which I thought was hilarious. He felt it made him look more important to attend nights with a P.A. on hand, but seriously, who takes their P.A. clubbing with them? No one!

One night, we headed out to the Aquarium in London, known for having an indoor pool. I wore a silver PVC zip-up halter top and matching hot pants, thinking a waterproof costume would be ideal. It didn't occur to me to take a swimsuit. When I sat on the side of the pool to slip into the water, a mean-spirited woman barked at me. "No clothing in the pool." I explained that it was waterproof, but she wasn't having it. After a brief interaction, Len said, "Can she go in if she takes it off and just wears her thong?" A tall, broad lifeguard waded into the conversation and grinned, "Absolutely."

Having been overruled by someone who was obviously her superior, the woman fell silent, but her scowl spoke volumes.

"I can't ..." I stuttered, feeling embarrassed. Andre and a couple of our mates joined in the banter, "Go on, show that snotty old boot! Get in the pool. She spoke to you like shit, don't let her ruin your night."

Emboldened by the pep talk, I slipped out of my top and shorts, so I was left wearing a tiny black thong. With my palms covering my chest, I quickly jumped into the water and splashed right under. When I came back up again, I was giggling manically. I thought of all the nasty jibes I'd had directed at me over the years and wished I could have been as brave back then. I'd stood up for myself; I'd not been put off by this harsh-faced, acid-tongued woman. I'd been given the loophole and had taken advantage of it. That's the thing, sometimes being with Len could be oddly empowering, at least in my mind back then. He would give with one hand, then take it away with the other.

The water was divine, and we splashed about for a while, giggling and joking. I had never been in a pool inside a club before and it was a novel experience, swimming while listening to the timely beats. Eventually, we got out and I slipped back into my clothing, the horrible woman forgotten.

Moral of this story: If someone bullies you and expects you to be meek, do the unexpected. It will absolutely confuse the hell out of them!

Chapter 11: Sicilian Swine

Various part-time jobs kept me on my toes, everything from working in the university media office through to waitressing at Ascot and Goodwood and silver service in fancy hotels. Silver service I was hopeless at and struggled with the heavy plates, being a size six and weighing around seven stone five (about a stone and a half less than I do now!). At a posh corporate do I was working at, I managed to drop a lamb chop in a well-to-do lady's lap. I couldn't apologise enough, but she simply patted herself down in the manner that frightfully posh people do and looked exasperated. While I wasn't great at serving, I was friendly, approachable and eager to help, so I was often found other duties to do, and I was never short of work.

Term passed quickly and summer had arrived. My student loan and part-time jobs didn't really stretch to covering my expensive halls of residence over the summer, and it was looking as if I might have to go back home till term started. The thought of being back with my feuding family, the drunken Saturday nights, arguments and hostility, gave me that familiar feeling of drunken butterflies crashing around my tummy.

"Why don't you move in with me for the summer?" suggested Len. "You can buy the food."

Len lived in a shared student house that was owned by his mother, and I was to share his small attic room. It sounded fair and so I agreed. I didn't realise that it would mean becoming Len's personal ATM whenever he wanted drink, drugs, food or money for God knows what.

He didn't change overnight, it was gradual, the demands, the bullying. He would start shouting about something, storm out and not come back till the next morning.

Then, one day he was full of smiles and suggested we fly to Ibiza for the summer to spend some quality time together. I assumed he was stressed about his exam results. He never showed me the paper and said he'd passed, but I still made excuses for his behaviour.

With Len nudging me and pulling my strings, I arranged a bank overdraft to pay for our flights and a place to stay. We'd sometimes go to the beach or would explore the island on mopeds, and over there we met up with Sarah and her boyfriend Ian, Andre and our friend Shenny from Gibraltar. We'd blag tickets into Pascha, Manumission and Space, headlined by the UK's hottest DJs. It should have been the time of my life, on summer vacation on a beautiful Spanish island, but Len was often unbearable. He would sink into a mood and then disappear for the evening. My suspicions were that he was sleeping with other women, but I couldn't prove it, as he hid every shred of evidence.

Keeping myself busy, I took a couple of jobs while I was over there, selling shots of Tequila in clubs and bars. I handed out flyers for various clubs and worked as a PR girl and security guard for an all-female club night called 'Charleys Angelz'. I know it sounds crazy, little me as a security guard, but I was good at it. There was a side room in the club where guys could buy lap dances with some of the girls, and my job was to organise the queue and ensure that the guys didn't get 'overexcited'!

Ibiza is a party island where people go to have fun, so often a little joke and a bit of banter were enough to keep them in line. I would say things like, "Come on, now, you are being a little naughty aren't you!" Occasionally, I would have to be firm and put on my strict voice (that I didn't even know I had), and it would usually work. If someone started getting lippy with me, I would usually appeal to one of their more sensible-looking mates, shoot them a 'help me' look and they would usually say, "Come on, mate, the lady is just doing her job, be nice," and then I'd crack a joke about being the smallest security guard in England and the situation would be diffused. I think the reason female security guards get less abuse is that they have a gentler approach and tend not to get drunken lads riled up with macho behaviour. Few problems were encountered and afterwards I would get to enjoy an evening in the club. It was only Len that ever had an issue with me.

He always wore a seething expression when things were on the up for me. He treated me as his property and wanted me to act like his inferior. When something started to go well, he'd say, "We are leaving Ibiza" and he had booked flights and would tell me to quit my job. Then he'd say he'd decided we were staying. If I think about it, most of the men in my life have felt the need to try and put me down or be in competition with me, even my own father. Perhaps there is something in me they find intimidating, and they feel the need to try and conquer my spirit. Who knows!

In those final weeks in Ibiza, I lived off stale bread and cheese, while Len bought Octopus and seafood for himself.

Chatting to a promoter in a bar one evening, he offered me a job. He had a flyer team and was arranging a parade of people in costumes to walk through the streets of San Antonia promoting a club. We would be decked out in crazy outfits and UV paint and would entertain the crowds as we promoted the brand. It sounded perfect! Len pulled me to one side and said, "What the hell do you think you are doing talking to that guy?"

"Just chatting, he said he might have a job for me. We need the money."

"What would he want with you? What could you possibly know!" he spat.

"He does a regular flyer parade for one of the club nights," I reasoned. "It would be handing out flyers, the same I've done for some of the other brands."

His lips curled into a vicious sneer and his eyes were black with rage. "He wouldn't hire someone like you, can't you see that. He just wants to fuck you and you are too stupid to see it."

With that, he stormed off and disappeared. I looked around to see if I could find any of my friends, but they'd all disappeared. I apologised to the promoter and said I would give him a call about the work and then headed off. The problem was I was in a part of town I didn't know. It took me two hours of navigating the streets before I spotted somewhere familiar, and I had no money for a cab because Len would always take any change I had off me to buy himself cigarettes.

When I got home, Len had already arrived back. "Where were you? You fucked him, didn't you?"

"What? I've been trying to find my way home after you abandoned me on the streets!" I shouted back.

Len slapped me round the head and smashed a glass on the floor. Trying to get away from him and leave the room, I cut my feet to shreds.

It wasn't the first time he'd stopped me from taking a job and raged at me. The last time I'd been asked to be a roller girl promoting a bar on the beach, and he'd told me I couldn't do it. Another time he lost it because he said I didn't cook his chicken enough and screamed at me till I cried hysterically.

The shouting went on for hours and I ended up sleeping in the bathtub that night with the bathroom door locked. The emotional agony I felt was unbearable and I started self-harming that night, lashing my arm with a razor blade, only content once I saw the dark crimson liquid sliding down my arm. There was something primal about it, something that told me whatever happened, my heart would still beat, and I was still human. It was comforting.

It may sound like such a bizarre thing to say, but it was an escape from the psychological onslaught from Len. This simple act of self-harming took me back to the present moment and helped tear me away from being trapped in my own head, which had become a war zone. I wish I had known other ways of achieving peace back then – meditation, exercise, mantras – anything but self-mutilation.

Self-harming is such a great taboo in our culture and most people think of self-harm as cutting of the flesh, but there are many forms of self-harm. Taking drugs is self-harm, eating too much food is self-harm, not ensuring your physical or emotional needs are met is a form of self-harm. In fact, most forms of behaviour that neglect or abuse the self are a form of self-harm. People engage in this behaviour for so many reasons. For some, it's a desire to regain control over their bodies; for others, it's a form of self-punishment. When you feel worthless, you can end up placing the blame on yourself instead of the person who hurt you, and you can only eradicate those feelings of worthlessness by punishing the self. The psychology of it is extremely complicated and it's messed up. There is still so much we do not understand about the psychology of the brain and how it functions.

After every incident, I would have every intention of breaking it off with Len, then the next day he was apologetic and full of excuses and promises of a better future. He would also appeal to my empathic nature by guilt-tripping me at every turn.

"My mum is in hospital and really ill," he would begin. "I didn't want to tell you and worry you, but I don't know if she'll make it."

I pushed back my feelings of rage and disgust for how I'd been treated and tried to reassure him. "I'm sure she will be OK," I soothed.

"We have to fly back tomorrow," he insisted.

I nodded. I'd had enough of Ibiza, or at least Ibiza with Len.

It's funny, I've allowed these memories to rise to the surface for the sake of this book, as generally I tend to bury all the bad stuff and think of all the fun times. Some of the nicer things etched into my mind are riding a moped past Bora Bora beach, lounging in a hammock in AC/DC, crazy boat parties, and reaching for the lasers in Manumission and dancing like a nutcase with Andre and the gang. What a place that was, with fire-eaters, little dwarves tumbling down the stairs, beautiful, elegant dancers and adults playing like children in dayglow clothing.

Closing my eyes, I can see myself dipping my toes in the sand, waves of euphoria crashing over me like a tsunami after dropping an E at sunset on the beach and feasting my eyes on that beautiful orange ball of fire in the sky. A sweet melody fills the air as the likes of Tiesto's remix of Samuel Barber's *Adagio for Strings* came on the decks, followed by "Castles in the Sky" and "Energy 52", and the corners of my lips raise. The music made me feel whole. I become awash with feelings and sensations, the citrusy tang of an iced orange juice and vodka, the warmth of the summer rays against my bronzed flesh. The feeling of my chest expanded as I laughed with hysteria at a shared joke. Reviewing it all, I now see them as experiences – some good, some bad, but all valuable lessons. I don't see myself as a victim. I see myself as someone who has learned what is important in life and what is simply noise, distractions.

When Len and I finally flew home, Lila turned out to be fine. She was probably in hospital with an ingrown toenail or getting some *work* done, and in time I realised that he'd hyped up the situation to excuse his poor behaviour.

Before we'd headed to Ibiza, we had arranged to return to shared student accommodation, which was a flat opposite the theatre and above an American diner. We would be sharing with Andre and one other.

On moving-in day, I spotted a sign on the door for Goodies, the American diner, which read, "Waiting Staff Required". I popped in and they hired me on the spot. I loved working at Goodies. It was so convenient being downstairs, and the bar staff and waiters were fun to work with and always joking around. We sometimes got to eat the food too, which was delicious and consisted of surf and turf, various types of stacked burgers, salads, and plenty of skin-on fries. I came to look forward to working at the restaurant, visiting the library and computer room and attending my lectures. Going home, however, I would dread. I never knew what sort of mood Len would be in.

It was great living with Andre, he was a lot of fun, and we'd often hang out listening to music and putting the world to rights. He was a real laid-back guy and probably kept me sane during that crazy year in the shared flat. Like me, though, he seemed

KAZ B

a little cautious of setting Len off. I think everyone was a little afraid of Len, not because he was tough, but because they never quite knew what he was capable of.

To make the flat more affordable, we rented out the spare room to a guy who went by the name of Tigger. He was skinny and pale, with thick, pebble-rimmed glasses, green hair and a bad case of acne, and always looked like he needed a wash. He'd often invite crowds of people round and it would be hard trying to concentrate on studying. Sometimes I'd head off to the library but when it was shut, I'd just join the party. When in Rome …! Some of them turned out to be great people, like Sam and Phil, the geeky tech guys. I remember Sam's icebreaker was, "Do you know your porn name? It's the name of your first pet and your mother's maiden name." I think I said mine was Pepsi Wows – there's nothing wrong with a little creative license, is there? We then went round asking everyone at the party while giggling like idiots. If I cast my mind back, most of the best parties happened long after Len had left the scene.

In those first few months, Len depended on me for money, then randomly got a job at a Mexican restaurant called La Cantina and persuaded me to get a job there too. The money was much better than working at Goodies, and while I loved working there, I could really use the money to be able to afford the expensive uni textbooks I needed. Often, when Len couldn't blackmail or extort money out of me, he would just help himself to it. I got into the habit of hiding money away. Sometimes I'd come home, and he'd ripped through all my drawers and left the room in complete chaos, with clothes everywhere. I then became exceptionally talented at hiding money away. Len wouldn't think twice about using up the pay as you go credit on my phone as soon as I got it so that I would be more isolated, so I learned various survival techniques, taping coins onto the underside of a stool or folding notes and slipping them into a book cover.

The extra money from La Cantina helped. Living with Len had put me in debt, and I had a huge overdraft, so I needed all the hours I could do. It wasn't as much fun as working at Goodies, but the shift seemed to go quickly, and they made a mean bowl of chili. By this point, I had surrendered to the lure of meat. It had a lot to do with being terribly poor, awfully hungover and the temptation of a bacon sandwich. I no longer eat red meat, but I'm still reminded of the flavour of the smoky meat and tangy tomato sauce that hit my tastebuds that morning, and my stomach growled, making me chew into the food instantly.

One night when I was off work, Len came home and told me he'd quit his job. The next day, I got a call from La Cantina, and they said Len had been fired for stealing and they had to let me go too because it was a conflict of interest. I was jobless again. Len of course denied everything, placing the blame on our various colleagues.

Scouting around, I managed to find some more waitressing work through a temping agency. Living with Len was akin to living in a mental asylum. He'd create arguments and disappear, and then come back reeking of perfume. He'd accuse me of being jealous and crazy. One day, I collected his club flyers for him from the printers and when I met him on the campus field, he just threw them all over the floor. He had turned into a complete monster, or more likely he was now revealing the full extent of his monstrosity, but I didn't realise that I deserved better.

Another time, my parents came to Southampton and took the pair of us out for a Chinese as a treat. He spent most of the night in the toilet, then got home and threw up in the sink. It was still there when my mum came around in the morning when I got back from my lectures. His Aunty May had kindly invited my parents to stay in her hotel so they could spend some time with me. My mother sent champagne, flowers and a note via Len. When they were invited by May the second time, my mum handed them straight to the night manager and said to me, "I wouldn't trust Len to go to the shops for a packet of crisps!"

My mother received a letter from Aunty May saying, "Thank you so much. Over the years, I have let many friends stay in the hotel and no one has ever said thank you or sent a gift!"

It seems that she had never received the first lot of gifts.

Len was bad news and I started to distance myself from him emotionally. What really made me wake up was when a good friend of his lent him £10. After months of the debt being overdue, the girl kept asking for her £10 back, and so he would clear her calls. Then he got angry and said he wouldn't pay her back because she was harassing him. It was so much easier to see how sick and twisted he was when it was someone else he lashed out at. I saw him for what he was, and he just couldn't hurt me anymore.

One evening, he broke the news that he was leaving to spend a year in Thailand. I was surprised at my own emotions. I expected that I would feel a sense of loss, but there was something else buzzing inside my tummy – a sense of freedom! It seemed unreal and I hoped with all my heart he wouldn't change his mind.

Len disappeared off to his mum's for a few days, which I thought was odd as usually he insisted that I go with him. I was beyond caring though. When Len left, there were tears from both sides, his – guilt, mine – relief! So, when the taxi pulled up and he stepped in, I dried my eyes and headed back into the flat. Far from sorrow, my heart pulled itself back up from the depths of my stomach and the sense of burden I'd come to feel dissipated.

"Are you OK?" Andre asked, giving me a big bear hug and wrapping his arms around me in a protective way.

"Yes, I really am," I replied with a smile.

Len emailed me from Thailand asking me to "wait for him". I replied that I didn't see us working out. I needed real closure though, to end this once and for all. I started doing some digging and asking questions to build up a picture. I discovered that when I got down to it, I was good at detective work, and knew what questions to ask and how to get people to reveal information without realising what they were doing.

Alexander was a Spanish guy that was always at our flat. He always had a bottle of whiskey in his hand and was as pissed as a newt at the bottom of a whiskey barrel most of the time. He was the obvious weak link in the chain and the easiest to exploit sensitive information out of. One evening, we were all having a party at the flat and Al was smoking a spliff. I made some small talk to start with and softened him up, then I switched conversational styles. "Do you ever miss Len, Al?"

"Ah, you know," replied Al with a flip of his hand, blowing smoke into the air in a manner which suggested that he was more likely to miss stepping in dog shit.

"Yeah, I've gotten used to it pretty quickly too," I agreed. "Still, I was a bit disappointed that he cheated on me with Sarah."

With anyone else, I would have had to be subtle in my encounter, but Al was as drunk as a skunk, and I had to quickly prod him for information before we were interrupted.

I don't know why I said the name Sarah, I think I was thinking he would respond, "You mean Sophie/Emma/Claire." At least someone I didn't know, not a friend, surely?

Instead, he took a swig from his bottle of JD and replied, "Yes, I am surprised his mother let Sarah stay at her house and share a bed when Len was seeing you."

This was more than I had bargained on. He had the loose tongue of an Irish fisherman and I felt both elated at my discovery and enraged at the cheek of that no-good cockroach Len!

"Well, that's Lila for you, no morals," I chuckled. "What was it, two to three weeks they had been sleeping together?"

"A few months."

It was impossible to hide the fact that this was news to me, and Al berated himself for disclosing things that had been sworn to secrecy. I'm certain he found solace at the bottom of his bottle of JD and didn't agonise over it for long. I didn't feel bad about using deceptive methods to get to the truth with Al. He had never felt bad about keeping such secrets from me, so now we were even, and nothing more was said about the subject.

If I'd have known, I'd have ditched the rotter. Still, I had the closure I needed. I knew what I had to do next. I typed out an email, "Dear Len, I know that you are a dirty, cheating liar and you slept with Sarah at your mum's. I have had this confirmed by witnesses. Please do not try and contact me again as I don't want anything to do with you. Have a nice life, Kaz."

I then blocked his phone number, his email addresses and threw away any trace of him left in the flat. Finally, I had managed to recognise him as a highly toxic individual, or what I know now as a malignant narcissist. Later, I discovered that he'd been seeing prostitutes while he'd been with me, so I was relieved to get a clean bill of health from the local GUM clinic. Other than that, I could no longer care less.

It was time to start living again.

Chapter 12:
I Move in with My Stalker

The parties became even crazier after Len had left for Thailand. There was always someone on the decks, and often there would be well-meaning people dragging me out of bed to join the party. Tigger was an absolute bugger for this; he'd get me up and insist I dress and come downstairs. Perhaps I suffered from fear-of-missing-out syndrome, as I usually obliged, after a few feeble protests! One time, Tigger was in bed when an impromptu party started. Phil, Sam and I reversed the tables, woke Tigger up and insisted he join the Pixie-eyes gang. We ended up frolicking down the high street, Tigger blowing on a huge three-foot didgeridoo. Another time, I made fairy cakes and the lads filled them with hash, so everyone at the party was spaced out, half asleep or mumbling into their cider with a silly, sloppy look on their faces!

Guaranteed, every weekend there were students sat on every space of floor, and more pills and piles of powder than a bloody chemist! There would be traces of white lines everywhere, then someone would walk past and lick the residue off the table, which nobody seemed to care about or notice.

After Len left, I tried to keep the club running for a while, then I became an events manager for the Palm club. We'd all pile out of the club and end up back at our flat. As the term ended, it was usually me and Andre, Bobby (an Irish guy) and a couple of others sat in Andre's room with a chillout mix playing. I started to spend more time with those guys as I felt safe and protected from all the madness after Len.

Deciding where to live for my third and final year was easy.

The constant parties at the house were a bit much and much as I had enjoyed living with the boys, I longed for some peace and quiet, so for my third year I decided to move into halls of residence called Emily Davis Halls. They were quieter and aimed at older students. I fitted in straight away and made good friends with a girl called Jen, who was studying photography.

Without all the stress of Len and with some solitude to study, I really came into my own and started getting 2:1s on my assignments.

Some of my lecturers were a bit strange; I had a Polish teacher who was unhelpful and when you asked a question, she would simply read the passage from the textbook again and again until you gave up asking.

There was also a teacher with floppy hair and an eye patch who could be quite brutal when giving criticism. At the time, I didn't like him, but now I appreciate his tough criticisms that forced me to become a better writer.

Seamus was an Irish teacher, and I couldn't wait for his lessons. He was in his mid-fifties and had a wonderful voice that I could just listen to all day long. He'd often pick me to answer his questions and I was thrilled when he'd remark, "Exactly! Very insightful, that's exactly what I was talking about."

At the time, I desperately needed validation from someone I respected, and his encouragement gave me more determination to study harder. For the third year, I was also given the most wonderful mentor. She was a red-haired lady in her fifties called Rosemary, and she was eccentric, intellectual and had a wonderful way with words. What I liked most about her was that she was gentle in her manner. She always had time for you, even though she was busy, and she was supportive and encouraging. She had kind, twinkling eyes that were slightly creased at the corners, and a smile that worked its way into your heart. I always left her office dancing on air and with a skip in my step. She brought out the best in me and I learned a lot from her about writing and structure and how to deal with people.

In the third year, I reduced my partying, allowing myself a trip to a club once every three months, and only as long as I had done all my work. Part of my dissertation was to write a creativity story, a journal about it and a thesis on the structure and style. This was exactly the kind of thing I loved to do and while my mates hung out in the student union, I'd head home to the sanctuary of my little room and write for hours, lost in a world of fairies, fantasy and mystery.

I still enjoyed a good drink with my friend Jen and would often go round to see Andre at his new place. He'd finished uni now and had a job and was sharing with a group of lads. I remember going round at the height of summer and there were big funky house tunes on the decks!

Andre asked me if I could put in a good word with my mate Jen and so I did, and soon they began dating. When I say dating, there were probably two or three dates before she dumped him. I can't really remember why she finished with him, I think they just didn't click, but he was pretty hurt at the time, and I felt torn as I really cared about them both. I decided to just listen to them both and not comment.

One night, Jen and I agreed that as we had worked so hard, we would blow off some steam at a club in Bournemouth called Slinky. It was a place you could watch the likes of Tiesto, Armin Van Buuren and Ferry Corsten playing some fantastic sets on the decks with everything from classic trance and hard house through to techno. It was at Slinky I met B, we had a dance and shared a kiss, and then he was just like a wart I couldn't shake off!

I used to post on a music forum back then, chatting about records with other clubbers on a site called Gifted Generation. I made the rookie error of saying where I was going that night and B would travel all the way from Windsor and just show up. He was persistent, and I just didn't know how to end things. One night, I was trying to do some work on my dissertation, and I just couldn't concentrate with him rolling all over my little single bed in the corner. When I asked him to leave, he refused and said he'd driven a long way. I said I hadn't asked him to, and he said he thought it would be a surprise. He was always hanging around me and when I confided in Jen, she said she would send him out with her friend Louis and some of the lads to give me time to study. It massively backfired when it turned out that Louis was trying to rent out a spare room and B told me he was quitting his job and moving to Southampton. It was a real comedy of errors and I tried to desperately claw myself out of this mess.

"No point," I said in a manner that Ricky Gervais would have been proud of, "my course ends in September."

"We'll sort something out," he said.

B was extremely clingy. One night, I said I was going to the pub with Jen. He sulked, pouted and made a fuss, but I just ignored him and said goodbye.

An hour later, I was sat in the local Wetherspoons with Jen, enjoying a glass of house white, when I looked up to see two eyes peering up at me over a newspaper. He'd only followed us to the pub!

When I had it out with him, he explained he thought he should get out too, and didn't realise I would be there. Of course, he was lying outright, but even telling him to get lost didn't work. Nowadays, there are restraining orders for this kind of behaviour. I was vulnerable and he eventually managed to wear me down. B was another one that never had any money and lived on handouts.

My little room in my halls felt safe, my own sanctuary, and I loved having time to myself. Sometimes I would go and hang out in Jen's room and chat for hours about life and the universe.

I holed myself up in the library when I could and eventually the time came, and I handed in my dissertation. I studied the beautifully bound document and was even more pleased with the contents. I couldn't believe that I'd created such a beautiful-looking document, and for the first time in my life felt proud of myself. Then came the tricky bit; I only had two tickets for family to come to my graduation, but both my parents and sister wanted to come. This caused a big row and once again I was caught in the middle of it. I was rather surprised my dad wanted to come and hadn't thought he would be interested, but I was secretly touched that he cared enough to come and sit through a boring ceremony. It consisted of waiting around for hours in a cape and gown like a kinky superhero, collecting a scroll and walking off stage. I wondered why they couldn't just post it to me instead! I'm not one for stuffy ceremonies. Dad obviously thought the same, as the minute I walked off stage, he was outside for a fag. He got a good telling off from Mum, but I secretly wished I could have gone and stood outside too.

I was awarded a 2:1 with honours, and my wish for a career in media was soon to come true.

B took me to his parents' house in Windsor one afternoon and his dad grilled me about what I wanted to do. I told him I would love to work for a media company, particularly the BBC. "Why don't you stay with us for a little while," he suggested. "We are an easy commute there and you can go for interviews."

"Oh, I couldn't put you out like that!" I began.

"Oh, you wouldn't be!" both his parents chimed in. "We'd love to have you here. It's the least we can do, as you have taken such good care of B!"

Not wanting to seem rude, I suppose I went along with it. It sounds utterly ridiculous now, doesn't it? Insane in fact, but that is how I was. Besides, his parents were so nice and kind, and his home life seemed so stable. Perhaps trying to make things work with B and focus on my media career was the best option. I had no money to rent a place of my own and I knew that if I moved back with my parents in Swindon, I would end up working at some crappy job in an office. I decided to go for it and started to make more of an effort with B. He was always jobless and moping around, so I decided that I would help give him some encouragement. Scouting for jobs for him, I then suggested he apply as admin staff at a local modelling agency. He jumped at the chance! *Things should start to get better now he has something to focus on*, I thought. How little did I know, and my appalling reasons for staying in a relationship my heart wasn't set on were punished.

Chapter 13: Nightmares Made of Pickled Egg and Pork

2003

Between writing to the BBC and applying for every single position that suited my skills (and a zillion other companies), I took a job at LEGOLAND in Windsor to keep the wolf from the door. The café had a cheesy name like 'Spud u Like' and was designed to look like a castle. Dishing up jacket spuds, I'd try and have a joke with the rest of the staff. They would stare back at me gormlessly, their lower jaws hanging, their eyes blank. They just didn't get me. This was not my tribe and my experience there made me work even harder to get onto my chosen path.

After dishing up hundreds if not thousands of spuds in between writing letters, I was finally offered some contract work at the BBC in Caversham. I was elated and couldn't believe I had managed to find some work so quickly. Our lecturers had warned us of the fierce competition and said that we may struggle to find suitable jobs, so this was like a dream come true. I think one of the reasons that helped me get work was all the voluntary work I had done for free while at uni. I'd worked at Star AM, BRMB in Birmingham, Fire FM in Bournemouth, Win FM in Winchester and more besides. I had faced criticism for doing work experience for free, yet I'd really worked hard to give myself the edge and given up my time to educate myself further in my chosen field.

I'd visit my family from time to time and B would have to tag along, as he didn't like me to go anywhere without him. My family all thought he was a loser. He would try to garner sympathy from them, saying, "I hurt my finger, I have a bad toe. I have a baddy." He sought attention in the same way a five-year-old child might. My family thought it was hilarious and for Christmas my mum bought him a medical kit with smiley-faced plasters in it, with a note attached, "For healing all your 'baddies'."

"I didn't think that was funny!" he seethed. That's the thing in our family, we all take the mickey out of each other, but we can take a joke back too – well, the female side anyway. B wasn't like us; he could dish it out but couldn't be the butt of the joke.

He was embarrassing too and followed no social niceties. He'd only met my parents a few times when we visited them one Sunday. Upon arrival, he declared he was "tired and going for a lie down". The look on my dad's face was a picture. He didn't need to say a word to me, I knew he was thinking, *What the hell are you doing with this guy?* I'm sure my puzzled face replied, *No idea!*

Another time, we stayed at my sister's house. He got engine oil on his clothes and sat on her new cream sofa, staining it. The next morning, he had no clothes on and wrapped himself up in her throw for the settee. Everyone was cringing with revulsion. He had no boundaries and didn't seem to notice when people were repulsed by his behaviour.

Another funny moment was Pickled-Egg Gate. B announced he was going to make us poached eggs. I wandered into the kitchen and saw him pouring half a bottle of vinegar into the pan. When he told us to collect our plates, the vinegar jar was empty, and he proudly presented us with plates of pickled, poached eggs. His face was a picture; anyone would think he had just got through to the final round on *MasterChef*. We roared with laughter at his rancid pickled eggs. Rather than join in the banter, he sulked and glowered.

As nice as B's parents were, I felt uncomfortable living there with them. Firstly, I wasn't comfortable with his dad collecting my dirty washing, it left me feeling a little violated, as well intended as it was. I also didn't want them to cook for me. Several times a week, his dad would cook pork, which I absolutely loathed, with hard boiled potatoes and peas. I'd be given a plate of tough meat on a tray on my lap, and a bread knife with which to attempt to saw through the tough old leather. As I sawed back and forth with my knife, a mound of peas would bounce off my plate with a 'boing!' and splatter surrounding parties. I was mortified and stuck for how to find a solution to the pork and pea nightmare. I would say, "Please don't cook for me," and I would get home from work to be greeted with a pork and pea ensemble.

A meltdown nearly ensued one evening in the safety of my bedroom after another pork and pea debacle. I insisted on moving into a little private flat in Maidenhead. Of course, B came with me. We had our own little place and freedom, and it should have been wonderful, but he was always moping around.

The first time we'd had sex all those months before, I'd been a little resistant. I had not wanted to and had also been put off by the rather odd-looking white stains on his sheets.

However, after a glass of wine I could be quite amorous, but he was never interested. He moaned constantly, like an old fishwife, and I couldn't connect with him; it was like he had a chromosome missing. B was one of life's victims that feels self-entitled and that the world owes them a living.

One night, I'd had enough, and I did something I'm not proud of. I got on a train into London and went to a club called Heaven. There I met up with some friends and a guy called Tad. I was sat with Tad and the DJ started playing one of my favourite trance tunes, "Holding On To Nothing" by Agnelli & Nelson, which seemed quite poignant as I really did feel like I was holding on to nothing. Tad leaned forward to kiss me, and I responded. He was a short South African guy and somewhat gobby and opinionated but had nice arms and a great tan.

I ended up hanging out with Tad and a red-haired girl named Kelly, who hated me because she had a crush on Tad. Also, she was an alcoholic then, but we ended up becoming the best of friends!

The next day, I finished things with B and asked him to move out.

When he left with his few things it was awkward; he pushed my things over to get to his stuff and deliberately made a mess. I had some loose change in an old jam jar, and he tipped all the change over the floor, then pocketed the jam jar and said, "This is my jar, I'm taking it with me."

I just shrugged, which seemed to anger him more. I had really tried to help B, but the truth was I never really loved him, and wasn't sad to see him leave. I just wished he would hurry up about it.

Soon, he stormed out and I thought that was the end of it, but then a few days later he returned to collect some things he'd "forgotten". He told me to come into the bedroom and then said, "You still want me," in a sinister voice, pulling me towards the bed.

"No, I don't, B, it's over. Get off me!" I snapped.

He pushed me onto the bed and climbed on top of me, using his weight to hold me in place.

"You do, I can tell," he groaned, pulling up my skirt and ripping my knickers aside.

"Leave me alone! Leave, I don't want you here," I cried.

"You are just playing hard to get," he said, and then he began laughing, a horrible, cackling sound in the back of his throat that was as vile as it was absurd.

This was insane; he had never wanted sex when we were together, and now feeling him against me, I felt sick, I couldn't believe he was doing this.

Trying to beat him off me, I struggled, but he was much stronger. He pinned me down, pulled his pants down and had sex with me against my will. Unable to escape, I turned my head to the side and screwed my eyes up. There was no one to hear me if I screamed. I knew I just had to wait for it to be over. I don't recall the physical sensation of it thankfully, only seeing the grey pallor of skin. My mind has blocked it out, though I recall the loathing feeling I felt when I heard his whiny, braying voice.

At least it didn't last long; he groaned and rolled off me, saying, "See, I knew you still wanted me."

Rage rose in my chest and before I could think about what I was saying, I screamed, "I hate you! You disgust and sicken me, and I wish I'd never met you."

The rage was flaring in his eyes, and I didn't know what he was capable of, so I took a few paces back and said in a calmer voice, "What would your mother think if she knew about all this?"

That seemed to do the trick. The angry glare in his eyes turned to panic; he dressed quickly and left. Bolting the door behind him, I made myself a hot cup of tea then sat on the bed cross-legged, nursing my cup. There were no tears; numbness filled me. Calling someone occurred to me but I didn't know who to call. My family would probably go ballistic and might try and get me to move back home. They would think I couldn't look after myself, and that was the last thing I wanted. Keeping my independence was essential. I'd just have to carry on and pretend it had never happened.

Chapter 14: He Tracks Me Down
Modelling at Max Power

I had hoped that B was out of my life for good, but he stalked me online for months. Even when I stopped using one music website and switched to another, he followed me there and would harass me online and shout about how I'd dumped him. About a month after we had broken up, he managed to hack into my email account and found out I'd gotten off with Tad the day before I broke it off with him. He then assumed I was seeing this other guy, which I wasn't, and wrote an embarrassing begging letter to the guy involved, saying "Please let me keep her, don't take her off me," as if I was his property.

It was pathetic. As if I'd ever want to be with someone who had done *that* to me. He was deluded.

Again, I reiterated that it was over, that I wasn't seeing anyone and had had enough of men and enough of him. In response, he closed my email account and stole a domain and website I had paid for, which were for a club night we had promoted together but which had been my brainchild.

I cut my losses and ignored his retaliations.

When I had moved into B's parents' house, I'd taken my dog Poppy with me, as I thought she'd have a better life there. My parents were always at work and so she had been on her own a lot. B's parents were besotted with her, and she loved their dog Jackie too.

When B and I had moved into the new flat, we weren't allowed to take pets, and we all agreed that it was best that Poppy stay with his parents, even though I missed her, especially now I knew

I couldn't visit anymore. It was a hard loss. That was the greatest trial in all of this, losing the companionship of a wonderful Cavalier King Charles Spaniel.

I was at work one day when a direct message pinged into my inbox on the social media music site I used. I groaned inwardly when I saw it was from B. It read, "Your dog's dead by the way."

It was an obvious attempt to hurt me, and it had the desired effect. However, I wouldn't give him the satisfaction of knowing this. "That's very sad," I replied, "how?"

"Mastitis spread through her body. She had to be put down."

I didn't reply again, but there would be comments directed at me daily on the message boards. I sought refuge in my sense of humour.

Buried thoughts would try to work their way to the surface. *He raped me. No – don't acknowledge the feeling! Bury it deep inside and make a joke.*

After a day of him giving me grief, sending me vet bills and various other horrible emails, he posted, "I'm so depressed and sick of everyone floating around my desk offering me cups of tea."

I should have stopped myself. I didn't. I wrote, "Do you see dead people?"

It was a quote from the film *The Sixth Sense.* The forum kicked off, and a stream of jokes followed, with B as the target this time. Up until now, some of our friends had been sympathetic towards him and they knew nothing of what he had done to me, but now they were saying, "Why don't you lay off her, man? It's been months! Get over it!"

He was seething and I took the flack. After this, I saw a post he'd written where he was bragging about how he was hanging out with models who were much better-looking than his previous girlfriend (me) and how they all wanted him. I sprayed my coffee over the screen. Humour was a great distraction from the unease I felt inside, and a little light release. He couldn't see how crazy he looked, and he genuinely thought he was making me jealous. I had to see the funny side. There is a great comfort and an even greater solace to be found in dark comedy. It's got me through some of the most challenging moments and I don't know where I would be without it.

I ignored B's comments and when he couldn't get a rise from me, he would call my sister and moan about me. She would tell him to forget about it and move on. He didn't. He was obsessed and wanted to hurt me. I was looking over my shoulder all the time.

A couple of months later, I started doing a little bit of modelling as a hobby while I was working at a media company. I appeared on the shopping channel promoting a bath spa, then I started doing some fashion shoots for local magazines. My friends had mixed opinions about my modelling and B was often popping up on the message board calling me all sorts of wonderful names – slut, slag, etc. – but I refused to let it put me off doing shoots. Being asked to promote at *Max Power* was extremely exciting. Word got around that I was getting some good jobs and everyone in my friendship circle seemed to be talking about it.

It was my first big job with loads of other people around, and I felt a little nervous, but I watched the pros closely and got the hang of draping myself over the cars and posing. Smartphones had become popular now and there was a blinding flash as a sea of guys stood clicking away taking pictures. I ignored my nerves and pushed them down and hid them with a smile. All was going well until out of the corner of my eye I saw B. Could I hide? Had he seen me? *Damn it!* He'd clocked me and was making his way over. *Shit, shit, shit!*

It's not a nice feeling to be confronted by your ex, let alone your rapist ex when you are muddling your way through a new job. You just couldn't make it up! *Of all the bloody days!* I considered running, but then that would make me seem weak. I didn't want to allow him that feeling of power or satisfaction. I stood my ground and allowed him to approach me. He was carrying a cardboard box, which he flung at me.

"Errr, what's this?" I asked, confused.

"That's your dead dog's ashes," he sneered.

He looked sicklier than ever. His face was now a real ashen grey, weathered and wrinkled at the sides of his eyes, his eyelids heavily hooded, as if he was permanently stoned. Looking at his visage made my stomach swirl with nausea.

My insides burned and my legs suddenly felt independent to the rest of my body, but I had to remain calm, I couldn't let him win. I have no idea how I managed to stay so calm or where the words came from that left my mouth.

"Well, it's nice to have her back and have chance to say good-bye to her."

Willing my voice not to break and my eyes not to leak, I stood my ground.

He just stood there, staring at me. God knows what he expected me to say. Maybe he wanted tears so he could be the hero and console me, or perhaps he thought I'd say, "Thank you for bringing my dead dog's ashes to me while I'm modelling on the stand. That's exactly what I needed to make this day go better! How could I ever have broken up with such a caring, thoughtful individual. Let's just get back together now, shall we, and have a celebratory shag over Poppy's cremated corpse!"

He looked at me expectantly.

"Well, I'll just go find a safe place for her then," I proffered, and turned away.

I ran off to the changing rooms and only when I was safe within its confines did I hug the box tightly and whisper, "I will miss you so much, Poppy."

No longer could I control the flow of tears running down my cheeks, and when one of the team found me that way in a state, clutching the box tightly, they kindly sat me down and made me a cup of tea.

Explaining what had happened, I realised that I wasn't making the best impression, but the words flooded out.

"He just won't leave me alone. He turns up at all these places I'm at and I'm trying so hard to make sure I'm doing a good job."

"Don't worry," said the guy, "you sort yourself out and dry those tears, and I will go and tell him to clear off."

Whatever the guy said to him I'll never know, but I didn't see B at the event after that. In the afternoon, my mate Smoky from uni turned up with a bunch of mates. I relayed the details to him, leaving the part out where B had forced himself on me some months prior to him bringing me Poppy's ashes at work. Smoky's eyes nearly popped out of his head.

"Are you serious? The guy sounds like a psychopath!"

"I just don't know what to do to get him to leave me alone?"

"Do you have any family you can talk to about this?"

I thought about the complexity of the situation. I could only tell my family parts of the story. It would have devastated them if they had known what B had done to me, and it was only a good ten years after the event that I finally told my mum and sisters.

"No, not really."

"Well, what about speaking to his family? Do they know he's bothering you? Are his parents nice?"

"Yes, I suppose I could do that. Yes, his parents are nice; in fact, his dad is a policeman."

The cogs started to whir in my mind – perhaps there was a way to finish all this for good.

"Why don't you think about that and come to the comedy club with me and the lads tonight. We'll cheer you up and make you laugh."

"Thanks, that would be great," I smiled. Smoky was a good friend; he offered good advice and knew how to cheer me up. I managed to get through the rest of the day without a hitch. Later, we enjoyed a night of comedy and a bizarre routine about a gay Eskimo over Tequila Slammers. It was just the tonic. Friends often have a way of making you see solutions when you thought you had exhausted all avenues, and Smoky's words stayed with me for a few days. Handling this all on my own was proving too much. B was showing no signs of letting up.

Phoning B's dad, I gave him the abridged version; I mean,

how do you say, "Oh, Mr Policeman, did you know that your son should be on the sex offenders register?" So, I omitted this part. I couldn't say it out loud. It made me feel like there was something wrong with me if I acknowledged it. I would rather push that part away, to some dark recess where I didn't have to think about it.

His dad listened gravely when I told him that B was stalking me and taking a lot of drugs. I mentioned him turning up to *Max Power* and that he was on a final warning at work due to his constant posting on the Internet.

"I don't want any trouble, I just want to move on with my life and not live in fear of B being around the corner," I said.

He apologised to me and said he would sort it. I was forever grateful to him for that. He and his wife had always been kind to me, and his dad did not disappoint in doing the right thing.

A few hours later, I was doing some work on my computer and decided to have a cup of tea and a quick skim of what my friends were up to on the music site. There was a recent post from B. It said, "I can't believe it! The agency where I work have said I need to buck my ideas up, and now my dad's only gone and grounded me! I'm on the work computer, but he's forbidden me to use a computer at home and I'm not allowed to go out until I sort myself out. It's so unfair!"

I sat there open-mouthed. B was a twenty-eight-year-old man, moaning on a music forum that life was unfair because his dad had grounded him. The banter started and people started to take the mickey, "You coming out to play mate? Oh, that's right, you are grounded aren't you!"

He replied, "This is all Kora's fault! She's caused these problems. If it wasn't for her, I wouldn't have been so upset and wouldn't have got into trouble."

I saw red and ignored the background cues from my brain telling me to remain calm. Before I'd had chance to think it through, I'd replied, "Well, at least no one *FORCED* you to do something that you didn't want to do!! You should understand what I am saying and stop this lunacy, as my patience is wearing thin."

I'm guessing he understood my hidden message about him forcing himself on me, as he left me alone after that.

Chapter 15: Dropping Acid and London Life

Living on my own in Maidenhead gave me a real sense of freedom. In the morning, I would put my headphones on, take the fifteen-minute walk to the station and head to BBC Caversham. Often, I'd pop into the gym before work and take a walk around the lake at lunchtime or sat in the café with my team. Life was good with all the B dramas out of the way,

Unfortunately, the job contract at the BBC came to an end and I moved in with my parents for a short while. It was hard being back home; every day I was on the computer filling out applications for jobs and I think my dad was a bit resentful that I didn't spend much time with him. I had just assumed that he wanted me out of the way, and so after that I always sat and had a chat and a cup of tea with him. He suffered from moods though, and I often felt a bit edgy around him. One minute you could be the golden child, and the next minute the black sheep, depending on which way the wind was blowing.

One day I was offered a contract at BBC White City, and I buzzed with excitement. My parents' reaction wasn't what I expected, and they didn't seem that happy. I suppose they had got used to me being around and hadn't expected me to leave again so soon. I couldn't just settle for a job in a bar or an office though – my mind was made up.

My mum was good enough to lend me the money and I put down a deposit on a room in a flat in Acton. This would mean I was only a short tube ride from work.

The day came for me to leave and looking at my parents as

I stepped into the cab, I felt a pang of sorrow. They both looked sad, and I realised, *They do love me in their own way*. Something must have shown on my face, as my dad started cracking jokes and recreating a scene from Laurel and Hardy where they keep saying awkward goodbyes because the car engine won't start. I laughed and waved, excited yet wishing I was able to connect to my parents on a deeper level.

Settling in Acton with several other housemates, I loved the London lifestyle. There were always things to do and people to see. You could get Vietnamese food at two in the morning or a pint of milk at 3 a.m. should you choose to! I was never bored and relished those quiet moments when I was alone in my room with a good book.

G was a drop-dead gorgeous Filipino guy that hired me to do some club promotion work for him. I fancied him from the offset, with his dark olive skin, sparkling eyes and stylish clothes. He was short but that's not really an issue when you are four-foot-ten like me.

At first, we had the most amazing adventures and dated for about six months, but I was somewhat insecure after my former relationships had gone so wrong, and he seemed detached. There were a few red flags; for example, he was often rude to taxi drivers, which made me cringe, but I overlooked his faults.

It came to a head when we were in bed one evening. He suggested I go on top, and we flipped position. After a few minutes, he screamed and I pulled away, shocked to see blood everywhere. At the hospital he told them he'd broken the connecting cord on his foreskin, which he called the banjo string, and he was banned from having sex for six weeks. He seemed to hold me responsible, and we started to grow apart. One night after a few drinks, I sent him a text complaining he was distant with me and not treating me well.

A few days later, he came to my house and ended things with me, and I sobbed my heart out. Three days later, I decided I was over him and planned to throw a celebration party. Perhaps it had been more lust than love, although I don't think I was over him at that point and was trying to fill the void with parties. He was a lovely guy, I reasoned, but we weren't suited to each other. Occasionally I dated, had a laugh with my mates, but didn't find anyone that I could really connect with. Telling myself I wasn't bothered, I focused on my work and my social life. My job as an assistant at the BBC was fascinating and allowed me to take various courses on offer, such as Broadcasting Law. It was a good time for me. Working in media in London was so different to working in an office in Swindon. Swindon had that small-town mentality where no one wanted you to succeed. The London office ran efficiently, and I learned a great deal about how programmes are scheduled, the day-to-day running of the office, and planning meeting and diaries.

Spending a lot of time at a friend's place, I came home one day to a vicious note from my flatmate, asking me why I had messed up the kitchen. There were about five of us sharing the flat and I hadn't been home for three days, so I wondered why she was blaming me. I felt ostracised and took it personally. Instead of talking it through with her, I made a rash decision and found another flat in Angel, Islington. It was a gorgeous flat and the other housemate was softly spoken, sweet and easy-going. When I had chance to explain the situation to my old flatmate, she was full of remorse at first, but I insisted my mind was made up and that I was leaving. Her feelings then turned to anger at the inconvenience of having to find another housemate. I knew I had made the right decision to leave.

Angel was far preferable to Acton, and I loved getting the tube home from work, seeing a few sights of London and reading my book. My flatmate Riya, a Chinese lady who worked with the BBC, was so much easier to live with. We took it in turns to cook and clean, and she introduced me to fish ball stir fries, which were delicious. I wish I had spent more time with her, instead of with some of the hangers-on and fake friends I used to hang around with. It's easy to say in hindsight now, and I often regret my choice of company when I was younger.

Settling into my new flat, it occurred to me that I could bring Pebbles my tabby cat to live with me. Riya wouldn't mind and the flat was suitable for an old cat. I phoned my mum and she said that Pebbles was a bit poorly and she wasn't sure. A couple of days later, she called and said that Pebbles had been put down and that she had been riddled with cancer. My heart shattered into tiny pieces; I was beside myself, full of guilt and self-blame … if only I'd been there for her instead of being caught up in my new job, maybe I could have known and saved her. Torturing myself with these thoughts day in, day out, I pictured her face all the time and the way she would sleep on my head at night. Never would I see her beautiful eyes again, and it was too much to bear. The guilt ate away at me, and I concluded that if I'd had money and my own house, I could have had Pebbles with me sooner. Now, I was more determined than ever to make something of myself.

Ploughing myself into every opportunity was a good distraction from grief. Pebbles had been with me since I was a little girl and even though I hadn't seen her for a couple of months, it was as if a huge gaping hole had ruptured its way into my existence.

To keep busy, I did a little modelling work, and I received an offer to do some shifts on a TV show called *Live XXX* that had come to me via a club promoter I knew.

The work was for a late-night cable channel. We would undress provocatively for the camera and talk dirty on the phone to the callers. Sometimes you would get lonely guys just call in for a regular chat about their day and they picked me as I looked the most innocent. One guy would ring me every time I was on and tell me about how he loved art, good food and wished he had someone to share his hobbies with. I provided a willing ear and built up some regular callers. With the sexy stuff, I was a bit useless to start with. I remember one evening, the producer calling out, "Kaz! You look like you are talking to your mum on the phone – make it sexier!"

I had no clue, so I paid attention to the other girls and followed suit, eventually picking up some sexy moves. It felt ridiculous pouting and pulling weird faces at the camera, totally not me.

Several months had passed when the guy who had put me forward fell out with Cellcast. He claimed that they hadn't paid him for some work, and they claimed he hadn't done the work. He sent them a filthy, angry email and they decided to fire me.

Disappointed but not overly bothered, I accepted the decision. There seemed to be plenty of opportunities around to expand on my range of experiences.

I was hanging around with a Malaysian friend of mine called Carlo when he invited me to a 'porn party'. We turned up and were given free drinks all night long. It was like a normal party apart from the fact there were girls all snogging each other and photographers taking photos of the girls posing.

Chatting to a lady, she said she wanted to get me into adult film and that she wanted to be my first.

Later, she snogged me in the loos and a photographer peered round the door taking photographs. Flattered by her interest in me, the whole thing felt so surreal. It turned out she was a famous porn star called Faye Rampton!

Producers kept coming up to me stuffing their business cards into my hands and girls were asking me to shoot with them. Giggling, I didn't take it seriously at first and popped them into my bag, thinking what a brilliant and funny night it had been.

My modelling hobby involved tame content, but the more I thought about it, I realised it could be fun to do a few racier shoots. Setting up a couple of shoots, photographers took photos of me clothed, in lingerie and nude. It just felt like a daring little adventure and an escape from my worries.

Life carried on and one summer's day I was invited to a BBQ for my friend Kelly's birthday. About thirty people showed up and I couldn't believe her parents were so chilled about it all. They came out and chatted to us before going back in to watch TV. My parents would have complained if I had two friends round the house at the same time! My dad didn't like people coming in the house.

I met my next boyfriend at that party, we'll call him Jorge, J for short! He had a nice smile, was a karate instructor and had a sense of humour. This was a must after B's total humour failure!

Later, he went home to Bournemouth, and I stayed at Kelly's in her bedroom.

We'd all dropped acid in the garden that evening and it had begun as a pleasant floaty experience, drifting into heavy visuals. I looked at the other partygoers in awe; some of them seemed to have beautiful glowing auras around them, a couple of them having shimmering halos round their heads as if they were blessed with angel divinity. While we were in the garden surrounded by nature, I was comfortable and relaxed, but once inside, I began to feel paranoid and curled myself into a corner. A horrible sense of dread filled me, and I felt as if everyone was annoyed by me. Hanging my head, I wrapped my arms around my knees, trying to shout out my inner and outer world. Then, the pain set in. LSD can give you some horrible muscle cramps and lying on a hard floor wasn't helping. Kelly and a few others eventually fell asleep, but I barely got any sleep at all as her snoring was intense! She sounded like an asthmatic warthog having an orgasm! I drifted into fragmented sleep eventually and was so relieved to wake up with the drug gone from my system, even if I still felt a little fragile.

The next day, J called Kelly and said he had forgotten his pager and could he come and collect it. He drove back and then offered me a lift home. Exhausted at this point, I agreed. We arrived at mine, and he asked if he could come in for coffee as he thought he might fall asleep at the wheel.

Making coffee, we got chatting. Soon we were laughing and joking, and I realised it was 11 p.m. and I needed to get up for work the next day.

"I'm too tired to drive, would you mind awfully if I stayed here?" J pushed.

"Well, I have a flatmate …" I started.

"I'll be no trouble," he insisted.

In my room there was a wooden floor, so I agreed he could

sleep in my bed. "No trying anything though or I'll scream for my flatmate," I said firmly.

He nodded. "I wouldn't dream of doing anything you were uncomfortable with."

We settled down for the night and J started cuddling me. "I promise I won't do anything else," he said.

"You'd better not, as I'll kick you in the balls," I quipped.

J was good to his word and didn't try to push anything more. The next morning, he left for work, and I went back to work at the BBC. That evening he called me, then the next day, then the next after that. I found it strange that he was so chatty for a guy, but I quite liked the attention. Our conversations turned more flirtatious and then he asked if he could see me sometime over the weekend. "I can't, I am doing a photo shoot on Brighton beach with some amateur models and photographers on Saturday for fun."

"No way? Really?" J sounded surprised.

"Yep, really, It's not that exciting," I laughed.

"I am at a wedding in Brighton on Saturday! I'll pick you up afterwards and give you lift back!"

I thought about it. He seemed nice, we'd been getting on well and flirting a lot. I guessed there could be no harm in it.

"OK," I agreed. "See you Saturday."

To this day, I don't know if there ever was a wedding or if it was another of J's ploys to worm his way into my life, to make it seem like the dots were connecting and then take control. I just saw it as harmless fun.

On Brighton beach that Saturday, we did a group shoot, dressed in bikinis and running in and out of the water. It was all amateur stuff, but the sense of freedom was wonderful. After the shoot, J picked me up and we had a good laugh in the car driving back. He stayed for dinner, then tea, then he ended up staying the night. This time we kissed, and we ended up sleeping together on the sofa downstairs. After that he called often, and then one night when I was out with friends, he called to say he was driving up to surprise me.

"Oh, I can't do tonight. I'm out with friends."

"I'm nearly there now," he said, "I'll come and get you, bye."

Half an hour later, he was ringing my phone.

"I'm outside in the white car," he said.

"Come on in then. I'm still drinking my drink," I said, annoyed he wanted to cut my night out short.

"I can't. I'm in my karate gear. People always try to start fights with me when I'm dressed like this, and I wouldn't want a scene. Can you come out, please, I can't find anywhere to park and I'm running out of fuel and battery on my phone."

I was irritated but agreed. This turned out to be one of those points in my life where I wished I'd switched my phone off, thrown it into the river or gone into hiding, because letting J into my life was the worst thing I ever could have done.

Chapter 16: Modelling and Crazy Stuff I Did

2005

I can't deny it, the first few months with J were an action-packed adventure. I'd visit him in Bournemouth, or he would come and visit me in London. We'd visit Camden Palace and dance to trance music and hard house until the early hours or meet up with friends. My rented flat in Islington was the prime location for a twenty-something in media. It gave me independence, I was a young, free spirit with my whole life ahead of me. Then a couple of things happened to change my destiny forever. My department at the BBC was closing and there would be no job for me, unless I was prepared to move to Manchester.

Although I didn't see my family that much, the thought of being so far away from them was too much to bear. We may have been dysfunctional, but they were my family, so relocation wasn't an option as far as I was concerned. On top of that, my landlord decided to sell the house I was renting and move to Spain. I needed to find a new job and a place to live. I started on the job search straight away but finding another job in media in London wasn't easy. J suggested that we look for a place together to share the costs, and he took a job at Sevenoaks. Although we hadn't been together long, it sounded like a fun, romantic adventure. Shortly afterwards, I was offered some work on the late-night cable channel Sport Babes XXX, which was similar to the channel I had worked on before.

"Why not just model full time?" J suggested. "You'd earn more in one shift than you would in a whole week in your current job." I thought about it, and as if the fates were pushing me in that direction, I started to receive more offers of modelling work. *Perhaps it could be a steppingstone to other things*, I thought, and I could save up some money while I found something more permanent, I reasoned, so I handed in my notice at the BBC and finished in September 2005.

J found us a flat in Forest Gate. He called me to say he'd accepted it before I'd had chance to look at it, but he assured me that I would love it. I'd never been to Forest Gate before and to say it wasn't what I was expecting would be an understatement. It was rough around the edges, but I concluded that it was within the budget and accessible to central London. Plus, I figured, it only had to be temporary.

The flat itself was spacious enough. While the kitchen and 'sitting room' were small, there was a large master bedroom with big bay windows, and a second bedroom that was a decent size. It was a little downtrodden and could have done with a lick of paint. The master bedroom was painted in a deep terracotta that made me feel dizzy to look at it. "Oh, I can soon slap some paint on that," J grinned. I spent around a year looking at those terracotta walls, and to think of them now leaves me queasy.

With an abode arranged, I could concentrate on modelling and Sport Babes XXX channel shifts. It took me a couple of shifts to settle in on the channel, but after that I found my wings. I loved the original format of the show before they changed it. We'd start with an intro which was like a raunchier version of *This Morning*. We would talk about the news and the girls would tell stories about their sexual antics and what we would be up to later on in the show. Initially, we read text messages from viewers and replied to them, but eventually the texts were replaced with phone lines so viewers could call in and speak to us directly.

We had to play it safe to get around the censors, so we would use a lot of innuendos. We'd also replace words like 'cock' with 'clock' and 'wank' with 'tank', and our conversations would get more risqué after the watershed. At 10 p.m., we would go encrypted. This meant that only paying adults with a pin number could access the show, so everything became a lot steamier. Lingerie would be peeled away; lips would explore each other; and limbs would tangle and become entwined. The toy box would also come out and we would act out role plays and viewers' fantasies. We didn't take it too seriously. The viewers loved to see us having fun and having a giggle. It was a different market to the babe channels you see on television now, which are all about the hard sell.

I was lucky enough to work with some fantastic porn legends on the channel. In the early days there was Faye Rampton, Angel Long, Amanda Pickering, Renee Richards, Bonnie Simon and more besides. Occasionally, there would be the odd tiff, but mostly everyone got on and enjoyed themselves. I had a woman crush for a while on Angel and turned ridiculously shy when she spoke to me, but she was so down to earth and lovely that I soon came out of myself and became one of the gang.

Working on the show increased my body confidence. Being among ladies of different shapes and sizes put everything into perspective. The airbrushed magazine models I'd idolised were not true to life. The women on Sport Babes XXX were gorgeous, confident and sexy, yet many still had cellulite, surgery scars and lumps and bumps. It made me see that perfection does not exist and that flaws can be beautiful.

Faye was one of my favourite girls to work with. She was so full of life and good humour, and so easy going. She was easy to bounce off and we'd be making wisecracks one moment, then would descend into a filthy battle of the wits.

Amanda often had me in stitches too. One night a viewer texted in asking her to use the strap-on on me. From nowhere, she adopted this Yorkshireman accent and adapted her posture to be masculine. It was all I could do not to laugh! Instead, I slipped into my best damsel-in-distress/nymphomaniac persona and played up to the camera. I always found it easier to play someone else rather than be myself, so role plays suited me perfectly. Amanda soon had her wicked way with me, and a barrage of texts came flooding in. "Wow, so sexy." "That's the hardest I've ever come!" We giggled as we read the texts out and knew we'd put on a good show for the guys and girls at home.

My first pro-modelling shoot was in 2005. It was a photography shoot in Portugal and was run by a lovely chap called Tony who ran a photography club, who has since passed on, rest his soul. The deal was that we would do a beach shoot in the morning and one in the afternoon. The rest of the time we'd be free to sunbathe, chill out or do whatever we wanted. In the evening, the group would take us ladies for dinner, all paid for by the photographers. I must have gone to Portugal about three times over the years for a week-long holiday. I worked alongside stars like Brooke Lee and Katie K, who were sweet and lovely people and professional. I'll probably mention a few names during this book, it's not to name drop, it's to give you a little insight into the industry and an idea of what it was like at the time. I will try to avoid saying anything too negative about anyone, but if they were utterly horrible, I will mention them and simply change their name.

For the stay, we were all based in a big villa or two, with the models at one end and the photographers the other. When you model, people always assume that everyone is sleeping with each other, but that could not be further from the truth. The photographers we stayed with were respectful, never tried to touch anyone and everyone kept to their own beds. Occasionally, you would get a few self-confessed perverts. I remember one poor chap, we'll call him Tom, who had a massive thing for taking close-up photos of the lady garden.

One day, I had a shoot with him by the way, and later, a grinning Tony asked me, "Has that old perve been taking close-up fanny shots again?" In response, I laughed and said, "I suppose it was fairly gynaecological!" I should have kept my mouth shut. From that moment, Tom's new nickname became 'The Gynaecologist!' Everyone ribbed him about it all week. He was not happy about this and sulked most of the time, throwing me a hurt look. I real-ised I would need to be more careful with my words in the future.

We were always well taken care of on those trips. We would be driven around, taken to the best restaurants and were told to order anything we wanted off the menu – steak, red snapper, bream, sea bass, whatever our hearts desired. I'd opt for a main, occasionally a starter too, but most of the girls would eat three courses including a huge pudding and copious amounts of wine! I was a little envious of how skinny they stayed, despite what they ate, but nonetheless I enjoyed their company and had a lot of time for them. I was always shyer in groups, so sat around the edges. I found the photographers a lot easier to talk to (they were usually quite geekier and had some interesting insights) and I would have a good banter with them.

Tony, the organiser, was a kind man and we would often have a banter with him. He was always spilling bits of food on himself and one of the girls presented him with a bib to wear. He laughed and grinned from ear to ear. It was decided that this would become a tradition and it was my turn to present the bib next time, except when I went to place it around his neck he looked really hurt and pushed my hand away. I spent the whole night tossing and turning over the thought of upsetting him. I wondered what I had done, but he was soon amicable with me again. That's how it was in those days, you never fell out with people for long. Perhaps fourteen years might not sound like such a long time ago, but life wasn't quite as fast-paced then; people had more time for each other, and the glamour and porn industry was in its glory. Everyone was making money and didn't stay upset for too long!

Upon my return to the UK, I sat down and made plans, organ-ising a mix of shifts on Sport TV and photo shoots. I became popular quite quickly, despite my shyness, and finding shoots wasn't hard. I always had time for people and was told, "I love working with you, you aren't a diva like some of the other girls." I can only hope that I haven't become too much of a diva since but can't make any promises!

I shot for various brands, including the naughty top-shelf magazines like *Escort*, *Razzle* and *Mayfair*. These tended to be striptease-style glamour shoots which culminated in some cheeky open leg shots. I also shot with amateur photographers, or hobbyists if you like, who enjoyed shooting photographs of women in various stages of undress. Some shoots would be clothed, while others hankered for lingerie and others preferred nude shoots. At the time, I had decided that the most I would do is pose open-legged with a toy or with another girl, but I had no interest in shooting anything with men.

I was open to most kinds of fetish and some of the things I shot you might consider outrageous. I did a 'flashing shoot' for a website called Dream Flash. The premise is that we would walk around public but deserted places – fields, roads, anywhere quiet – and I would quickly pop a boob out or lift my skirt up and the photographer would take a quick snap, then we'd move on quickly so as not to create any attention or cause a stir. Later, I shot with a similar brand, and we did the same kind of thing around London landmarks. One of the places we shot in front of was Buckingham Palace. I would quickly open my long coat for a saucy photo, then we got the hell out of there as fast as our legs would carry us! We never got caught as we were cautious. The aim was not to cause offence.

A couple of times we were taken unawares by a cyclist or a jogger, but I'd cover up in time. Sometimes they would see the camera and stop to watch, and so we would move on. We always had a laugh on these shoots, I'd get to explore London and we would always go for a drink or a meal in between photosets. It was a relaxed affair.

Soon, I was popping up all over the Internet and in the magazines, and the fans began to recognise me. My success was growing, and success can be addictive. I started to overstretch myself and take on too much, which led me to start feeling tired a lot of the time.

I also realised that with my face appearing all over the place, I would have to break the news to my mum. I faced this with absolute dread.

Chapter 17: A Confession and a Bum

The whirlwind romance I had experienced with J started to become fraught. He never seemed to have any money to contribute when we bought anything or went out, and when I challenged him on this, he admitted that he had massive debts. I was fuming he'd hid such an important thing from me. He was also a hoarder, chaotic and messy. He would wake up and go to work before me, and I'd get up to cereal, bread and butter all over the floor, food packets all over the side, and the dishes and mess he'd left out. Countless times I implored him to be a bit more thoughtful, and it always ended in arguments, with him accusing me of being hurtful and making him feel bad. It was exasperating and I coped by concentrating on my work.

For my birthday in November, J had gotten me a kitten and I called him Blade, after the sci-fi film starring Wesley Snipes. I had wanted a female cat but fell in love with Blade the minute I saw him. He was a cute little scrap off white fluff with black patches and was adorable. He was such a little character. Once I caught him on the sideboard stealing leftover curry. He looked up at me with a turmeric-stained face, with the most sheepish expression. I couldn't help but laugh, before gently reprimanding him and lifting him down.

If I stroked Blade, J would always take over and pick him up; it was like he had to be in control of everything. Often, I was travelling the country and Blade ended up going more to him, so he was more like J's cat, and I really missed my cat Pebbles and having that strong feline energy around me. I have always felt deeply attached to animals. They don't hurt you like humans do and they give you unconditional love. Pebbles was always on my mind and J suggested we get another cat as his birthday was coming up. J phoned around and it seemed that all the cats were gone, then he managed to talk a lady into selling a kitten she was planning to keep. I have no idea how he did that, or whether he made it up, but he came home with a black-and-white kitten with beautiful green eyes. I named her Tinkerbell, bought her a sparkly pink collar and worshipped the ground she walked on.

Blade and Tinkerbell became firm and fast friends and were always wrestling and racing around in a flurry of fur. While Blade was technically my cat and Tinkerbell was J's, it was the other way round. Tinkerbell would curl up on my lap and gaze up at me. I'd stroke her and sing to her, and we were instant buddies. With my new playmate to entertain me, I wasn't as interested in bars or clubs, and loved evenings in, cuddling the cat and reading a good book. All these cozy nights in meant I had to start being a bit more careful with my weight and became even stricter with my diet. I went through phases of cutting out carbs and trying faddy diets and extreme diet pills that left me shaky and jittery, but with Blade and Tinkerbell I finally felt like I had a little family again and felt a little more content for a while.

After a few months of living together, J seemed to resent the fact that I earned more money than him and expected me to pay for everything. He'd come home moaning about his job, how hard it was and how unfair it was that I could earn more money 'easily'. Meanwhile, I was travelling to Manchester one day, Southampton the next, all over the country for shoots, and in my spare time responding to emails from photographers. I was busier than he was and sometimes didn't get back till late, so I found his slovenliness frustrating.

One day he came home and told me he had been fired, although knowing what I do now, perhaps he walked out. From that point, he made little effort to get a job and sat around the house eating and watching porn movies. It was the beginning of a long end. I think back to that Laurel and Hardy scene where they keep saying goodbye, but the car won't move.

***

I invited my parents to come and visit me in Forest Gate. My dad was otherwise engaged, so it was my mum that came. I cooked dinner and made sure there was plenty of red wine. After dinner and several glasses, I broke the news about my new job. My mum was obviously shocked and didn't know how to take it. At the time, she asked lots of questions and for weeks after would call me up saying, "Whatever will my customers think?"

"Who cares, it isn't their life," I would reply defensively.

Mum stayed for several days and was unimpressed by my choice of boyfriend. He'd been out of work for a while and seemed to have no intention of finding another job. I'd managed to push him into getting an interview, but he had no money and so I bought him a new shirt and a suit to wear. The night before the interview, despite being a self-confessed teetotaller, he drank a litre of vodka. The next day, furious, I couldn't wake him up, and so when my mum suggested I tip some water over him to shock him into waking up for the interview, I took her advice. His version of the story later turned into me being drunk and throwing a lager at him. He forgets my mum was witness to this event.

That morning, he reluctantly dressed and disappeared for a while, then returned saying that the tube had been cancelled and he couldn't get to the interview. Another time he had an interview lined up, he dropped his phone in the sink and said he could no longer get the phone number or address for the interview. Of course, being naïve, I believed him. It was preferable to the reality that my boyfriend had a work phobia.

Still, there were other problems going on in my personal life. For a while, there was some backbiting and rumours between my family about my new career, and I distanced myself, now the black sheep of the family, isolated and alone. J would encourage me to hang up the phone if it got heated. On occasions, they would call my phone and I'd be in the bath or at the local shop round the corner, and he would tell them I was asleep, and then would 'forget' to tell me that they had called. I just assumed that they didn't really care much about me and isolating me from my family helped J burrow in deeper and cling on like a parasite.

Chapter 18: Struggling Mentally

Mentally fighting a battle with my family that didn't really exist, I became troubled. J's erratic ways were a struggle to cope with, alongside the pressure of modelling. It's hard to look great when you are sleep-deprived and stressed out, and I became more conscious of my looks and more insecure as a result. The confidence I had found was slipping away.

Taking the tube into London one day, my heart started to race and I came over in a sweat, filled with nausea. My mind spun with negative thoughts and I didn't understand what was happening to me. Trying to clear my brain, I got to the shoot and did my best to carry on like a professional. I can't even remember what I shot that day, most of it is a blur. I plastered on a fake smile and pretended that everything was OK. This was to become a habit and I relied on my acting skills to hide my personal problems, of which I felt deeply ashamed. I didn't know a great deal about anxiety at the time or realise that it's quite common. I felt embarrassed and that I had to 'hide it and appear normal', which is mentally draining. I felt like I was going crazy, and that people would find out and then everything would be ruined.

Time passed and I hid my feelings well, until one day I was at home and had just cleaned up when a little over an hour later J had turned the place into a squat with computer parts everywhere and food packets all over the floor. His behaviour had become increasingly chaotic. He had started to buy amphetamines and told me to dab it for weight loss and energy. I complied, taking small amounts, which staved off my appetite, but he would consume monstrous amounts that made his behaviour more erratic.

He was constantly taking apart computers and putting them

back together, leaving screws, nuts and bolts on the floor for me to tread on. Where he sat was a sea of debris and crumbs, and there was always porn playing on his working computer. It was too much, and I screamed at him that he was selfish, unreasonable and making my life hell. He went quiet for a while, then he told me he had realised that he had depression and he was convinced I had too. It seemed plausible; after all, I felt incredibly unhappy. I suppose at the time I loved J, and so I let myself believe that my unhappiness was down to depression. J made us both a doctor's appointments and as I was never comfortable with talking about symptoms, not wishing to come across as a self-obsessed malingerer, I wrote bullet points of my feelings down on a sheet of paper. The doctor took one look at what I'd written and filled out a prescription for Fluoxetine.

Taking the tablets felt like another dirty secret to hide, and I was terrified it would make me look incapable and not the strong career woman I wanted to be. When my family discovered I was on them, they urged me to flush them down the loo and told me that only weak people take antidepressants. J retorted that they were clueless, and I felt torn in all directions.

I concur that many people do need antidepressants, but in hindsight the only thing that was making me so deeply unhappy was J. I wish I'd had the wisdom then that I do now, but then that's what life is, it's a journey of exploration.

With the tablets came other side effects – lethargy and apathy, and my usually sharp mental vision become muddied. Everything seemed a lot more effort. It was as if someone had stolen the sunshine from my soul and pulled in dark, foreboding clouds around my head. I returned to the doctor, but she insisted I give the tablets time to take effect.

I'll never truly know if the tablets ever helped, as life was soon to become a great deal more challenging.

Chapter 19: Assaulted on Set

2006 was an interesting year for fetish shoots. I remember feeling insecure about my figure a lot and striving to lose weight, but looking back at photographs now, I was tiny! If my calculations are correct, this was the year I took part in a promotional movie for a naturist resort in France. It is only thanks to Gmail that I can put the history of these shoots into order, otherwise I'd be lost! The plan for the naturist shoot was for me, a popular spanking model called Jocelyn, and another well-known model called Sammie B to present pieces to camera about the resort and all the different activities on offer. We would be doing normal things that naturists on holiday do – sunbathing, eating sandwiches, joining in sporting activities and even bouncing on the trampoline.

Like I said, I wasn't particularly happy with my figure, so the idea of going completely nude all week was something that made me feel anxious; however, I was determined to put my vanity aside and to try and immerse myself in the experience as much as possible. The guy who was filming the video, Reg, was a relaxed, easy-going fellow and made us all feel extremely comfortable. The only thing was he was nude too, so I didn't know where to look and tried my hardest not to let my eyes wander. Sometimes though, you just can't help it; you see an appendage swaying in the breeze on a windy day and you can't help but glance at the movement, like a cat watching a dangling string. Jocelyn admitted to me that she had felt the same the first time she had been on naturist shoots, and it turns out that it's a common worry that you might accidentally look at someone's bits! I started to relax a little more and eased into it.

Naturists are hygienic people – well, they have to be really, don't they? They always carry a towel with them and sit on the towel wherever they go. I approved of this a great deal, as really I didn't want to sit where someone else's sweaty posterior had been placed previously. Other than the fact we were all naked, it was pretty much like any other shoot. We played sports – archery and tennis – we swam, and we ate lunch and drank wine in the evenings.

The most challenging part for me was bouncing on the trampoline without a bra. I'm not going to lie, it bloody hurt my boobies! I was between a B and C cup at the time, which is enough to cause discomfort when you are making them fly into the air with force, then crashing them down again with gravity. This was my least favourite bit of the whole week. I think I would have enjoyed the archery, had I been strong enough to pull the arrow back, but sadly my arms were not strong enough. Being a naturist resort and an over-eighteens affair, they didn't have any children's bows I could improvise with either, although I did do quite well on the crazy golf!

In Manchester for a girl-girl shoot, I was on set with a girl called Anya. I got long glittery acrylic nails and curled my hair and was still tanned from my naked week in France and feeling optimistic. On arrival, the photographer poured us a little glass of wine too, which helped chase away the worries. It's a tough call giving models alcohol on shoots. A glass can be great to get them relaxed, but too much and they start losing focus, acting out or looking dreadful. I have seen many photographers push too much wine on models and the resulting photos have been dreadful. In fact, I did a shoot in Hungerford with an old boy that kept topping up our glasses and I am afraid to say I got rather legless. Knowing one's ever-changing limits for alcohol (depending on body weight, time of the month, etc.) is no easy feat.

Anyway, I digress. It was a glorious, balmy summer's evening and we began the shoot in the gardens of a mansion. We posed in metal cages, and I did my best impression of a feral tiger growling through the cage. We did some interesting things with a flowing garden hose, certainly not things you are meant to use it for! The shoot was going well, with the photographer making all the right sounds, "Oooh yes, that looks good, perfect!"

Then we headed inside and took some shots of us, showing an alternative way to enjoy a cucumber. I will let your imagination do the work!

Most of the shoots were relatively easy, it was the travel that was tiring. Occasionally, you would get a grumpy or demanding photographer, more rarely a total perv or sometimes a bitchy fellow model, but overall it was good.

Unfortunately, life is full of ups and downs and soon there was a downward spiral that affected me for some time. I was contacted by a photographer called Jon who asked me to pose for a spanking magazine called *Spankaholics*. Firing off a dozen questions, I implored how hard will the spanking be? Will it just be a hand used and not a paddle? What other models are going? Do you have references? Jon assured me at every stage that it would be a soft shoot with no marks left. One of the models attending would be Jazz, a model who I'd shot with before, so that gave me some comfort and the guy's references checked out. I still had a strange gut feeling about the shoot, however, and I was on the verge of cancelling when J talked me out of it. "Don't worry, I'll drive you down to Brighton and sit in the next room. I'll make sure nothing untoward happens."

I decided to go for it and put it to the back of my mind until the big day arrived. However, it did not go as planned. I was packed and ready to leave when J said, "Actually, it's going to cost quite a bit to get to Brighton and back. Plus, I checked the motorways and there were a few accidents. It will be much quicker and cheaper to go on the train."

I wasn't happy about this and started panicking. I considered cancelling the shoot, but also didn't want to be seen as a flaky model. I argued my point to J and told him he had promised he would come. "You have references and it all sounds legit!" he reassured, and so eventually, with little other choice, I headed off on the train to Brighton on my own.

Eventually, I arrived and the shoot was in an old run-down building. Jazz greeted me with a friendly smile and the other girl Lilly seemed nervous but friendly. Jazz was the only one who had done spanking shoots before, so we decided to take her lead.

I was concerned when we reached the set and saw a sea of faces looking up at us. I was confused about why there were so many people watching, but as I had never done this style of shoot before, I thought perhaps this was what usually happened. The premise for the shoot was that we were fashion models, but we were acting too haughty and would get punished for it.

In our diva outfits, we sauntered up and down the stage, getting into role, and waited to be called. One of the cast then told us our behaviour was unacceptable and that we would need to get spanked. I watched Jazz get spanked by the master and she sounded like she was enjoying it, with plenty of ooohs and aaahs! By the time the director yelled cut, she was giggling and returned to her place. It was my turn next and feeling assured, I took my place over the master's lap. His palm connected with my buttocks and other than a bit of a sting, I thought, *This isn't too bad!*

"Cut!" the director yelled.

Lilly took her turn, and it was time to get spanked by the blonde Russian mistress. I placed myself over her lap then WHAM! Her palms came down on my backside like a rain of fire. I wriggled and squirmed and tried to escape, but she pinned me down. "Try to escape and I will hit you harder," she threatened. This didn't seem like role play anymore, this felt out of control and fear rose in my chest. The sad thing is, I didn't even know about safe words at the time, and all of us models should have been given one at the start of the shoot. Had I known that, I would have been yelling, "Red, red, get off me, you fucker!" Instead, I wailed, "It hurts too much, I don't like it, please stop."

She didn't stop; the angry, fiery blasts across my flesh continued and I felt like a mouse in the beak of a hawk. My bottom cheeks didn't just sting, they felt raw. Tears stung my eyes and the humiliation of it burned away at me. I know for many subs, they love this feeling, but I was not a sub. I was a model engaging in a so-called role play. Finally, after an age, it ended and I tried to stop myself crying, although tears were threatening to spill down my cheeks. The worst of it was having an audience watch and see my reactions.

I should have just left there and then, walked out. Jazz seemed to be acting quite normal though and Lilly seemed shaken but coping OK. I didn't want to be the one diva model ruining it for the other girls, so I took my place and sat down.

That's when Jon said a caning would take place next. "You said no canes," I protested, aghast.

"Yes, but unfortunately the fans require it now. Our main funder dropped out, so we are using a different one and he wants caning. It won't hurt much, don't worry."

Of course, this was all absolute bollocks and manipulation, but I wasn't sure enough of myself back then to argue it. I looked to the other girls for reactions, but there were none.

I can't remember the exact order of who got caned first as it was all a blur; my emotions were running high and I was paralysed by shock. Often in life, you get the fight or flight sensation, but I was like a rabbit in the headlights, frozen to the spot. When I was called up, it felt like walking to my death sentence. Every slow step took me closer to that wicked witch and her cane. When the caning began, it sent me straight back into shock. The pain level was unbearable. It was not a fleeting sting. It was a cascade of brutal and vicious strikes intended to cause maximum harm. I remember screaming a high-pitched wail, and then fearing the threat of harder punishment if I persisted.

"If you don't take this like a good girl, I will hit your friends even harder too," the woman sneered.

I should have seen that this was a manipulation tactic, but I felt genuinely worried for the other girls I was on set with. My whole body tensed. I wanted to stand up and smash her in the face with my fist. I was frozen between doing something crazy and going completely limp when the producer murmured, "You are doing so well, not much more now, you can do it."

This has taught me a great deal about femdom. I insist that all my slaves have a safe word, whether they want one or not. If they refuse, I don't see them, it's simple. A safe word is paramount for everyone's safety. Also, sometimes one of my slaves may want to experience more pain, but when they are on the verge of breaking, a soft word can egg them on. I am never relentless in my approach and can see when someone has reached their upper limit and I know when to stop. This devil woman had none of that foresight, training or compassion, and she smashed the cane down with full force. The moment she paused, I bolted. I pulled myself up and fled across the stage, my eyes red and bloodshot, tears flowing and mascara running down my cheeks. As I ran, they called me back and I shouted something like, "No, leave me alone!"

Making for the stairs, I ran to the toilets. Once there, I dived into a cubicle, slammed the door behind me and locked it.

After a few moments, Jon and the two models came upstairs breathing soothing words through the door. "Go away!" I yelled. "I'm not coming out. I don't want to do your stupid shoot anymore!"

Jon was extremely persuasive and eventually talked me into unlocking the cubicle and finishing the shoot. While I have summarised the shoot and the main details, it had taken place across three hours, and I was feeling broken. Reluctant, I came out of the cubicle and sat on a wooden bench. Jon was calm and talked slowly, his eyes big and wide behind his thick glasses. The strangest thing happened next. He turned to me and said, "I feel really happy. I started on these new antidepressants, and they are really helping." I thought to myself, *Mine aren't.*

To this day, I have no idea why he said that to me or what his agenda was. I don't know if it was a cry for pity or to make me see him as less of a threat. It was all peculiar.

Against my better judgement, I agreed to return to set with the other girls and to take some more caning. Someone had obviously had a word with the woman, as she seemed to tone it down a little, but the wooden cane still seared into my flesh. My backside felt bruised and battered, as if I had sat on a hot grill. I think I managed to zone out for the remaining time. I could still feel the pain of the implement she wielded, but I told myself it would be over soon; I pushed my brain to float away and detach itself from the experience, so then it was only my physical body that suffered.

When it stopped, audience members called to me, "You did so well that time." I looked at them as if they were completely barmy, which they obviously were. They were praising me for allowing someone to physically assault me.

The whole experience was horrendous, but the thing that remains so vivid and terrible is what they did to Jazz next. She was a pro-spanking model and had done many of these kinds of shoots before, so to see how they savagely beat her and how it affected her shook me to the core. If I had thought my caning was brutal, by God! This was something else. The usually calm Jazz began to shriek and sob. Her previously perfect backside was covered in overlapping bright red lines and blood blisters. Angry black bruises rose from her flesh. The most disturbing thing wasn't so much seeing the inflicted wounds, or the thrash of that heavy wooden cane on her rump, it was the sounds of agony she omitted that tore into my heart. They were the wails of someone who had given up. I prayed for her to call it to an end, but it continued, I don't know how long for – ten, maybe twenty minutes – but those minutes felt like hours.

When Jazz had finished and we were flashed fake smiles and 'well dones', we were all sullen and subdued. The energy had fled the room and I couldn't wait to escape. Jon passed us all a cheque for £200 for the assault that had taken place and we scarpered. Outside us girls fell into each other's arms crying. "I'm so sorry," Jazz cried. "I've never known anything like that. That's not how it's supposed to be."

We agreed to alert the police; after all, they had told us it would be a soft shoot and had coerced us into taking a beating.

On the train back home, I couldn't even sit down. I found J in floods of tears and had to endure his fake concern. "I feel like it's my fault," he said to defend himself against any perceived backlash.

Arriving home, J must have been feeling guilty, as he poured me a lukewarm bath (my raw skin couldn't take heat) and made me food. I looked in a mirror to see how damaged my skin was and the whole of my backside was red and black with cuts across it. It seemed Jazz had fared worse. She sent me photos of her bottom and she had deep welts and cuts across her cheeks.

J walked me down to the nearest police station as requested by the police and I made a statement and filed a report. When explaining it all to the policewoman, I could see tears welling up in her eyes and she was trying not to cry. In a way, this was soothing. I had half expected them to say that I had agreed to it and that it was my fault. This is rare and would be victim shaming. Abuse is taken seriously by the police, but it does sometimes happen.

My bottom was black for two weeks afterwards and I had to cancel all of my shoots as no one wanted to shoot evidence of an abuse that had taken place. It just doesn't portray the right image.

In time, my flesh healed. It was the emotional scars left behind that took longer to heal; it re-opened all my old wounds from the bullying I'd suffered from at school, and I struggled to trust anyone. Perhaps a lack of trust can be a good thing though and I made sure a situation like that never happened again. You take experience and lessons from everything in life and so despite how awful this situation was at the time, it made me mindful about the safety of others and myself. Many of my slaves call me a nurturing domme, because I coax out of them what lies within, but I don't abuse the power. That is my personality though and I doubt I would have ever been any different, even without that experience. If I have only taken from that awful day a lesson in caution and trust, then that is still something I have gained.

Chapter 20:
Empty Threats from a Bully

Two things I have always been are independent and resilient, and while I carried the scars around on the inside, I wasn't about to let anyone see them. It was me against the rest of the world. Try to break me and I will rise up harder. Right after the spanking incident, I had put a warning out on a model's forum called Net-Model, with pictures of my bottom, warning other models not to make the same mistake as me, to get a safe word and always speak up or leave if they were uncomfortable. Part of the emotional healing for me was looking out for other models and ensuring that they didn't have to suffer the same fate.

I still expected comments like, "Well, what did you expect?" which I got from my mum. Fortunately, no one else said anything like this. There were hundreds of replies to my warning, messages of support, outraged models and photographers who had urged me to go to the police and make the people involved culpable for their crimes. I had strangers messaging me offering support and I began to meet a lot more people in the modelling community. I now had new allies.

Lilly had dropped out of filing a police statement and Jazz did, too, as they feared the repercussions it would have on their careers. I thought about what they said but decided to press charges anyway. The thought of the production company finding a girl – perhaps even younger than myself – and harming her spurred me on with the prosecution and the need to stop those people from repeating their crimes. Far from harming my career, it actually made me more popular in a bizarre kind of twist. Every photographer seemed to want to shoot with me and congratulated me on "doing the right thing and looking out for other models". I hadn't been looking for gratitude or thanks, and I felt a little embarrassed at the attention, but the extra shoots certainly didn't hurt and made up a little of the money I'd lost.

In time, I had news from the Surrey police and it transpired that the Russian domme had been cautioned for assault and charged with ABH. It was extremely disappointing to learn that this producer Jon had escaped a conviction. A couple of years down the line, however, he pulled the same stunt and ended up in prison. Upon his release, he sent me an abusive email, which I shall copy and paste for you to peruse:

Jon White

Mon, 8 Feb 2010, 16:43

Hello Kaz

I came across your services for bdsm on the net. You do realise that by providing such you are legally and in print described as a 'prostitute'. The services you offer may bnot involve penetration but that does not exempt 'us' describing you as a common prostitute in print. Whilst there is nothing wrong with that I will however be keeping this on record and should your real name be published Katherine **** as prostitute you will have no legal recourse, unless you can prove that you have not engaged in such practises but as we have client feedback that may prove to be an issue for you if you dispute your role.

A copy of your website may be sent to Customs/Revenue for review.

I have also listed your activities with another agency and a well known national newspaper.

I do hope you enjoy being classed as a common prostitute.

tahnks

Jack Jims

Aghast at the poor grammar and typos in the letter, I wasn't prepared to let that slide. This is what I wrote back:

Hi John,

The Collins English Dictionary definition of prostitution is:

1. a woman who engages in sexual intercourse for money

2. a man who engages in such activity, esp in homosexual practices

3. a person who offers his talent or work for unworthy purposes

vb (tr)

1. to offer (oneself or another) in sexual intercourse for money

2. to offer (a person, esp oneself, or a person's talent) for unworthy purposes

You may notice that contrary to your earlier assertion that none of these apply to me. Hence your entire un-intelligible monologue is inapplicable. Furthermore, you may contact Customs and Excise just as often as you wish as they will be able to check their records and find my up-to-date tax and national insurance payments and full accounts for all aspects of my business.

Your language and tone in this email, I have no option but to take as highly threatening, particularly given that this is your first communication to me since the last time I had to report you to the police! Therefore I have copied this email to the original case officer for his information and advice.

Furthermore, please be aware that should you attempt to cause any harm to my business prospects by any method – including but not limited to electronic dissemination (e.g. Internet/email), newspapers and 'mysterious agencies', I will pursue indicated legal action to recover all possible costs and losses.

Yours Sincerely,
Kaz B/PrincessKaz
(Model/porn star, actress, dominatrix and cam girl) (and proud of it!)

Of course, I knew that if he were to send my information to a newspaper, there would be two possible outcomes. 1: They would have absolutely zero interest, or 2: They might run an article and it would be fantastic publicity. I preferred not to allow him this insight. A few more messages went back and forth, him accusing me of "persecuting innocent people" and posting "peppercorn attacks" by posting online about his company assaulting me. He wittered on about it being unfair that I wouldn't agree to meet him in person after the shoot – duh! – or accept compensation. He finished by saying, "Don't be a fishwife and chill out," and claimed he had been "duped" too and would "never have worked for those people if I had known".

He also claimed that *Spankoholics* had nothing to do with the shoot, until I took a screenshot of the Who Is page that listed him as the owner and sent it to him.

This was over four years since the shoot had taken place and I wasn't the naïve little girl that I had once been. He was trying to scare me, and the big bad wolf impression just didn't hold any weight anymore. With age comes wisdom. I closed the chapter swiftly and moved on.

Chapter 21: Hellos, Goodbyes and a Police Raid!

2006

Every day was different – one day I'd be posing against a backdrop in the latest England football kit and then the next day I'd be modelling jewellery or doing a raunchy shoot. Another unpleasant shoot I did was a sploshing shoot in Wrexham, North Wales. The photographer was an amicable-enough chap, but we were shooting in a freezing-cold barn. The aim of the game was for me and another girl to pour food products over each other while the photographer took photos. We started with yoghurt, then cream which stunk to high heaven after a while.

Towards the end of the shoot, we were given cartons of melting ice cream to pour over each other. We were trembling with the cold and had to hold on to each other for warmth by that stage. I looked at her and could see her lips were blue and knew mine would be too. I had never felt so cold in my life. The worst of it was that there was no shower, and we couldn't wash the sticky residue off ourselves properly before taking the four-hour train journey home. Over the years, I have caught the train home in many states of disarray, with custard in my hair, mud smeared across my face and even fake blood. The funny thing is, when travelling around London I never got one single funny look off anyone when I got on the tube like this. Even when I went home from a horror movie still covered in fake blood (that wouldn't come off in the shower), no one batted an eyelid. Londoners certainly mind their own business, and I suppose if I did look like a mass murderer, they weren't about to make eye contact with me. Thank heavens for small mercies!

It was spring 2006 when I met Diamond on a shoot. As I will be going across some rough territory throughout my memories of Diamond, I have changed her name and will change any obvious features or locations that might link her to the real person. We were on a group shoot down in South London when we met, posing for soft girl-girl photos. She giggled a lot and hid behind a sofa when she got changed, but on set she was a different girl entirely. It was only meant to be a soft (not hardcore) shoot but she seemed determined to snog my face off and head into my knickers, and the photographer kept telling her to behave herself. I thought that the whole incident was hilarious, and I didn't take it too seriously. We got chatting and after the shoot she came back to my place in Forest Gate with her husband Micky for some pizza. Micky got on like a house on fire with J, and us girls carried on chatting about the industry. Diamond hadn't been around that long and was only doing BDSM shoots, so I said I would help her promote herself and give her some contacts. Overhearing Micky's conversation with J was hilarious; when referring to Diamond, he said, "She's mad she is. I'm always telling her to calm down, stop getting your pussy out. Behave yourself, woman."

Perhaps I should have taken heed at these words, but I just found it funny. The thing is, Diamond was a great deal of fun to be around; she was as mad as a hatter on acid flying a teapot, but entertaining. In time, we became good friends, and I got her some shifts working with me on Sport Babes XXX. We worked together well on the channel as we were both upbeat. Her confidence grew and, with that, she became more outrageous. I'd know that when she started to yell, "I'm a squirter, I am," that would be the cue for me to duck to the side as she shot urine everywhere. The channel of course didn't allow this kind of behaviour and she was told off, but the truth was it was good for ratings! Everyone loved our double act, and perhaps my gentle, calm energy offset her outrageousness.

Unfortunately, the channels were in a ratings war with each other, and Sport TV was eventually fined by Ofcom for 'obscenity', or at least that is what I was told. This meant there were strict cutbacks on what was permitted, and the show started to become more formatted. Eventually, the text messaging service was dispensed with the phone lines that came into play. This transformed a brilliant entertainment show into a catalogue of bored-looking models, waggling phones at the camera. Most of the stations follow this rigid phone-waggle format today, and I always giggle when I see a bored-looking woman waggle her phone at the camera. I know exactly what she's thinking, *What shall I have for breakfast tomorrow?*

In the golden days at Sport Babes XXX though, we did pretty much what we felt like and got away with it for a while! We could be serious, silly, fun; whatever we did, the audience seemed to love. Diamond and I started to do more shoots together and I found work for the two of us through some of my photography contacts. We went on shoots abroad together and even took a holiday to Alanya in Turkey together eventually. Diamond had gone back for her hair straighteners and missed her flight then called me up, sobbing. I paid for another flight for her and Mickey to join us, and we spent a week hanging out in the villa, visiting bars and exploring. Diamond had said she had no money for a flight but always seemed to be going on trips with Mickey. Deciding to let it slide, I said nothing.

It all flew by and a week later we were back at Sport TV. When I had started working on the station, I took the tube to get there. Then they sold their London offices due to increasing rents and moved up to Milton Keynes. It was a lot more challenging getting there and back, and often I'd end up getting the train there. J would usually promise to drive me then conveniently lose the car keys or house keys, or have a migraine or a bad toe, and so I'd be lugging my huge suitcase on and off trains. He was still jobless, and it annoyed me that he couldn't even get off his backside and drive me to work when he wasn't paying any rent.

CONFESSIONS OF A DOMINATRIX

I'd finish my shift at 1 p.m., everyone would leave and I'd be waiting alone on a cold dark trading estate in the early hours of the morning for up to an hour. One time he didn't answer his phone at all and I was stranded. Visions of him getting into an accident haunted me, so in a panic I called the police. An officer said they would send someone round to the house, then called me back to say that eventually he had answered the door and had been asleep. J then called me furious, "Why did you send the police round? I had some gear [drugs] on the side."

"Because it's the middle of the night, I'm on a dangerous dark trading estate on my own, and I thought you might have been injured."

"I was tired, I fell asleep. The policeman wanted to come in and you could have created a big problem."

When J screwed up, it was always my fault. He would never apologise or admit his error, and instead would always try to make me feel it was my fault. After a while, I started believing him. I didn't realise then that this is a manipulation tactic called 'gaslighting'. Gaslighting is when an abuser twists, bends and distorts facts beyond all reasonable recognition. They will rewrite history, change events and make you even question your own reality.

Amid my growing angst, I lost a friend that was dear to me, Joe A, who I met at the porn party in 2005. He had been somewhat an advisor to me during my career and he would often invite various porn producers and porn stars round to his flat in London and would cook a lovely meal for us. He'd got sick a couple of months before. He had a terrible cough and kept throwing up after meals. Everyone would urge him to see a doctor and he would refuse. The fear in his eyes was clear. I think he knew what was wrong with him. One night a few weeks later, my friend Terry rang me up to say that Joe was in hospital. He had throat cancer and it was terminal. He had requested to see us.

In denial, I couldn't accept he was dying and wrote a long letter to him praying for a miracle and bought an angel pin to give to him. When we arrived in his ward, the first thing that hit me as we entered was the smell. It was a smell of urine and sickliness, overpowered with bleach. The sight of my friend looking so tiny and withered in his hospital bed shocked me to the core. He was refusing all food and medicine; he just wanted peace. Tears stung at my eyes, but I knew Joe wouldn't want pity, so I smiled and said, "Hey, Joe!"

"I've seen you looking better," J joked.

Joe was struggling to breathe but he managed to lift a finger and waggle it at J, "Don't you start."

What do you say to someone who is dying? The shock of it all had taken the words out of my mouth. Joe was Jewish, but I didn't want to start talking about death and the afterlife, it seemed so final. I started talking about what we'd been up to that week, and he struggled to lift his head and listened. Doing my best to be upbeat, I talked about what we would do when he got out of hospital. I was deluded, but perhaps it was for the best. What do you say to a dying man? The last time I'd seen him he'd been ranting about a performer who he believed had screwed him over years before because she went off and did her own thing. I'd told him he needed to get over it and stop moping. That being our last proper conversation felt awful.

Eventually, the nurse told us visiting hours were over. I pinned the gold angel pin onto the end of his bed, gave Joe a kiss on the head and said, "Seeya later." I couldn't bring myself to say goodbye.

Later that night, J was in the study watching something online and I was in bed when I had the strangest feeling come over me. It felt as if there was a presence nearby, then I heard Joe's voice say, "Goodbye, pet."

The tears that had been threatening to spill all day came and I whispered, "Goodbye, Joe, I'll miss you."

Then the feeling passed, and I was alone in the dark again. I lifted back the covers and ran into the study.

"Joe's just passed," I blurted to J.

"What are you on about? How do you know?"

"He just said goodbye to me!"

"Don't be silly. There is no such thing as ghosts and spirits. It's your imagination playing games on you," he scoffed, a look of scorn on his face.

Returning to the bedroom dejected, I tossed and turned for hours before I slept.

Terry phoned us the next morning. Joe had passed in his sleep.

"See, I told you he'd passed," I told J. "It was real. He said goodbye to me."

"It's simply your brain's way of processing the information and a coincidence. It's just not possible and I don't believe in the afterlife."

Whatever I said, he would try to convince me otherwise, so I decided to avoid the conversation and keep hold of the small comfort from my belief that Joe had passed onto somewhere better.

Joe's death hit the UK industry hard, at least for the many who knew and loved him. He was such a kind person and helped so many new models learn about health and safety. For me, the loss had a great impact. He'd been like a father figure and I didn't cope well with losing him.

The next day, I had a shoot and didn't know how I was going to get through it. Cancelling was not an option; we didn't have much money. Our rent in London alone was around £800 plus bills, and the cost of living in London was not cheap.

The shoot was for a panty fetish site, talking to camera and flashing your panties. I was working alongside three other girls and when the camera turned to me, there was a fleeting moment of panic. I could barely even raise a smile, let alone be bubbly and inviting. Without even knowing what I was doing, I slipped into the softest, most Marilyn Monroe-esque voice I could summon up, giggled and lifted my skirt. The cameraman was smiling and nodding, and I realised that I was somehow pulling it off. I continued in this vein and managed to get through the day by being this other person. That's when I learned how to get through tough on-camera situations by creating personas. If I had no idea what I was doing, I played a ditsy character and would giggle through it. I now had a way to escape reality when I needed to, and it also gave the scenes a little diversity. I was no Grace Kelly, but it certainly helped me become a lot more comfortable with my on-screen presence. In my youth, I often dumbed myself down when around others. It was easier to blend in that way. People didn't feel threatened by you if you played the dumb blonde.

Role playing was exactly what I needed at the time, as I seemed to start experiencing episodes of what I presume now was psychosis. I have mild tinnitus and often hear white noise, drifting words and snatches of music. I often quite enjoy it to be honest and start singing the words to the music I can hear, but during the period after Joe's death, it became unbearable. I would often hear disembodied voices hurling insults and criticisms at me, telling me I was fat and worthless, or that bad things would happen to me. I had this unbearable sense that something in the darkness was hanging over me and waiting to devour me whole.

Starting to feel as if I was officially crazy, I now had an even bigger secret to hide. My brain would often summon up the worst-possible scenario in every situation and feed it back to me tenfold. Trying to reason with my brain and shut it all out, I couldn't escape my own thoughts. Reading a lot of self-development books again and studying mental health videos gave me a small amount of clarity and stopped me from descending too deep into the abyss. Returning to the doctor, she said not to worry and that auditory hallucinations are common with certain types of antidepressants. I switched my medication again; I think it was citalopram she put me on next and I was relieved to have a technical term for this phenomenon, but in my lowest points I thought that I was being psychically attacked by demons. I couldn't even discuss that with my doctor. How do you do that big reveal? "Hey, Doc, what's up? By the way, there are demons in my attic and they are trying to give me a hard time. Any tips?"

I was sane and lucid enough to realise my thoughts and notions were not real, that they sounded utterly insane, and I knew that if I vocalised them, it would make them more real, so instead I kept quiet.

I found some solace in music; it seemed to sweep the audio hallucinations away on a blissful wave. During those years, I always had the radio playing music or comedy. Silence was my enemy. It's funny how your perception shifts over time. Now I find silence idyllic – to hear nothing except the odd pitter-patter of a cat's paw, or the song of a bird.

The rest of 2006 sped by in a blur of shifts at Sport TV, arguments, and the struggle to survive. Soon, 2007 was upon us and there were a lot of problems with the flat. The hot water stopped working and everything started to break, and it was becoming uninhabitable. "Why won't the landlord fix anything?" I'd complain.

"Oh, he isn't fussed," J would reply.

Christmas came and I had foolishly let myself be persuaded to stay at home in Forest Gate for Christmas. I don't blame J at all for this; part of me wondered what it would be like to be a proper grown-up at Christmas and spend it in your own home. I let the fantasy take over and imagined it full of laughs and entertainment. In reality, I had a foot-high tree, no decorations, no television (we didn't own one), no Christmas songs (J couldn't stand them) and zero Christmas spirit. I gave J a few small gifts. He didn't have any money to buy me any. I'd bought some pre-cooked lobsters from Asda for our Christmas dinner, thinking it would make a nice change to treat ourselves to something a little more exotic. They were tasteless, and I wished I'd gone home and spent the day with my family, laughing and joking, sipping wine and tucking into a roast dinner. My first Christmas away from home was not the exciting foray into adulthood I had anticipated, and I realised that Christmas is all about family and the company you keep.

The new year came, and I became increasingly frustrated and insisted we move. We found a house in Hitchin which I fell in love with. It was a simple two-bed terraced house, but it had a small patch of grass out the back, a log fireplace in the sitting room and bare wooden floorboards in the top bedroom, which I felt gave it character.

When I asked J to tell the agency we were leaving, he said he didn't have their number and couldn't remember the name of the agency. No wonder the landlord wouldn't help us, he didn't even know we'd had problems!

It was too late to do anything though. We had accepted the new property; though I felt terrible that he hadn't informed the agency that we were leaving, I had no idea how I could find out who they were or how to contact them. Later, J came up with a letter saying that we had absconded. I was mortified!

Moving our stuff to the new house proved a lot more difficult. J said he had backache and halfway through putting the boxes in the van said he couldn't do anymore that night and would go back for it. He bundled Tinkerbell and Blade into the van, and they started to get distressed. I didn't want to drag it out and was so concerned that the cats would escape I agreed.

Half of our things were still in the old flat and J was going to go and pick them up the next day, but still claimed he had a backache and migraine that wouldn't allow him to drive safely. This became his default excuse over the years if he couldn't think of any outlandish excuse.

The next day, I was working down in London. I had been given a film extra part on the set of *28 Days Later* and was taking part in a crowd scene where everyone was running around screaming. It was a great experience, though freezing cold and I started to feel worse for wear by the end of the shoot. My nose, toes and hands were frozen. I was trembling from head to toe and felt weak. J was due to pick me up about 4 a.m., but of course he didn't arrive until much later. When he did arrive, he said he'd forgotten to put insurance on the car, so parked up and went off to "find an Internet café". I couldn't believe he had driven without insurance, but I was exhausted and laid down in the back of the car. It was hours before he came back, and he had stories about cafes being closed and walking to one and then another. For all I cared, he could have claimed he had been kidnapped by aliens! I just wanted to get home to bed, in the warm.

By the time we reached our house, it was around 8 a.m. Going straight to bed and slipping under the covers, I breathed a sigh of relief while J faffed around with the car. He returned and climbed in beside me. Then I heard a voice, "Hello? Police!" I thought I must be imagining it! Was it my tinnitus? It probably hadn't helped spending years standing next to the massive speakers at festivals and in clubs. I was used to hearing strange sounds. When you are slightly deaf, your brain tries to find patterns and match them, so often it creates sounds within your ears and antidepressants can exacerbate this. So, of course I ignored the voice, thinking it was my imagination. The voice came again louder, "Hello? Police."

This time I knew I wasn't hearing things and jumped out of bed and threw on a jumper! J had left some white powder on the side, so I threw a mug over it and rushed to the bedroom door.

"Hello?" I called with a bewildered expression.

There were two policemen and a policewoman walking up the stairs. "We have a warrant to search your property."

"Really?" My eyebrows nearly flew completely off my brow.

"What are you looking for?" J asked.

"A hydroponics plant."

"What sort of plant is that?" I asked J, puzzled.

"They mean they are looking for a cannabis factory," he said matter-of-factly.

My expression changed from puzzlement to astonishment to amusement, and I started laughing. I studied their uniforms and badges to see if they were real, which they seemed to be. I was still expecting someone to pull out a camera and to shout, "Ha-ha, got you!"

Back in those days, there may have been the odd packet of powder in the house from time to time, personal quantities, but neither of us smoked cannabis and wouldn't have had the foggiest about hydroponics plants. On top of that, we had only just moved in!

The police were serious, however, and insisted on searching the place. I offered them tea and biscuits, which they politely declined and said that they were not allowed to accept.

While the whole thing was ridiculous, I understood that they were only doing their jobs, so I was as polite as possible and helped as much as I could. I've always had a lot of respect for the police. They have been helpful in the past and they do their best to uphold the safety of the community, so I wasn't about to start making protestations.

The female officer asked to search my wallet. I fetched it from my bag on the sofa and handed it to her. When she pulled out a paper wrap, her eyes lit up and she looked like she had won the policewoman's bonus lottery! Her expression changed from excitement to confusion as she pulled a wad of fur from the paper.

"What is this?" she asked, looking at me as if I was the biggest weirdo on the planet.

"It's cat fur," I explained.

She looked confused and I wanted to put her out of her misery, so I continued, "When my cat Pebbles died, I took a locket of her fur and I always carry it around with me."

She looked disgusted but respectfully put it back in the paper wrap safely and handed me the purse, before saying, "I'm allergic to cats. Can I wash my hands please?"

"Just through the kitchen on the right," I said, pointing helpfully.

A smile was trying to break through the corners of my mouth. I certainly didn't want to make their jobs any harder, but it was funny watching her expression change as she had discovered my cat fur wrap!

J then wanted the toilet and a policeman said he needed to watch him in case he was trying to flush anything. J told me later he did the loudest poo in front of the policeman, making groaning and straining noises. I was completely disgusted and thought it was completely unnecessary to be so awkward and barbaric. They finished searching the house and wanted to look in J's car.

They found, belonging to J, some empty food packets, a half-eaten burger, some cake and a box of flyers with me on advertising my adult website. They were most bemused at this and left most likely thinking we were harmless, but a pair of nutcases!

By the time I got into bed, I was drained and starting to feel ill. I started sneezing and there was no way I'd have been in a fit state to return to the set again that night. Whenever I became over-exhausted and emotionally drained, it affected my health and, as a result, I lost my part on that movie, which is a real shame, but that's all history now.

To make matters worse, it transpired that J still hadn't collected our stuff; he said the locks had been changed (probably a lie). So, we had now lost half of our belongings. None of it was particularly valuable – we didn't even own a TV or a radio – but there were many nostalgic items that were irreplaceable, photos and memories lost. Sometimes, just when you think it can't get worse, it does. It seems he had left the van, which still had loads of our stuff in it, outside a police station, claiming he'd run out of fuel. Instead of getting more fuel, he'd left it there, hence the intrusion in our new rented house. The police had called the van hire company and they had taken it back to their depot. We had to travel down to London, and they made me pay £1,500 on a credit card under duress to get my property back. Combined, the lot probably wasn't even worth anywhere near that, but it was our clothes, the cat stuff and again items which had a sentimental attachment to them.

For months, I had been trying to scrape some money together to attend my sister's wedding the following year, which would be held in July 2007. This had wiped out all my existing savings, plus would eat into future rent and bill money. It was now October 2006. I had nine months to reduce the debt and replace the money. Why did I have such a sinking feeling in my stomach? Would I make it to the wedding? By nail or by tooth, I'd do my darndest!

Life On a String

Spilling like rancid honey
Words so sweet, fall from your tongue
So why do I feel like I'm on your bottom rung?

Saccharin words
Devoid of emotion and empty
Like the cavernous heart in your chest
You always say that I'm the best
So why does it always feel like a test?

Actions speak louder than words
They always shout the loudest truth
So don't tell me that I'm aloof
When action is the real proof

They say listen to your heart
That's the biggest lie
Your heart is blind and stupid
It will only make you cry

Listen to your inner voice
It always makes the perfect choice
So why do we ignore it?
Why do we endure it?

The heart is a fool
The heart is cruel
The heart sees you played like a tool
It's that heart that we must overrule

But is it fair to blame the heart
When all it's done is to play its part
If life is a stage, the play's begun
But I have no script, no lines, I'm done

Dancing in the lights
Like a broken marionette
These strings are not mine
So I'll just dance off set

I'm not a puppet, I'm not a toy
I'm someone that you won't destroy
My song may be done
But the truth will live on
In simplicity, we find the sweetest joy

Chapter 22: Goodbye Dear Blade

After the initial setbacks, I enjoyed living in Hitchin. When I had a peaceful moment (which was rare) I would curl up by the fire with the cats and listening to the crackle and spit of the logs as they burned, which was therapeutic, and I was at my happiest when it was just me and the cats and J was in bed, or otherwise disposed.

The prescription tablets I was on made me sleep more than normal, but I needed healing and sleep was perhaps the best way to achieve this.

Sport TV was nearer to me now but still a pain. The owners knew I was reliable and repeatedly called on me at the last minute to make the journey up to Milton Keynes. I'd try and protest but Nessa the schedule planner would try every tactic under the sun, "Oh please, you are our top girl!" (I'm sure they said this to everyone.) "We'll pay you £180 for the shift!"

Of course, despite dropping all my plans last minute, racing off to MK and battling with public transport, they never paid me the promised amount. It was a long journey, which would sometimes get me there ten minutes after the shift had started. They would then refuse to pay me any extra, fine me £50 and after all that travelling and messing around, I'd come out with only around £80. £80 might sound great for a shift, but if you consider that was an eight-hour shift if you include travel and it was one wage split between two people, it's not really a lot and it didn't go far. Whenever I tried to speak to Nessa, she would either be out of the office or would tell me to send an email, which was ignored. I started to lose faith in the channel and had my doubts about staying. I knew in the future I would be exploring alternative options.

I had made some good friends there and I enjoyed working with a Brazilian girl called Rio. She was down to earth and genuine. Sometimes, you would get girls come on to the show and within weeks the fame would go to their heads, and they would believe all their own hype, resulting in them becoming difficult, deplorable people to work with. I kept my distance as much as possible from these types.

2006 had been a dramatic year of ups and downs. I had won Best Newcomer at the Adult Film Awards in Hammersmith (that caused me no end of trouble with other girls who felt that they should have won it). It's only a matter of the judges' opinions and not based on facts, and while it's nice to win, it's just a trophy made out of glass. It's the promotion that leads up to it that is of true value, but some don't realise that and just want to be seen as the best.

One of the highlights of the year was an amazing portfolio shoot in France. I spent a week in St Tropez soaking up the local culture and had now gotten my website up and running. The photographer Rory and I hung around in little bars by the harbour with million-dollar yachts yards away. We did some brilliant glamour shoots in some old ruins and enjoyed some French meals on the azure coast, sprinkled in sunlight. Working holidays with photographers were often a great escape. They treated me well and life felt lighter, easier.

Webcam was now becoming popular, and I started to talk to guys online, and they would pay per minute. Life seemed to constantly see-saw though – if it wasn't one thing, it was another.

Upstairs writing on my computer, J called me down. Clocking the expression on his face before I saw the blanket in his arms, my heart stopped. "I'm very sorry to break this to you, but the neighbour has just found little Bladles in the road and he didn't make it."

Bladles was our nickname for our cat Blade. I looked up at the neighbour, who looked morose, and I mumbled a thank you as I took the blanket gently from J's arms and cradled Blade. I did a complete body scan to check and be 100% certain he was gone. *Perhaps they are mistaken. Perhaps he is unconscious*, but in my heart, I knew that the freezing cold form I held no longer had Blade's spirit dancing around inside it. Another part of my heart shattered and dispersed out into the universe. There was no stopping the tears that came, and I was unable to speak. Clutching Blade tightly to my chest, I disappeared upstairs and sat softly sobbing on the futon in my bedroom. I'd been out most of the day and again blamed myself. Perhaps if I'd been there, Blade would have been inside the house.

We showed Blade's body to our cat Tinkerbell so she wouldn't be confused and keep looking for him, and then I whispered my goodbyes as we buried his little body in the garden by the rose bush.

Chapter 23: Fetish, a Blow-up Doll and a Chinese Meal

Often, I'm asked what my favourite fetish is, and it's so hard to choose. There is so much variety and I'm certain that if I focused on just one discipline of femdom, I would grow bored of it. Therefore, I usually answer with role play, as it can always add a new and exciting dimension to any dynamic.

It isn't something I would advise on a first meet between a mistress and her submissive, or indeed a submissive and her master. There needs to be some element of trust built up first and the mistress or master needs to be certain that the slave is assertive to use his or her safe word if need be. A role play can confuse the situation and a new submissive may feel reluctant to use the safe word when their boundaries are being pushed. I should know, I was afraid to speak up in the past.

Assuming though that sub, and mistress have become acquainted, role plays can be extremely useful in helping a slave overcome their shyness. They can step outside of the situation and exist in a carefully controlled and safe fantasy world. It takes them away from thinking of their daily stresses, obligations and routine. That's another thing I've learned from my past experiences.

Over the years, I have played a strict headmistress, hell-bent on punishing an unruly pupil; a bitchy boss that threatens to fire her employee if he doesn't do as she says, a kinky masseuse, a secret agent, a Russian spy, an assassin, a friend's wife, the list goes on.

All my role plays have one thing in common, I am the Boss and I wield the power. The slaves that visit me are desperate to experience submitting to a woman, and often crave punishment. That's the one thing that they have in common, other than that there aren't any defining features of a submissive male. They can be tall, short, old, young; they come from all walks of life and background.

You can never guess what someone is into from the way they look or speak. One day, after a double domination session with another mistress, my friend said, "You wouldn't have expected a big six-foot guy to want to dress like a woman and be feminine, would you?" I simply shrugged. I have had footballers, rugby players and builders visit me, wishing to be dressed in sexy women's clothes, feminised and given a makeover. One of the services I offer is a feminisation service. When my slave arrives, we sit down and talk about what he would like to experience, and I always ask how they want to feel. They normally say either sexy, vulnerable or slutty. This gives me a good idea of how I will structure their session.

For those who want the full treatment, I blend their foundation, apply either brightly coloured or smokey eyeshadow, glossy lips and lashings of mascara. I have a choice of wigs for them to select from if desired. I'm always curious about whether they will opt for sexy blonde, naughty brunette, a quirky blue or feminine pink. Next, we look through my 'sissy box'. This is a cross-dresser's heaven and contains pretty panties, stockings in every colour and design, suspender belts in multiple sizes, slinky dresses, tutus, petticoats and even 'chicken fillet' boob enhancers.

First-timers are usually nervous, and I can see them visibly trembling. If I am putting on their make-up, I explain what I am doing and how they will look, as it helps to relax them. If they are dressing straight away I will playfully comment that the wig or undies suit them and tell them they will make a very naughty girl, or words to that effect. Some cross-dressers and sissies are into BDSM, but some just want to experience feeling like a girl, so it is essential that they feel relaxed and understand that I will not surprise them with a whip or spanking paddle!

You might be wondering what the difference is between a cross-dresser and a sissy. A cross-dresser is a man who enjoys dressing in women's clothing, whereas a sissy wants to feel as feminine as they can. They are more likely to enjoy wearing some make-up and acting like a female as well as dressing like one. This is important for me to establish with a new slave early on, as a sissy would get a different session from a cross-dresser. With my sissies, we will do some work on the way they walk and hold themselves. I will ask them to walk as if they are on a catwalk, then I correct their posture and movement until it is more feminine. Sometimes there will be voice training and I will have them practise softening their voice and even changing their body language and mannerisms. I recently taught a sissy to act like a shy girl, glancing at me through eyelashes, then peering down coyly and giggling and pulling his wrists in tight to his chest. To see such a sudden change in their demeanour is rewarding and I know they are getting a lot out of the session when I praise them and they look pleased with themselves.

A lot of my sissies enjoy something called 'slut training' – this basically means teaching them how to be slutty! It may involve them pouting or blowing kisses, practising a seductive lap dance and parading around in front of me, or at the more extreme end they may suck my strap-on, or I will use the strap-on on them. Apparently, sucking a rubber cock isn't as easy as you would imagine, and first-timers often grasp the rubber shaft with a limp hand and half-heartedly suck on the end. I teach them to twist and curl their tongue around the end and tell them that a lot of it is about sensuality and anticipation. I teach them how to grip the dildo properly and to look up with big wide eyes as they explore the dong with their tongues. If they do this well, I giggle and tell them they would make the perfect little porn star. They always love hearing this, but I don't give out compliments if someone is not trying. If they don't seem to be enthusiastic enough, I coax them and throw in the odd sound effect that I encourage them to imitate. I often get them practising moaning like a girl and sometimes they are good at it, but from time to time I have laughed raucously when they sound like a cat being strangled!

The ultimate in oral training is to see how far they can take the dildo in their mouth. At this point I may throw in a reward for either getting to a certain point or going deeper than on the last visit. It's not all about depth though; if they can hold it midway for a longer time period that may qualify for a reward too. My sissy sessions are more reward-based, whereas a session with a 'pain slut' would be punishment-based. More on that in a moment.

A suitable reward for a sissy may be letting them worship my bottom, letting them keep a pair of panties to wear at home, or even just verbal praise. I rarely need to deny rewards, they are always beautifully behaved and I don't stand for any nonsense.

Pain sluts can be a little more challenging, though a great deal of fun! Pain sluts are slaves who enjoy a certain level of stimulus beyond the norm. They tend to be attracted to more extreme punishments such as caning, electrics wired up to their genitalia, hot tabasco sauce or chilis in delicate places or nipple torture, to name a few examples. I have some pain sluts that lie there and go into sub-space, and I know I must keep a careful eye on them and look out for things like excessive trembling. It means their body is overrun with adrenaline and that they will experience a drop afterwards and feel depleted. Other pain sluts may be cheeky and say things like "Is that all you've got?" or "It wasn't as bad as I thought it would be."

They know that is my cue to give them another hard whack or increase the current on the electrics that they are wired up to. It's not serious and I find it amusing. Friends will often say, "How do you stop yourself from laughing?" I don't stop myself from laughing; if I find something funny, I laugh. That's one perk of being the boss – I live only by my own rules and attract the clients that like my personality. If they don't want a giggly domme, they will go and find someone more serious in personality and that is fine by me.

Safe play is essential and I ask if slaves have any medical

conditions before entertaining into extreme play. I tend to hear 'bad knees' a lot as I have some older gentlemen who visit me for BDSM, and so I ensure that they are not on their knees for long periods. Also, I never use electrics powered by the mains on the chest and I do not work without a safe word. Their special word can be 'aardvark', 'bananas' or 'Geronimo' for all I care, but I insist all slaves must have one. I've only had a few slaves argue that they don't want a safe word. I remind them, a safe word isn't just for when they are feeling they have reached their limit, it could be used in an emergency if they felt ill, started experiencing extreme cramp or any other kind of ailment.

One of the sissies I film with regularly tells me that I am a 'nurturing domme,' meaning that I am encouraging with my slaves and coax them rather than forcing them, and I always provide aftercare. This might sometimes just need to be a bottle of water, a sit down and chat, but it's essential for any kind of extreme play.

It's lucky that I've not had many experiences of slaves feeling ill during a session. I did have one slave that obviously didn't clean out well before a strap-on session. Without going into too much detail, it reminded me of the Russell Howard sketch where the black woman shouts, "Liquid ass!"

One slave threw up during a session too. Often slaves find that using poppers (which are legal in the UK) during a session relaxes them, but there is a fine line between relaxing and feeling ill! He inhaled the poppers too quickly and then started belching, then tried to get up from the bed and escape to the loo. He looked like a trapped animal flailing his arms against the restraints as he tried to hold the vomit back. Without thinking, I grabbed a towel and said, "Into the towel!" The slave complied and the towel was swiftly thrown in the bin. He was given a bottle of water and a ten-minute breather and then was fine. It's crucial not to panic in these situations. The slave is relying on you to be the authority on every matter, and he puts his trust in your judgement. If you start flapping around and panicking, so will your slave! I always start speaking in a reassuring and calm voice and get them to rest and take deep breaths. It doesn't take them long to start relaxing again.

It's more common for people to suffer from mental health issues these days and I find a lot of my slaves will open up to me about their mental health and concerns. I am by no means a counsellor, but often they just want someone to listen to them and be able to express themselves freely. Modern life is busy and more narcissistic in the age of selfies, Tinder, Facebook and Instagram, so a lot of people don't have time for each other. I provide a non-judgmental, safe environment where slaves often tell me their innermost secrets, and I'm sure that I hear more than their hairdressers do! They reveal their early sexual experiences, or lack of, their hang-ups and insecurities, their worries about life and even their guilt about having a fetish.

A sub is more likely to experience guilt after a session, and no, these aren't all married men. It may be a career-driven, single guy that just happens to feel guilty after he's been spanked. I tell them they are experiencing sub drop. During a session, a sub's serotonin levels, adrenaline and endorphins will be racing around, so when the excitement stops, they suddenly drop and feel low; this is where aftercare is important and I tell them to look after themselves, take a hot bath, eat some good food and relax.

Slaves who have been experiencing BDSM for years do not always require aftercare. They understand their bodies' limits and how to cope with the after-effects when they feel drained. In my twelve years as a domme, I have only ever had two slaves get close to everything becoming too much for them emotionally.

The first time was during a double-domme session with a slave called Latex Trooper. I had taken Diamond to double up with me and she had fisted Latex Trooper and then caned him for around ten minutes on his rear end. He was struggling somewhat, but enjoying it, nonetheless. After some time, I got the feeling it was all becoming a little much for him with the impact play. He had previously asked for "lots of humiliation", and so I had instructed him to buy a blow-up doll and have it blown up for some humiliation.

As the other domme repeatedly lashed the cane down hard, I could see the tell-tale signs that he was physically at his limit. His whole body was shaking, and he was struggling to stand; instead of whimpering, he had gone deathly quiet and looked pale. I took over and said he would practise 'pleasuring a woman' so he could gain some experience in this area. Of course, my intention was to give him a break from the physical demands of the previous activity, but I should have gone in with something softer than humiliation. I had him practise kissing the blow-up doll, micro-managing his every move and criticising his errors. If he wanted extreme humiliation, that was the dish I would serve. "Move your lips to the nipples, no, not sucking, just a gentle lick. This is why you are single, do it properly or you will never find a girlfriend." We got as far as advising him on how to fellate the blow-up sex doll, before he wailed "Please can we stop?" and broke down sobbing, his head in his arms.

We did not need a safe word to know that it was time to curtail the session for the evening. We wrapped him up in his dressing gown, made him a cup of tea and sat him down to talk. I think he had been going through some emotional problems at the time, and this had somehow triggered it. Once we reassured him that we were happy to just sit and chat and wouldn't just leave him on his own, he was fine and seemed to appreciate the aftercare. Soon we had him laughing and joking, and he ordered a Chinese for us all and put a film on the TV. Slaves often think you will be disappointed if they ask to cut the playtime short and 'don't want to let you down', but to develop a strong domme/sub relationship, the sub must be able to call time when he needs to.

Another time, Bob, a twenty-year-old slave, wanted to experience small penis humiliation. "Don't hold back, I want an extreme experience," he informed me. So, of course, I mocked his appendage, told him I could pleasure a girl more with my little finger than he ever could with his sad, shrivelled little dinky, and asked him if girls laughed when he stripped naked in front of them. I had started with my pretty generic repertoire before upping the ante, and about twenty minutes in he asked if we could just chat instead. He admitted he wasn't ready for extreme humiliation but was enjoying my company. It's always finding that balance, and it's a craft that takes time, care and patience.

I did have one slave, Jarvis, who nearly left before the session had even started. Jarvis asked for a shower and then came back out of the bathroom dressed, his eyes bulging in fear and making him look like a scared rabbit.

Strict mistress Kaz was put back in the cupboard temporarily and reassuring Kaz took her place. Two things had taken place that had put the fear of God into the slave. He had grown his own weed plant and had apparently been peeling the leaves off it that day. Some of the THC had soaked into his skin, leaving him a little bit paranoid. He had then arrived at mine, taken a shower and as he stepped out, he'd seen a massive sixteen-inch monster of a dildo drying on the rack. He then became convinced my plan was to use it on him!

Laughing my socks off, I explained that those kinds of toys were by request only, and that I would not even go near his bottom! He visibly sagged with relief. He learned to trust me and visited a few more times after that, until I moved away. I left him with one valuable piece of information, "Make sure you wear latex gloves next time you are messing about with naughty plants!" My job is not to judge, it's to create a fantasy in a safe space where I am their queen and they are my subservient.

To me, slaves are just normal people with desires that are considered 'kinky' by many of the populace. For some slaves these kinks aren't even sexual. They are simply searching for *a feeling*. They may wish to feel safe, vulnerable, scared or feminine, but for them the kink is about feeling certain emotions and exploring themselves. It's not always about a physical release, it's about growing and uncovering their identity through a serious of emotional events.

Kinks are such a taboo topic, and we are so incredibly British about it in England. On the continent, they have sex shops in the high street with all kinds of films and paraphernalia in the window displays. It isn't considered anything out of the ordinary. Perhaps this stems from Queen Victoria's reign, which had the effect of oppressing the English sexually. I suspect we have never recovered from it. However, whenever something is outlawed or forbidden, it tends to push it underground. Back when the first magazine presses were invented, risqué images would circulate in secret. Then of course there were the 'What the Butler Saw' machines, which one could look through and see a saucy image. This was how people got their kicks. They couldn't talk about it in public, but it certainly happened!

When you think of spanking, if you are not a kinkster you may think of elderly chaps who went to public school and want to find a reminder of their schooldays being bent over the head-mistress's desk. The Internet has changed all of that though. There has been an explosion of BDSM films that have played their role in persuading much of society to crave these things. If you put it into context and see it as healthy exploration of the human body, it doesn't sound so terrifying, does it? Yet the government are quick to label fetishes and many forms of BDSM as obscene. The hypocrisy of this is apparent. For some time in the UK, face sitting was banned (the act of a women straddling a man's face, whether clothed or unclothed). Meanwhile, videos of women performing deep throat on men and being ejaculated on were deemed as 'acceptable'.

It doesn't take a genius to work out that this is a sexist law that intended to oppress women and spread the message that women should be submissive to men and serve them. There was outrage when this law came into practice, and sex workers, mistresses, producers and performers petitioned against the law and staged protests. The most amusing protest that springs to mind was a face sitting protest outside parliament. Women straddled men's faces in a controversial bid to prove once and for all that face sitting did not pose the risk of suffocation or place the submissive party into a position of danger. The law was revoked soon after and women across the world rejoiced!

Unfortunately, government prohibition does not focus on the safety of the populace, it focuses on scapegoats and using prohibition as a form of taxation. In 2019, we faced the possibility of a new verification law known as the 'porn ban'. If the bill had been passed, it would have prevented everyone in the UK from accessing over-eighteens websites, unless they bought a porn card from their local newsagent. That would certainly have been interesting when you spied your neighbour asking for twenty Silk Cut, a Twix and a porn card!

The law would not have affected porn tube sites or social media sites such as Twitter, where pornography is rife, so would have done little to prevent minors from accessing explicit material. It'd simply have been a form of taking a second layer of taxation from pornography. Furthermore, many experts in social sciences stated that this would push pornography underground, that it could cause teenagers to create hacks and start using the dark web, a dangerous place where they may be exposed to crime, drugs and paedophiles.

Eventually, the whole idea was dispensed with as those in power encountered many obstacles in trying to create this totalitarian regime, although Mastercard and Visa have since brought in their own restrictions. One good thing to come of it was that it created a strong sense of community between all the producers, models and performers that create films to sell online. A lot more people now are willing to help one another and share resources. There is always a silver lining in every situation, should you choose to see it. We can apply that to everything in life and if I look back at a lot of the stuff I went through, which was extremely troubling at the time, I don't feel angry or resentful now, I see what a valuable lesson it was and how much I learned from it. I've learned that you grow from mistakes, they teach you how to be a better person. Enlightenment is not something I've yet reached, but I am content in myself; I know who I am, what I stand for and what my values are. If this is all I achieve in this life, then that is no bad thing.

Chapter 24: Conflicted

2007

We both missed Blade, though J's approach to death meant that he didn't experience all the 'what ifs' and 'whys' when our cat died. He used the word 'pragmatic', whereas I would have said 'shallow'. He believed that "Once you are gone, you are gone," and that "There is no point being upset about it."

A dreary soul I must have been in those following weeks, as one day he came home with a tiny, black male kitten we named 'Sneak'. Sneak was by nature shy and would hide in the strangest places, hence his name! We would panic when we couldn't find him, only to eventually discover him curled up in a sock drawer!

He was such a timid little thing and would shy away if we tried to touch him. We would have to be patient and gain his trust.

One day, J left the lounge window open and Sneak escaped. For three days, I was beside myself! I imagined the tiny little scrap of fluff, scared, alone and hungry. I scoured every inch of the house, the garden and the local area to no avail, and had started to think we had lost him for good.

Then one night, I was in that distant place somewhere between consciousness and sleep, when I felt something batting me and little claws digging into me.

"Sneak's back!" exclaimed J, and I sat up to see a little black scrap of fur prancing around on the bed and attacking my feet. I giggled happily and reached out to tenderly stroke his head. To my amazement, Sneak let me pet him and proceeded to enjoy keeping me awake half the night by attacking my toes! I had no idea where he had gone, but his behaviour had certainly made him a little braver. Soon he was coming to us for affection and rubbing up against my other cat Tinkerbell. I had two fur balls to focus on and I was as happy as a pig in mud!

Our home in Hitchin had a cosy fireplace and thick shag pile rugs, and I was content there, but it was quickly becoming obvious that the neighbours were not happy. By this point, Sport TV had purchased a house in Milton Keynes for the girls to stay in when they had shifts on the channel. Often, I was away for days and would come back to J's complaints about our rental agency. One time, J had left loads of rubbish sacks out the back and the neighbours had complained to the agency. There was always some sort of drama happening.

Then another time I returned home from three days on the channel to discover that Tinkerbell had been let out and was pregnant. I had always intended to get the cats neutered and had asked J to do it. I should have cancelled a shift at work and taken them myself in hindsight, but of course I'm glad that wasn't the case now for reasons I will come to soon.

One day in spring 2007, the agency said that the landlords were returning home, and we were given a month's notice. I suggested moving to Brighton, but J wasn't sold on the idea. I liked the idea of living somewhere a little more bohemian, where people were less judgmental. In an area like Hitchin, J was bound to rub people up the wrong way, and then of course there was my job. I had friends in the same industry who lived in Brighton, and no one there batted an eyelid.

J argued we wouldn't get a big enough house (for all his junk) in Brighton and so he found a dilapidated bungalow in Horley. Surprisingly, it was a good find. It was a detached place with a river running right next to it, fields behind us and no neighbours for about half a mile! I knew it would be isolated, but I had already started to picture myself sat by the stream, walking across the fields and sitting in the garden with the cats. I was prepared to accept that the place was run-down. It was a trade-off.

Moving was tight financially. J had left his car on the road and not insured it, so I had to pay to get it out of the impound again and bills just seemed to mount up, plus having to keep moving to a new house was proving costly!

About a week before we were due to move, Tinkerbell gave birth to four beautiful black-and-white kittens. I later named them 'Bibby', 'Pinky', 'Crackers' and 'Piskie'! Bibby had a white bib on his black coat; Crackers was named after I left some Jacob's crackers on a plate on the floor and he started munching on them, much to my mirth! Pinky had a pink nose, and Piskie was originally 'Pixie' because she was so tiny, with an elfin face. She was always tumbling over and walking into things though, so soon became Piskie! J always claimed he named her after me as I was a Piskie after a few drinks. Of course, there is as much truth in this as in a party-political broadcast.

I put a box in my front bedroom for Tinkerbell and the fur babies; Tinkerbell hopped into it straight away. It fascinated me to watch how the two adult cats interacted. Sneak would come in and sit by the kittens, as if to say to Tinkerbell, "I'll watch them while you go to the loo and eat," then Tinkerbell would get up and go and see to her business. Sneak would sit there patiently watching them and would put them back into the box if they tried to climb out. It was beautiful to see, and I felt so privileged to be witness to this.

Soon, the moving date was upon us. The big cats were put in a crate in the back of the lorry with a blanket and water, and the kittens would sit on a blanket on my lap for the duration of the journey. It always took an age to drive anywhere, as J would always drive at about thirty miles per hour. He would do things like stop to check the oil, brake lights and re-fit the radio on route, then he would drive slowly and keep going to garages to get sandwiches, sweets and Red Bull. It was frustrating, but on this journey, I had the kittens to focus my attention on. During the stops they were fed, watered and popped into a little mini litter tray we'd fashioned so they could go to the toilet. I loved to watch them crawl around and tumble over each other, but I was worried about Tinkerbell being separated from the babies, so I was eager to arrive.

It took at least three hours to reach our destination and it was around 5.30 p.m. when we got there. We called the agency to say that we had arrived, but they said they were going home now and wouldn't be able to bring a key until the morning! We were homeless until the next day.

The only thing for it was to check into a local hotel. I withdrew £40 from my overdrawn bank account and booked us a cheap Travel Lodge for the night. It wasn't possible to sneak two cats and four kittens in, so the only option was to give them extra blankets and do constant checks to make sure they had plenty of food and water, and a chance to go to the loo. I hated being parted from them and wanted to sleep in the van, but eventually agreed to sleep in the room. To give him his due, J insisted I stay in the warm and he checked the kittens at regular intervals.

The next day, we drove to the bungalow and J parked the moving van down the road so that the agent didn't see our family of cats and throw us out straight away! Eventually, he left and we took the kitties into the house. There was a small front garden behind a quiet road, which led up to the house. Everything was painted white and there were two bedrooms, a study, a lounge, kitchen and a small bathroom. One bedroom would be for sleeping, and the other was to spend its life being a junk room for J's hoardings. I had discovered by this point that he had a terrible inclination for hoarding useless items. He owned boxes of books he never read, pieces of tech that were broken, and all manner of unusable junk that he refused to part with. Over time, this habit grew worse, and he not only hoarded his own stuff, but mine too. I would put something broken in the bin and I would see it in the kitchen or in the study a week later! It could have been a pair of ripped stockings, a broken toy or an old Walkman. He would get it straight out of the bin the minute my back was turned and would stash it away. Our house became cluttered quickly and I was always at war with trying to de-clutter!

We were also having serious money problems with me being the only wage earner. He'd been out of work a year and a half now and had no intention of getting another job. One minute he would say he was going to train to be a Corgi engineer and in the next breath it was something else. He talked at length about all his grand schemes, but nothing ever came to fruition. He had started to upload some of my home-made videos for me online and tried to convince me that this alone was sufficient. The videos pulled in a few quid here and there, but not enough to live on. He convinced me that it took him hours to format the videos, edit them and upload them, and not being technically minded at the time, I believed him. Now I edit myself and do all my own uploads and realise that it's a simple process. I upload to about five or six websites; he was only uploading to one and convincing me that it took all the hours under the sun. He would tell me that he was going to edit a video for me, but then I'd walk in the study to find him naked and 'enjoying himself' while watching a porno. He'd suggest I 'join in' and couldn't understand why I was annoyed that he wasn't editing. The difference is, he never saw it as a career and could never look towards the future, he was only ever capable of living in the moment, unable to think of the consequences or to act responsibly.

We were both on antidepressants still, but despite my daily challenges, our new location brought me a sense of calm in some ways. When J's behaviour was erratic and he was stumbling around, leaving food packets everywhere, watching porn or otherwise behaving like a degenerate, I would head outside and walk round the gardens. I spent hours sat down by the stream and basked in my escape. As the kittens started to grow and get big enough to go outside, they would follow me, and often I had six cats sat with me. I felt like Snow White with all the animals around me.

I remember the first time I opened the patio doors and let the cats out. I laid a big blanket on the ground and sat down, and they all joined me, tumbling and wrestling on the blanket and playing with blades of grass. It really was like a little sanctuary with all my favourite people – my cats.

Studying Sneak one day as he rolled on his back, I noticed his stomach was distended and his nipples were protruding. My eyes widened and I gasped and called to J, "Err, come and look at this. I think Sneak is actually a female, and erm heavily pregnant!"

J looked at Sneak's stomach and for once agreed with me. We were going to have more kittens!! I knew I had to get some more jobs sorted so I could·afford to feed them.

The first few months were hard to establish myself as a model in a new area and a few things happened. Sport TV decided to pay my agent Tim my fee, instead of me directly. This was done to save them paying tax. Tim then failed to pay me and, ultimately after much debate, refused to do so, justifying that he shouldn't have to pay me because J was rude to him.

Sport TV was unwilling to get involved in the situation and so regretfully I handed in my notice. The MD wrote back, "Sorry to hear that, you were always one of my favourite girls."

He probably said that to everyone. I couldn't have been one of his favourites if he was willing to stand by and see me not paid my wages.

Another day, I had a shoot with an agency, we'll call them D-Pole. J had gone to see a friend but was meant to come back and take me to the shoot in London. He called to say he was stuck in traffic and wouldn't be able to make it. I was halfway across London and twenty minutes late when the boss Dan at D-Pole called me up, angrily telling me not to bother turning up. He screamed down the phone at me, threatening me and telling me that he would bad-mouth me to everyone I knew and would stop me from getting any work. I was in tears as I turned back to take the train home. This wasn't my first run in with D-Pole. Another time, J and I had shoot for *Playboy* and the receptionist at D-Pole rang up asking for J's passport I.D.

"I'll send it now," he said. Then we'd gone up to the Peak District to shoot for a photographer's website for a few days, where there was no phone signal. When I had gotten back, I was just on my way home from a local shoot, when I had the strangest phone call. The man appeared quite irked initially and seemed nonsensical, "Were you hiding behind your sofa or something?" he snapped.

"Sorry, who is this, I really have no idea what this is about?" Puzzled, I thought it was a prank call.

"Sorry, I haven't introduced myself. My name is Larry, you did a shoot for us a few weeks back for *Playboy* and we didn't get J's I.D. on the day, so we have been calling you, but you didn't answer. We even went to your house and knocked on the door, but no one answered."

"Well, we haven't been at the house. We have been shooting in the Peak District, and J has said he sent his I.D. over."

"So, you weren't out of it?"

"Yes. We were out of town and out the signal area, yes," I responded, confused.

"Ah, that makes a lot of sense. See, Dan said you were out of it on drugs and were probably hiding behind the sofa. It's all becoming clear now. You actually sound really nice, sorry about this misunderstanding."

I was both annoyed and incredulous but tried to keep the anger out of my voice as the gentlemen on the end of the phone had been misled. While we did dabble from time to time, we had been shooting in the Peak District on a normal shoot, and the thought of hiding behind the sofa was laughable!

The phone call ended amicably, and I reassured Larry that I would find the I.D. and send it across myself. Larry sounded like a nice chap, who had just been given the wrong end of the stick.

I had heard a lot of horror stories about D-Pole from other models; they even sent girls (including myself) to an alleged sex pest, Fifi Capper, who was supposedly related to Peter Sutcliffe, the Yorkshire Ripper, but being the only adult agency in the industry, they were a necessary evil.

Previously, they had begged me to shoot with Fifi Capper, and when I voiced my concerns, they promised to have a word with him and make sure he behaved. On set, I had all my barriers up.

At one point, Fifi threw me a pair of worn, crusty knickers and I chucked them straight back, quoting health and safety at him, which he evidently didn't like and acted like I had an attitude problem. He touched my ankle during a scene, and I barked, "Your hand will not go higher than that, will it!" We got through the day and while he was quite grumpy, he didn't attempt to grope me.

Anyway, I decided to forget the D-Pole incident and move on, but I knew that I couldn't work for someone that not only spread vicious rumours and lies, but also threatened me. That was another avenue of work down the pan.

***

I decided I would start doing more webcam instead. I could work from home, so it was safe, I could set my own times and hours, and I wouldn't have to pay out for travel. J set my computer up, all the while acting as if he were a magician weaving magic. He often liked to remind me of how super intelligent he was and could do things I wouldn't have a clue about.

Around this time, Adultwork launched a piece of software called Justcamit, which meant you could webcam with multiple people in a webcam room at once. I decided to give it a go and I logged on, not knowing what to expect. I was amazed by how many viewers came into my pay per minute room. I danced around, giggling, chatting with the guys, giving them flashes and pulling out a naughty selection of toys. The clients could also phone a special number and talk to me on the phone too. I began to webcam regularly, and I would dominate kinky-minded and submissive men online. It proved lucrative, but I wasn't such a fool that I was willing to rely on one stream of income based on a few days of busy shows, so I applied to work on Babeworld.

By now, I had worked on various channels such as TVX, Babe Chat, and Babe Star, so had a lot of experience.

Attending an interview in London, I glammed myself up and

chatted with a lovely lady in charge of recruitment. The interview was more like a chat than an interview, that's always a sign it's going well, but I didn't allow myself to get my hopes up. I was halfway home when they rang me to say I'd been successful. I was delighted. Unfortunately, I didn't know what to expect when I got home and never knew what sort of mood J would be in. Sometimes he would be sulky and ignore me, while other times he would be hyper and knocking everything over or telling me how brilliant he was and how he was going to create some amazing new project that ultimately never materialised.

Whenever I had a 'success', I learned quickly not to make a big deal of it. It would trigger J's insecurities and his mask would slip and his nasty side would take over. It was never obvious enough for me to point it out. It would be subtle – back-handed compliments, mocking me, implying I was brainless and incapable, and calling me "stupid little fluff" as a nickname when I had an opinion about something. He would also try to repeatedly correct me, tell me that I was wrong and that "this actually happened", contradicting my every word. He would rewrite history and it was only later that I found out the correct terminology for this kind of abuse. It is called 'gaslighting' when someone tries to make you believe a false or different set of events from what happened. He'd interfere in emails I sent and tell me my grammar was poor, or that I shouldn't word things a certain way. He was highly critical, and I felt as if I could never do anything right. The more often good things happened to me – such as getting shoots or shifts on the channels – the more derogatory he became towards me. He started to make me feel as if I wasn't capable of anything and crushed my confidence.

By this point, I wanted to exit the relationship. I was paying for someone to exist who not only made no effort in the relationship, but also put me down constantly and made me feel miserable. It was a one-sided relationship, with me giving everything and only receiving back heartache and emotional torment.

Finally, the consequences of it all came to a head. Babeworld paid me late and I went £50 over my overdraft and was slapped with massive charges. Bank charges weren't a set rate back then and banks could do whatever they wanted. Every time I paid money into the bank, it only paid off the charges and I was sinking deeper and deeper into arrears. I organised several amateur shoots with photographers, but once I'd paid the rent and bills and the charges, I was left with little else. Soon it was a couple of weeks before my sister's wedding in Cyprus and I couldn't even afford a sandwich for the plane! I had to borrow some money but knew it wasn't fair to ask without some way of paying it back. I put out some adverts on model and photography forums saying that I would be in Cyprus on set dates and would be available for shoots. In the past, I'd chatted to a photographer that was based in Cyprus and so I contacted him asking if he still wanted to shoot with me. He was happy to hear from me and luckily interested in organising a shoot. With the promise of enough money for a flight and a cheap hotel, I asked my sister to loan me the money temporarily. My sister was annoyed that I didn't have any savings and said she couldn't lend me the money as she'd had to pay out for friends to fly out there. I could see her point; I'd had a year to save, and she was unaware of all the events that had taken place to sink me into debt.

Dejected and full of guilt, I called my mum and asked her if she would loan me the money.

"Yes, that's fine, on two conditions though."

"What are the conditions?"

"One, you pay me back when you have the money, and two, you will come out alone. I'm not paying for that lazy sponger to go on holiday. He is the reason you are in this mess!"

I thanked my mum profusely and reassured her that I agreed to her terms. Relief swept over me. I'd have felt awful if I had missed my sister's special day.

J was lurking, waiting to hear what my mum said. I told him, but obviously left out the bits where she said he was a sponger and it was his fault. I was diplomatic in my delivery of the news, but his reaction stunned me! He was livid that my mum wouldn't pay for him to go. He said we were a couple and that she was trying to get between us. He said all manner of awful things about my family, and I saw his mask slip again. In his rage, his true colours were showing and he felt entitled to bum around and rely on others to fund his way through life. For once, I refused to be beaten down by his verbal antagonism and I was resolute that I was going to the wedding.

"Without even going into the details about why we are skint, such as you abandoning the van and letting your cars get impounded, J, the truth is, if you had even got a part-time job, you would have the money to go. You've refused to work and now this has happened."

He had nothing to say to that, so stalked out moodily, a thunderous look on his face.

Chapter 25:
A Wedding and an Illicit Liaison

July 2007

The big day had finally arrived and soon I was boarding a flight bound for Larnaca in Cyprus. Butterflies danced a merry jig around my tummy as I thought of a whole week in the sun, just relaxing. You might think that taking a flight alone to another country might be quite terrifying for someone who suffers with anxiety, but this was not the case. The thought of escaping my home life for an entire week filled me with an incredible sense of freedom. It wasn't until I stepped on that plane and popped my headphones in that I realised how free I felt. There was no one to criticise me, tell me what I was saying was wrong or try to butt into my conversations. I didn't have to worry about imminent chaos or catastrophe, and on that plane surrounded by strangers, I felt safe.

I'd stocked up on glossy magazines for the journey and read about the latest trends and who was doing what in the celeb world. J had always mocked me for reading women's glossies and for wasting money, so I made sure I bought several and read them cover to cover. When I'd read those, I read the in-flight magazine and then studied the map. Before I knew it, I had reached my destination.

Flying fills me with wonder. I'm not one to worry about crashing; humans are scarier than anything natural or mechanical. That moment the plane takes off and soars above the clouds, I wonder at the brilliance of it all; the part when the plane comes in for landing and you see beautiful new landscapes, tiny, jagged islands, and huge expanses of sea. That feeling as you get closer and closer to the earth – knowing that a new adventure is about to begin – is insurmountable!

We landed and I waited impatiently as passengers took forever taking their luggage down and pushing their way to the front. Walking down the gangplank, I reached the exit door, where the portable stairs stood. The dry heat hit my face and a warm feeling of happiness radiated through me. I had done it, flown to another country on my own, and felt rather pleased with myself. It might sound quite trivial, but when you are told how stupid and incapable you are all the time, things like these feel like little victories.

Having spent the latter part of my teenage years in Cyprus, it felt like returning home. Aboard the coach, I was excited to watch out of the window as we drove past cobbled streets, viewing the scenery, little white villas, olive trees, beautiful pink Bougainvillea flowers and Greek coffee shops. This side of the island was new to me, only having been once for a reps cabaret, so every time we stopped outside a ropey-looking hotel, I prayed it wasn't mine! Eventually, we pulled up at the hotel I was staying in, the Silver Sands Hotel, and I felt relieved that it wasn't a building site! I returned to the Silver Sands several years ago, sometime around 2018, out of pure nostalgia. It was looking a little shabby and in need of a serious revamp, yet it felt wonderful to be back and I walked round savouring every detail and getting lost in the memories.

Anyway, back to 2007, I checked in, immediately showered and changed, then headed over to meet my family at the Capo Bay Hotel, luxuriating in the feel of the warm air and delicious smells from all the restaurants wafting up. My mum, dad, sisters, brothers-in-law and nephews were all there and we spent the next couple of days lounging by the pool or running into the sea and screaming that it was freezing, but "all right once you are in". We visited many bars along the strip, including the Friends bar, the

Only Fools and Horses pub and various other places you could buy 'cheap as chips' toasties and cocktails. I barely thought of J while I was there and started to realise how much better my life would be without him in it. One evening, I went to a bar with my sisters and they both interrogated me, asking me when I was going to dump him. They couldn't stand him and were pleased he wasn't there answering for me and not allowing me to speak.

A couple of days into the holiday, I did my photoshoot with the photographer I had been emailing and we spent a day shooting photos at his villa. Later, he took me down to the beach in his moon buggy to get some beach shots. It was incredible racing across the sands, bumping across the rocks and feeling the breeze in my hair. I giggled and realised that this was what life should be like, feeling free and experiencing new things. When the shoot came to an end, I thanked the photographer for a great shoot, and he dropped me home. He'll never know how much he helped me, not just with the cash, but with making me feel empowered and that wherever I was in the world, I could survive. I didn't need anyone.

I used the money to pay my mum back straight away and I think she was surprised at how quickly I managed to get it. I still had a little bit left over, which would be enough to keep me fed for the week and buy a few drinks too. I had some cash in my pocket for once and no one to spend it for me, and I was in high spirits. I was on top of the world and felt once more as if I could achieve anything.

I couldn't help noticing a young lad always on the edge of our group. He was a friend of a friend of the family, and I saw him looking over sometimes. He had a lovely smile and stylish blond hair. I couldn't remember the last time anyone had really caught my eye and realised that he was attractive. I didn't have the courage to speak to him, and thought it wasn't the best idea anyway, so I just pushed it to the back of my mind.

There were many hilarious moments that week. My sister's friend Gareth and his son Jack joined me and my sister on the beach. Jack was fifteen and had a pint in one hand and a fag in the other. Meanwhile, Gareth phoned the school to say Jack wouldn't be in that day as he was having a pint on the beach! We were in stitches and couldn't believe how brazen he was.

Another evening, we went to a club called Rainbow. I was trying to have a (pretty tipsy) conversation with Gareth and couldn't hear a thing over the booming speakers. I beckoned him to step into a doorway and tried to shout in his ear. All of a sudden, a pair of bouncers pushed into us! It seems we had tried to have a conversation in the doorway of the men's toilets, which obviously isn't a great idea. We started to argue with them, and then one of them got a bit rough with Gareth. Before I knew what was happening, one of the guys from the group who was on crutches started hitting the bouncers with his crutches. Suddenly, we were pushed back about twenty feet. It was so surreal – one minute I was stood there watching a guy whack this solid six-foot guy that was built like a brick shithouse, the next minute I was flying backwards, smashed through the fire exit doors, and landed on a big pile of rubbish sacks next to Gareth. We'd landed with quite a force, but as we struggled to sit up, I giggled, and then we both fell about roaring with laughter! It was such a ridiculous situation and every time I thought about that kid rushing to our defence with his crutches, I fell about laughing again. The main thing was that no one was hurt and so we made our way back to our hotels laughing about how crazy it was.

The next day, we all sat round the pool laughing at the absurdity of the evening before. It was a blissful day, the sun was scorching hot, and everyone was in high spirits. My dad sat drinking a beer and smirking with amusement, and even my mum laughed. I think she was a little concerned but saw the funny side and knew I was safe with the lads, so didn't lecture me on visiting nightclubs thankfully.

Soon, my sister's wedding day had arrived. Everyone was buzzing and excitement filled the air. My sis was feeling anxious and didn't even get her hair done in the end, but when she slipped into her black corset dress, she looked simply stunning. It was floor-length and she looked like she had stepped out of a fairytale. Her husband Mack looked extremely smart, and I was so excited for them! My dad had even dressed for the occasion, under duress. He had wanted to wear shorts and a T-shirt, but my mum and sis had forbidden it! Instead, he wore cream shirt and trousers, and looked extremely dapper. All my family looked beautiful, and I felt so proud of them.

The vows took place just in front of the ocean and I listened intently as my sister nervously took her vows. She just couldn't wait for the ceremony to be over so she could relax and has never been one to enjoy the limelight. I'm not one to cry at weddings, but her Mack is such a lovely guy and so good for my sister, so it was emotional. She is an anxious type and he is calm and stable. Over the years, he has been a fantastic influence on my sister, and vice versa.

The wedding banquet was next, and we feasted on a traditional roast, which was quite hard going in the heat. We necked plentiful bottles of wine, which proved not so hard-going, and soon the sun was sinking low in the sky. Some of the girls decided to jump in the pool fully clothed. In went Debra, squealing as she hit the water, her dress billowing out. Next, my sister jumped in while still wearing her expensive wedding gown! It was crazy yet seemed so fun at the time. I was about to join them when the manager started bellowing, "You no swim! Pool closed now!"

They climbed out of the pool laughing and a little sheepish, my mum chiding my sister for jumping in with her wedding dress on. The girls decided to change and while they were distracted, I decided to slink back to my hotel and get a nap. After all the emotional highs, socialising, drinking and being in the hot sun, I felt like I just needed to lie down somewhere cool and close my eyes. I was all peopled out! Finally sinking onto my bed, my head hitting that cool pillow felt so blissful and I fell asleep quickly. I must have slept for a few hours as I woke up around nine or ten o'clock, my mobile ringing loudly and pulling me out of my slumber.

It was my sister. "Where are you? I'm worried."

I explained that I was exhausted and didn't want to get more drunk, so went home for a nap.

"It's my wedding day though, you have to come back. It won't be the same without you," my sister said mournfully.

Wiping the sleep from my eyes, I agreed and went for a shower, re-did my make-up and changed my clothes. I arrived back at the Capo Bay Hotel soon after, as it was only five to ten minutes' walk down the strip from my hotel. We decided to go to a bar and get cocktails. My mum and dad had decided to stay home that night and my dad was a bit short with me when I said I was going out. "You really should spend this evening with your mother!" he scolded.

"I've spent every day with Mum and most evenings. It's my holiday too," I protested.

"Don't worry, it's only because he doesn't want to have to make an effort himself," Mum snapped.

Later that eve, I drank colourful cocktails with long straws, enjoying the feeling of my skin glow from the sun that day. I noticed that the young lad with the blond hair was there with his friend. Let's call him Aiden. My eldest sister soon engaged Aiden in conversation and started telling him about my awful boyfriend and how she wanted me to dump him. My sister was quite drunk, we all were to be fair, and I remember thinking how sweet he was for chatting away with my big sis and not thinking it was sad to speak to someone older in a bar, and we all eventually became engaged in conversation.

When the bar closed, the boys declared they were going to the club, and I found a confidence I didn't know I had and invited myself along. They didn't seem to mind at all and soon Aiden, his friend and I were all laughing and joking. God knows what I said, but I can remember Aiden kept laughing and saying, "You are mad, you are!"

At first, it was like we were all old friends, joking and laughing, then after another drink I got a bit flirty with Aiden. We had all been drinking all day long and were in high spirits, so I felt a little emboldened by this. He held my hand and we walked around the club like that, which felt super cute. We were both sun-kissed and blonde, and I thought we matched well in personality. Often, I felt too fat or too short, and had some other obsessions with my face or body, but right now in this moment I felt fantastic. I had been swimming all day long and getting the sun on my skin, my hair was kissed by the sun, and I felt a million dollars, especially when he looked at me the way he did – that soft, gentle look in his eyes, it made me feel special and more than a little naughty!

There were no dramatics in the club that night, no scary bouncers to accost us, and we simply talked and danced or "threw some shapes", as Aiden said.

Aiden was funny, down to earth and had a nice accent. I liked that. He mispronounced certain words, so didn't correct me on my pronunciation or grammar, he didn't mock me, and the conversation flowed, at least from my point of view. In hindsight, I probably rambled quite a bit of nonsense given the number of cocktails I had drunk, but he didn't seem to have any issue with this.

Later, as we walked across the beach, I suggested we paddle in the sea. His friend sat on a lounger while we waded into the sea up to our chests. Aiden wrapped his arms around me, and we held each other, feeling the heat of one another's bodies in stark contrast to the coldness of the sea. We stood there floating, the moon reflecting on the surface of the water, gently rocking as the tide pulled us to and fro. It felt like being wrapped in a cocoon. The last two years of misery seemed to dissipate and get snatched away on the waves, which pulled all my worries far away from me. For a long time afterwards, I used to think back to that moment and remember it fondly. My eyes would glaze over and I would picture us frozen in time, the world so still under an inky black sky with only the gentle sounds of the waves beating on the shore.

I ended up going back to his hotel room and things certainly got fruity while his friend was passed out on the bed opposite! At least, I think he was asleep! I remember waking up the next day and asking Aiden if he had any toothpaste I could eat. As much as it was a strange question to ask, he simply pointed towards the bathroom and I raced in there to chew on some toothpaste, aware of my morning breath, tainted with last night's alcohol. When I felt sufficiently minty, I slid back under the covers and as he faced me, my hands wandered to his tight stomach, which boasted washboard abs. I couldn't help running my hands over them and commenting on what great abs he had. Then the three of us chatted, casual as anything, laughing about the previous night. Then it was back to my hotel to change, and then I headed to Capo Bay to meet my family.

Chapter 26: How I Met My Best Friend

I ended up spending quite a lot of time with Aiden that week and my sisters adored him. He kept asking to be my boyfriend and while I wanted to agree, I realised I would somehow have to deal with J. The thought of going home to him filled me with dread and so I pushed it as far to the back of my mind as I could.

I suppose part of me felt a little guilt. When I explained this to my sisters, they said words to the effect of, "Don't feel bad, ditch the loser! Aiden would make a wonderful boyfriend!" They made it sound so easy.

All good things must come to an end and soon it was time to go home. Aiden had flown home already and so I was stood at the entrance of Capo Bay waving off my mum and dad. When it was time for them to go, tears rolled down my face and my dad comforted me, "Don't worry, we'll see you soon," but I knew J would find a way to keep me struggling, away from everyone.

My sister and her hubby had decided to stay on and so at least I didn't have to wave them off tearfully. The journey home is a haze. A black cloud descended on me; the threat of my old buddy *anxiety* had started to creep its way in, winding around my chest and crushing me tightly like a serpent, squeezing the life out of its prey, and I found distraction in a book.

Arriving home, I became distant. The previous week had contrasted greatly in the way I was treated and with how J normally treated me. It had made me aware that there was something seriously wrong with my relationship with J. He didn't seem to notice that there was anything amiss, or at least didn't care. I'm not sure which. I had saved Aiden's name as Slave X in my phone, a sneaky thing to do, and while it was wrong, I didn't want to let go of the little bit of happiness I had felt. Aiden called me and I would walk down the lane outside my bungalow and talk to him. He would tell me that J was using me and I should finish with him, but I was weak and scared. I didn't know what to do or how J would react.

Then a couple of days later, something else happened to distract me. Sneak's kittens were born. I heard her giving birth in the cupboard and the poor thing was squealing in pain. Eventually, she gave birth to eight kittens. We gave her space so as not to worry her, but she seemed to want our attention, so despite J's protests, I would lean into the cupboard and stroke her glossy black head and reassure her. On the third day, disaster struck and Sneak disappeared and never came back. We called the RSPCA, who said they had no space for the kittens, then we phoned the vet's, who said we would have to feed them with little syringes and special formula. I put the kittens on a heated electrical fleece to keep them warm, and J insisted on making the formula, arguing that I would only get it wrong. We fed them with milk, and I stimulated their bottoms (as their mother would have done) with a cotton bud to make them defecate. It felt like the most natural thing in the world to care for the kittens as if they were my own flesh and blood.

One night, J kept snatching the feeder from the kittens' mouths and shoving other kittens at me. He insisted I stop feeding the one in my hand and fed the next one. "But they are hungry!" I retaliated.

He started shouting, saying he was tired and didn't want to heat up more milk. That he had been getting up every four hours to feed them (this was most likely another lie). He angrily stormed off to bed and left me there sobbing, desperately trying to comfort all the kittens and share out what was left of the milk. He had me so convinced I was incapable of making formula that I didn't dare try. I felt terrified that I might get it wrong, not sterilise the feeders properly and inadvertently kill the kittens. Psychologically, I was back to being a complete mess, within less than a week of being back at home.

A day or so after, the electric blanket stopped working and the kittens were all cold. I cuddled them into me and stroked their soft fur, trying to give them warmth. We found a warmer spot in the back room for them, but then they developed diarrhoea.

I knew they would need to go to the vet's and that I would need to make more money for the rent and so on, so I found myself having a conversation with J about me escorting. I think I instigated it out of desperation, as I was so worried about our finances, but I don't think I actually thought it through, and didn't realise that J would use this to control my body as well as my mind. He arranged it all, found a client and then told me I would be having anal sex. "No, I'm not!!" I retorted.

"Oh, don't worry, I've written to him as you and I've told him he has to be gentle, as you are not experienced." I couldn't believe he was making decisions as to what I would have to do with my body and could have punched him in the face there and then. We argued and I ranted, but he sat there as calm as anything telling me all the reasons why I was overreacting. I was livid and started to panic, but I pushed the feelings down and packed my suitcase for a photoshoot, happy to be able to leave the house for a day.

The photoshoot was the next day, so in the morning I told J to take the kittens to the vet's. I'd been paid by Babeworld at this point and left some money in the kitchen. I couldn't wait to see the back of him.

My shoot was in a hotel in Colchester with a black model called Danica and a Scottish model called Amber. The photographer David suggested various outfits and poses for the three of us and got us a bottle of wine. Danica didn't drink so Amber and I shared it between us. We really hit it off and seemed to click with one another. When the photographer had enough photos, he said he was leaving. Amber asked if we could keep the room and he readily agreed. We headed down to the bar and she treated me to a bottle of champagne. We sat enjoying the bubbles and Amber poured out her life story and soon I was confessing my secrets about J, that I was having to escort with a client the next day and didn't want to do it.

"You shouldn't have to do that, and not to financially keep a man!" she exclaimed in shock. It felt good to have someone to confide in and the more I talked to her, the more I knew she was right. It felt good to have someone on my side who didn't just want me for what I could do for them.

The more I thought about this guy that wanted to meet me, the worse I felt. Instead of going home, I stayed at the hotel drinking with Amber. Eventually, we headed back to our room but couldn't remember our room number, so we had to ask the rather nervous guy on reception to show us the way. He let us in and ran off sheepishly. When we closed the door, we burst into giggles like naughty schoolgirls. It felt good to misbehave, drink champagne and laugh at silly things.

At some point, Amber pulled me in for a kiss and I ended up whipping one of my vibrators out, which I used on her. I don't think I'm bisexual as such, but I did enjoy playing around with girls, and if I am being honest, getting attention from pretty girls. When I was at school, the popular girls always beat me up and humiliated me. So, when I was in my twenties, I loved the fact that gorgeous girls wanted to sleep with me. In a way, I suppose it validated me and made me feel attractive, whereas I'd felt so ugly and worthless at school.

It might sound sad, but this generally happened on a shoot when I was being paid to do so and when you are in that world, it just becomes normal. Occasionally, things might happen off set with another girl, but it seemed like innocent fun. They would generally come on to me to start with and then I would whip out a toy and be the one doing them. The other way around felt a bit more awkward without a camera there, so I tended to be the one in charge. J was always around when this happened and he would try to get involved, but generally they weren't interested in him.

I was quite thankful for this, as while I didn't realise why at the time, I rarely enjoyed sex with J. There was no genuine intimacy, it felt flat and empty, and I felt like a rag doll being used, but anyway, I digress! Amber and I woke the next morning still drunk and called down for room service. The reception said they didn't do room service, so giggling, I said it was my girlfriend's birthday and wanted to treat her. Amber and I then slid into a couple of PVC costumes and waited for the door to knock, while trying to stifle our giggles.

To give the staff their due, they brought us up a lovely platter of breakfast! They looked quite uncomfortable when they clocked us still tipsy and looking like we were on our way to a fancy-dress party. It had been meant as a laugh and not to make them feel uncomfortable, and so I dug through my purse for a good tip to make up for it.

After we checked out of the hotel, we hopped on the train to London, and only then did I realise that I must have left my purple vibrator in the bed! If you were the staff at the hotel and you are reading this, I'm so sorry you had to find that!

Hopping off a tube at Camden, we found a pub. The kind of working men's club that had been refurbished into a trendier bar but with carpets your shoes stuck to and a strong smell of ale in the air. It was the perfect place to hide away for the day! We carried on drinking, and I realised that I was putting off going home. It occurred to me that if I stayed out and kept my phone switched off, I would miss the escort booking, and rather than sitting there anxiously waiting for the time to pass, I ordered another drink and pushed it to the back of my mind. Oh alcohol, my sweet friend and enemy! How doth thee bring me relief, then fill me with dread.

After a day's drinking, I contemplated over the timings and considered it safe to go home, ensuring to take my new best buddy with me for moral support. Amber was happy to accompany me and was excited to meet the kittens! We chattered excitedly all the way about all the cats we had known in our time, and it was the start of a beautiful friendship.

When I got back to my little rented bungalow in Smallfield, I was in good spirits, for the first thirty seconds. Then J coldly broke the news to me that two of the kittens had died!

"What, why, how did this happen?" I exclaimed, my heart sinking and my eyes welling up with tears.

"Well, you knew they needed the vet's and yet YOU didn't bother coming home!"

"What? I left money for the vet's?" I answered, confused.

"That was already spent on other things," J snapped.

Somehow, he always had a way of twisting things and making it out to be my fault, and with my spirit so crushed, I started to believe him and wept for those poor little kittens that were dead now, feeling that I could have changed their fate and didn't.

J was extremely angry at me for not coming home. I was "selfish", "thoughtless", "unreliable" and a whole host of horrible things. Amber interjected a couple of times and explained that I hadn't come home because I didn't want to face what was supposed to happen that day, but it fell on deaf ears.

I'd assumed that returning home late meant I'd escape having to do the booking, but J corrected me in that self-assured, overly cocky manner of his, "I've told him you are running late from a shoot and have put the meeting back. He'll be at the station in twenty minutes."

I was in shock. I was feeling horrendous after learning two of the baby cats had died – they were just a little over a week old – a little disorientated from the alcohol and knew there was no way I could let some stranger put his whatsit in my back entrance. I felt sick inside.

I just seemed to shut down at that moment. I turned to J and said, "Then you will have to tell him he has had a wasted journey."

Asking Amber to stay with the cats, I went into the spare room and climbed under a duvet and refused to come out or speak. J pleaded relentlessly with me to meet the client, but I had no energy left in me to argue or shout, so I met his protests with silence and ignored him. I may as well have been catatonic.

I shut down completely. He kept coming in and out of the room, saying I would look unprofessional. Still, I refused to speak. He asked me if the guy could just talk to me, and this was met with more stony silence. He kept coming in and out of the room using different tactics to try and break me, and I knew my only defence was silence. Eventually, J said he was giving the guy a lift back home and he disappeared out of the house. At the time I believed him, but no doubt he was off buying drugs with my money.

As soon as he had left, I went to find Amber and we carried on playing with the kittens and feeding them formula. There were four black ones left and a large tabby and a small tabby. One of the little black ones (Furkin) loved to climb up my sleeve, then he'd pop out the top of my dressing gown and stare at me and mewl. The large tabby (Tabstick) would sit in my sleeve and sleep. The other kittens were quite listless; I didn't realise this meant they were unwell.

The next day we awoke, and I bid my farewell to Amber with promises of seeing one another again soon. Then J and I discovered four more of the black kittens had died in the night. I couldn't bare it and felt this was my fault too. "We are going to the vet's," I insisted.

"That will cost money," J said.

"I don't care. I want these babies to live," I declared stubbornly, and so eventually we made our way to the vet's with Tabstick, Little Tabs and Furkin. The vet was extremely short with us to start with and said that little Tabs was suffering and had to be put down. She hadn't got enough liquid and was suffering from hypothermia and an infection. I was bordering on hysterical as the vet pushed the needle of death into little Tabs. She squealed loudly as she was injected and my heart shattered into a million fragments, tearing at my soul and taking it to a dark abyss. I was teetering on the edge, feeling like I wanted to scream. Tears were pouring down my face and I felt panic rising in my chest as that little soul slipped away.

The vet turned to me. "She's not suffering anymore," she said a little more pleasantly. I later found out that kittens who lose their mother at such a young age often struggle to survive. The vet I spoke to later said we'd done extremely well for even two kittens to survive, yet I wouldn't know this for some time, and it was an extra weight on my heart I carried around with me.

Little Tabs was buried under a rose bush in the garden. The bush was a gift from my mother and I liked to think that when it bloomed, Little Tabs would always be part of the rose bush, her energy fortifying it and making it strong and beautiful.

Tabstick and Furkin came home, and I insisted we up the feeding regime. While I couldn't stand up for myself, I felt that I had failed these kittens and there was no way I was failing them again. I prayed with all my heart Tabstick and Furkin would live, and I would rush off webcam to check them, ensure they were fed and that they had enough warmth. Tabstick would lick Furkin, eat his poo poo and cuddle up to him. It was a little gross, but I understood that she was helping him learn to go to the toilet. Cats have an instinct for these things, and she became the 'mother' of the two. It was as if she was helping to keep him alive. Every day I woke up, dreading that I would wake up and find one or both dead, but thank the heavens, that day never came.

The kittens, while still small, were growing and starting to wobble about on their little legs, play-fighting and bumping into one another. Days passed and soon they were scampering around. I weaned them onto cat meat as soon as it was safe to do so, being careful to mash it up into a paste so that they didn't choke on it, and they ate with monster appetites, much to my joy. My heart melted when I taught them to drink water by themselves for the first time. I set the little bowl aside and they plopped their whole faces in the water, then pulled their little heads back, their faces full of surprise and bewilderment. It took a few goes, but they learned to lap the water after I demonstrated with my own bowl of water, lapping it with my tongue as their mother would have done. They were so cute; they'd still get their faces a little wet in the beginning and I would have to dry them with a towel.

Every day they grew stronger, I had more hope that they would live, but there was still a part of me that thought they would be cruelly ripped away from me. I had really started to bond with them on a deeper level now. Tabstick especially seemed to think I was her mum and followed me everywhere. Furkin soon started to follow Crackers everywhere and they became best friends. Wherever Crackers went, Furkin followed. Crackers didn't seem to mind at all and groomed Furkin's ears with long, loving licks. He would then run off and stop to look over his shoulder, as if to say, "Come on, buddy, catch up!"

A deep bond grew between Tabstick and I, she trusted me completely. One day she ran up the curtain and got stuck at the top. I threw my dressing gown on for protection then stood below, pointing at my shoulder. A moment later, a wide-eyed kitten was on my shoulder, her little claws splayed out, looking shocked at her own bravery!

Every milestone filled me with happiness – Tabstick eating my leftover boiled eggs, Furkin jumping onto the sofa, the kittens' first adventure into the garden and climbing their first tree. I was a proud and devoted cat mum.

Whenever we sat outside, there would be a parade of cats as they all followed in unison and came and sat in the long grass with us, Tabstick always by my side. I felt like I was in a Disney movie. My life had felt diabolical before and now it seemed as if I had been sent a special gift to focus my attentions on. The gift of unconditional love. I saw it in Tabstick's eyes as she sat and gazed up at me, and I loved her back with all my heart. To this day, Tabstick and I are soulmates. Sometimes she'll just give me a knowing look, that she understands me. She's a real character and at night as I settle down into bed, she lies on my head, stretches out her paws and sighs peacefully. She's the only cat I've known to sigh! She always loves to throw looks of disgust at people she finds annoying, and squeaks like a mouse whenever she hears the word chicken!

The calls from Aiden were petering out; although I still

thought of him, my main focus was on the cats and doing everything I could to keep them all safe and with me.

Often, I've wondered if my life would have turned out differently if I would have left J sooner and if the kittens hadn't been born. They seemed to be the only thing that really connected us then, but then I can't imagine life without Tabstick. She is the best thing in this world that has ever happened to me and so for that reason alone, I wouldn't change the past. Well, that's not entirely true. If I could go back in time, I'd skip back to the part when the kittens were born, end things with J and take care of them myself. Time machines don't exist though, and our history makes us who we are. I'm no longer ashamed of some of the things I did to survive. I understand that I did my best to keep surviving when life became difficult, and I'm still here, so I obviously got something right. Evolution, baby.

Chapter 27: The C Word

Saturday, 25 August

It was the day of my sister's second wedding reception, for all the guests who couldn't make it to Cyprus. Our family love to have jolly good knees-ups, so why not have two parties! J insisted on giving me a lift to the train station but faffed around with the van for ages. He had brought this bright red van that looked like Postman Pat's van. It made a dreadful noise and was always full of rubbish, and it was embarrassing being seen in it. He was always complaining about the battery and when I announced I was ready to leave, he decided to charge it for an hour. I had booked a photographer to come and take some photos of the reception and I had promised to help him get people into groups, so it was frustrating knowing that I was now running late. Once I reached the station, I would have to travel to London Victoria, down to Swindon and then get a taxi out to the village, so it wasn't a quick journey. As I arrived, the photographer was packing up to leave, as he said he'd struggled as people didn't seem to want their pictures taken, although he'd tried his best. I apologised profusely for my lateness and thanked him for coming along.

Then my big sister Melanie asked me to come into the pub and have a word. She wore a serious expression and so I started to feel worried. Seeing my face drop, she said, "Don't get all silly, it's all going to be OK so don't get upset, but Mum's got breast Cancer."

I felt as if I'd been punched in the stomach and my heart started to pound.

"She's OK, it's treatable, I just wanted to mention it to you first. You need to be strong for Mum, so try not to get too upset."

Tears had already started welling up in my eyes, but I wiped them away and nodded, resolute that I would not make things worse by being a cry baby. She took me in to see my mum and middle sis, and Mum reassured me she was fine.

"I don't understand, why didn't you say anything on holiday?" I implored.

"It was Clarissa's big day and I didn't want to ruin it."

I couldn't believe she'd kept it a secret! Only her and my dad had known. After the initial shock had worn off, I asked lots of questions and it turns out the hospital had wanted her to cancel the holiday and have a lump removed, but she'd refused point-blank. She was due to go back soon and have the op and radiation therapy. She was so brave and acted like it was no big deal, but I'm sure she was doing that for us girls. She wanted us all to carry on as normal, so we did as best as we could. We headed to the bar, got some drinks and did some karaoke. I was back on the emotional rollercoaster and knocked the drinks back swiftly.

I'd invited Aiden, or my sisters had, I can't remember now, but anyway he came along and I introduced him to my dad. "He's a handsome fella, isn't he," my dad said, and they exchanged compliments. It felt like such a normal exchange, and different from the conversation J would have had with my parents. J would have called my mum "an institutional racist" or would have effed and jeffed and told my dad he loved swearing while using as many expletives as possible. He'd always figure out which buttons to press with people to antagonise them as much as he could. It was nice not to stand there wishing that the ground would swallow me up for once.

My sisters and I drank, we sang karaoke and we laughed, a lot. The night wore on and we were all quite squiffy. I remember being sat on my dad's knee while he played Elvis Presley's 'Angel' on his iPod and sang it to me. I loved moments like this, where I felt like a child again. I felt safe. I'd had my ups and downs with both of my parents, but family is the most important thing in the world, and we never held grudges for long. My sis Clarissa came over to join us and started on at my dad about his health. Mum's diagnosis had been an awakening for us girls and made us realise that no one is invincible.

Later, Dad laughed his head off as he told me I had turned to my sister and said, "And you need to look after yourself too, you aren't getting any younger."

Apparently, she didn't look too impressed at that statement! I'd insisted that they mustn't die and that I loved them. Later, when some of the lads joined us, I insisted they agree that my dad was pretty, much to their amusement. We had a good laugh that night, despite the circumstances, and I enjoyed spending some quality time with my mum. In all, it was a success.

Later, Aiden and I went back to his tent. The nicest thing was cuddling up and not feeling anxious. With him, what you saw was what you got, there were no snide comments or hidden agenda and I fell asleep quickly, something I rarely did.

The next morning came all too soon. I said my farewells to everyone and made Mum promise she would keep me updated with details. Then it was time to head back home. I remember wishing that the party would never end and that I didn't have to go home.

Chapter 28: Dante's Inferno

All good things must come to an end and summer was over as soon as it had begun. Bibby, Crackers and Pinky had gotten big now. Even Piskie had grown a little, although she never grew to full size and always looked like a kitten. Tabstick and Furkin were strong now and I was so proud of my little warriors.

We'd had a scare recently. My mum had come to visit for a couple of days, and we had headed off to Camden to shop and eat tapas. I'd gotten a call from J saying the two kittens had pulled a pallet down on themselves and were on oxygen at the vet's. My heart pounding, I raced home and was furious, as I had been telling him relentlessly to get rid of the big, heavy pallets he'd brought inside the house. God knows why he'd brought dirty pallets inside.

Now, Piskie and Bibby had almost fully recovered from their incident with the pallet, except sometimes Piskie would almost walk into a wall, then stop and shake her head, confused. She would also sit in a corner staring at the wall for ages. She had definitely lost a few of her marbles when that pallet brained her, but she seemed a happy little chappy at least.

Contact with Aiden had fizzled out completely. I hadn't found the courage or energy to leave J and so I suppose he felt I was stringing him along, and who could blame him.

Work had started to pick up and I found myself doing various photoshoots alongside TV work and webcam. HSBC now had a debt collection agency hassling me day in, day out and so I was trying to spend as little as possible. One time someone from HSBC phoned me up and said, "Why don't you stop spending?" I argued that I hadn't spent anything apart from around £50 on food from the supermarket. He then proceeded to point out my Internet bill had increased. I explained I needed Internet for my work and if they hadn't slapped on ridiculous charges, this never would have happened. I wrote letter after letter to HSBC and the Ombudsman, but nobody was interested. In the end, I closed my account with HSBC and opened a building society account. To this day, my new bank has been an absolute pleasure and I wish I had banked with them in the first place.

Life was stressful with debts mounting up, but my career (on paper) started to go from strength to strength and I appeared in glossy magazines, on Bravo TV and even in *Homme* magazine. I even saw one of my previous critics online saying, "Wow, she is in *Homme*. Looks like she is doing well for herself." On the outside I was. If I'd have had the balls to go it alone, I would have had a good standard of living, but with J at my side, life was chaotic at best. I was just thankful for my cats and my beautiful garden by the river that brought me peace when life felt like Dante's inferno.

Chapter 29: Chasing a Burglar with a Platform Shoe

Winson Green, Birmingham, 2008

Just as I seemed to be falling on my feet again, we had a letter from the rental agency saying we needed to vacate the house in two days. I was furious and insisted they couldn't do this. They insisted they'd sent a letter three months previously to give us notice. I wondered if J had been up to his old post-hiding tricks again. He came up with some story about the cats peeing on a load of letters, so he'd had to throw them out. I had never known the cats to pee on letters. Perhaps he had though, it wouldn't surprise me.

We met the agency representatives at a civil court to contest the matter in hand. This culminated in them giving us a notice period and we had about two weeks to find a new home. J wanted to move up North, claiming it was cheaper. I didn't want to feel more isolated than I was already and argued against this. He told me he was going up North to look at houses regardless and went alone. Perhaps he was seeing a woman, a prostitute, a drug dealer, or was just being obstinate, but I didn't go.

While he was out, I started googling, "My boyfriend is trying to isolate me." I clicked on various articles and the same word kept coming up – "NARCISSIST". He seemed to match most of the traits on the checklist, but even though I knew in my heart that he wasn't normal, I wasn't ready to face the truth and I would to and fro between my thoughts, feeling conflicted for many years after finding this. You can learn more about traits of narcissism here:

https://www.mayoclinic.org/diseases-conditions/
narcissistic-personality-disorder/symptoms-causes/
syc-20366662

When J arrived home about midnight that evening, he returned without the Postman Pat van. He claimed that someone had driven into him and written it off, not far from the house. He said he'd left it in a car park and walked home. At the time, it didn't ring quite true, but I didn't know what to believe. It seemed odd that he never contacted the police or chased this up. In hindsight, he probably didn't have insurance and the van was impounded. It wouldn't have been the first time!

So, now we had to find a house and had no transport. We scoured the adverts and the only place we found that we could afford was in Birmingham, which happened to be the street that appeared on *Benefits Britain*. By this point, I was drained of all energy as well as resources and was going along with things, so we drove up in his white Peugeot and accepted the house on the spot. He left the car behind, and we took the train home as we would need a transit van to move. I hired a van and we packed it up half full, J insisting he would come back for the rest of the things the next day. We left behind my treadmill and a lot of my books and clothes, and that was the last I ever saw of them. He claimed he went back for it, but none of it was there.

His Peugeot he took to a local garage and abandoned it there, then refused to take phone calls from the garage. I didn't know what he did, but I could never get any sense out of him. One minute he said they couldn't get it over their pit, the next minute he didn't want it anyway as it wouldn't pass its MOT. Every statement was confusing, conflicting and made my head pound. It wasn't so much word salad as word puree.

Moving to Birmingham was a huge culture shock for me.

Before I'd been able to escape the chaos of the house by sitting by the river or walking across the fields. Now I was in a concrete city, in a three-level terraced house. There was a garden, but it was uninhabitable. The grass was six feet high and you couldn't mow the lawn as there was rubble and rocks under the grass, so I was now stuck inside and it was a pretty rough area, so going for walks wasn't an option. I was now on a different kind of antidepressant, and this combined with the lack of exercise made me balloon and put on two stone. I was disgusted with myself, but just couldn't seem to lose weight. I even tried the Ali supplements and went on a restrictive diet. I lost a few pounds, then put it all back on again. I did weight training, but this just made me look bulkier. In the previous six months, I was lean and had gotten into walking, bouncing on a trampoline and using dumbbells. Now I was drinking more alcohol to cope with my emotions, which didn't help my figure. Drained all the time, I always wanted to sleep.

Britain entered the recession, shoots were sparse and there was little reason to leave the house. I threw myself into webcam and decided to do more Femdom sessions. We'd left most of the furniture behind in the old house and so I didn't really have much in the lounge, where the sessions were to take place. My first couple of slaves were quite baffled when I instructed them to lie on the hardwood floor. To be honest, I was quite baffled myself about where to put them, but I had to try and make this work! After this, I informed my slaves that I was waiting to buy furniture and they were understanding. They didn't seem to mind at all as I ordered them to their knees on the hard floor, with only a towel below them. As soon as I had enough money, I bought a strong metal futon which could easily be transformed from a sofa into a bed. It was great for restraining people as well and wrapping ropes around the metal bars!

I bought a lot of my initial props on the cheap. I visited places like B&Q and Homebase, and bought good-quality metal rings, hooks, chains, tow rope and items I could use for BDSM for about a quarter of the price I would have paid online! I even bought silicone spatulas for spanking bottoms. These cost about £6 and delivered a lovely sharp sting! A proper spanking paddle can cost upwards of £20, so I managed to avoid spending money I didn't have in those early days. I even made a few items myself … I collected some pieces of birch and tied them at the base to make a suitably stingy punishment tool. I did something similar with some strong mini bamboo canes and an elastic band. It looked quite impressive too.

No longer did I need to worry about photoshoots; it seemed there were a lot of submissive men who wanted to be dominated by a four-foot-ten blonde and didn't seem to mind the extra curves I held at the time. I squeezed myself into tight corsets and sexy black nylons, making sure I looked the part, even if I felt like a blob.

This side of things was still quite new to me, and I was fascinated by all the different scenarios that slaves wanted to partake in. One slave called Sindy became a regular. I would dress him up in my stretchy clothes and make him wear tutus and suck my strap-on. He loved to be told that I would make him take part in gang bangs and pimp him out. Of course, I never did pimp him out. I'd never actually done a forced bi shoot at that point – I'll talk more on this later!

Another slave was a policeman. He used to turn up on his motorcycle and dress in full rubber from head to toe, then I would humiliate him and tell him he was a filthy pig (he prompted this), and the irony of a policeman wanting to be called a filthy pig wasn't lost on me. I couldn't imagine any other scenario in the world where I would speak to a policeman this way and the thought of it sent me into fits of giggles!

Towards the end of each session, I would order him to strap the plastic funnel he brought with him to his face. I would pee into it, and he would be forced to guzzle it down, then I'd instruct him to go and clean my bathroom. He always did a great job and got the tiles sparkling beautifully.

Other slaves wanted to be whipped; some enjoyed role plays

where I was their bitchy boss who blackmailed them into carrying out humiliating tasks, and others wanted to kiss my feet and be my footrest. One slave, Sven, used to like lying under my desk while I answered my emails and ignored him. Occasionally, I would rest my heels on his face or grind the toe of my shoe into his cheek. He never even masturbated once. He just wanted to feel controlled and dominated entirely.

I found the sessions therapeutic and a good outlet for some of the stress I was feeling, but I was careful never to overstep the mark. It would have been easy for someone like me to have become a man-hater, but I understand that it was a power exchange, and as Spiderman once said, "With great power comes great responsibility". Many of my slaves were kind to me. They seemed genuinely interested in my life and brought me gifts. They made me feel like a real person instead of a free ride through life. It would never have made sense for me to have negative feelings towards them.

I met Latex Trooper around this time, and after a few meetings, we started to do overnight domme sessions. At first, I was a little taken aback at the extreme punishments he wanted to indulge in, but we got on well and so slowly I ramped it up, pushing further through his boundaries each time. Financially, he was a big help to me; an overnight paid my rent and bills and took some of the pressure off me. He even sent me off on a luxurious Champneys spa weekend to recharge my batteries. It was exactly what I needed at the time and lazing around the pool after a massage was divine.

It was great to be building up my client base. I knew that I couldn't stay in Winson Green for long, it would drive me mad. I'd walk outside the house and there would be mattresses thrown out on the street and people hanging out on their doorsteps all day long as they didn't have jobs. I don't want to come off as snobbish, and I will happily mix with people from all walks of life, but to be honest, I felt a little embarrassed having people over to the house, and so other than slaves, I rarely invited anyone over. J would pile up the kitchen surfaces with fag ash, food and empty packets, and I was trying to be breadwinner, cleaner and caretaker. I just couldn't keep on top of it all. I have a real thing about cleanliness, so I found this really depressing.

Sometimes he would even take my BDSM props off and leave them scattered all round the house. When I went for an item such as my electro-stim kit and it wasn't where I had left it, I felt like it made me look so unprofessional in front of the client. Once, I even found a dildo J had 'borrowed' and left under his desk. He hadn't put a condom on it and it was caked in whatever he had eaten for dinner the day before. I rushed to the loo and threw up! The wedge between us was growing more and more. I was beginning to find him an utterly deplorable and revolting creature.

Even my sister said to me, "When J opens his mouth, you don't hear him. You just switch off and go into your own world." It was true. I had started to create unconscious survival techniques and found myself often detaching from reality and my surroundings. I would dissociate, safe into my own little bubble where he didn't exist. Sometimes I would dream of magical lands with talking animals. Now and again, I would dip in and out of creative writing projects. J did not like this at all. Most of the time he was happy to ignore me, but the minute I started writing or talking on the phone, he would be in and out of the room distracting me and talking nonsense. He resented me having any personal time. I have since learned that this is a classic abuser technique to sap your energy and take away your sense of identity. He wanted to feel that I was reliant on him for stimulation and didn't approve of me being independent in any way.

Work was a great distraction. I had started to do some work with a porn star called Tallulah Tease as she was local. She was a real down-to-earth Brummie and a lovely lady. One shoot we did, we dressed from head to toe in nylon pantyhose for a fan. Another time, we did a girl-girl shoot where she played a rock star and I was a fan. We also did various duo domme sessions together and terrorised the subs, who cowered before us. Not that they were complaining.

A dungeon space called 'The Facility' popped up on my radar. It was on multiple levels, had a schoolroom and a fantastic dungeon room on the top floor. There was everything from a St Andrew's Cross and a spanking bench through to all manner of crops, canes, floggers and medical equipment. I loved being in the dungeon. J never came in with me, so I felt I could relax, be myself and escape reality for a few hours. Venturing out again lifted my spirits and I attended some of the adult networking parties. They were events organised by companies such as the UK Adult Producers Society, now known as SNAP – Support Network for Adult Professionals.

The meets consisted of networking in a bar or nightclub with other industry folk. Being so detached from everything now, I thought that no one would remember me, but people always came up to me hollering "Kaz! Long time no see!" and would hug me fondly. J always skirted on the edges like an outsider. It was the one time where I was the confident one. These were people I knew and admired, and I enjoyed catching up with many of them. Like me, many of them were survivors for various reasons and worked hard to get where they were. J didn't approve of anyone giving me attention and so he would keep tapping me on the shoulder mid-conversation saying we had to leave. He'd always be twitchy as he'd generally be on the sherbert and wanted to go home and take more, but these little outings helped preserve my sanity.

One day we had a huge row. He'd trashed the kitchen and it was filthy, then during a conversation he started talking down to me and I flipped. "Get out! Just leave and get out of my life will you. I hate you!" I screamed.

Unwilling to give up his meal ticket and his parasitical lifestyle, he simply refused to leave. A week or so later, I'd calmed down but insisted he get a job. He took a job in a hi-fi store and for a while I tried to be positive and encouraging, but he would come home saying he hated it and that everyone was awful to him. I pointed out that over the years I had done jobs I didn't want to do to keep us afloat, and that led to another row. Again, I was the bad guy for putting him down or making him feel bad. Everything I said was twisted and used against me. After that, he punished me with silence. He would come home in a foul mood and go and sit in the bedroom in the dark, binge-watching TV and eating, leaving wrappers everywhere. While he was watching anything, I wasn't allowed to talk, and he refused to help me around the house or with anything else going on in my life.

Retreating, I decided it was probably a blessing in disguise. He would break these long silences to intervene if he suspected I was planning something that might be successful. I invited a photographer over to chat about organising a group photographic day. J charged into the room and bamboozled the photographer with nonsense information, convincing him that he should run up some figures and costs for the day. This was utter nonsense of course. The only cost would be the venue costs and the models, which the photographer's fees would pay for. It wasn't rocket science and I sat there glaring at J while he wore a self-satisfied expression on his face, having convinced a stranger he was an expert on all matters. If this happened now, I would say, "Thanks but I don't think we'll take financial advice from someone who can't hold down a job and is in colossal debt." I just didn't have the nerve at the time though, as I was soft and most likely suffering from some form of Stockholm syndrome, where the captive empathises with their captor.

The photographer rang a few times asking me if the figures were ready, and J would say they weren't done yet. They never would be done. His intention wasn't to help, it was to sabotage any effort to better myself. We never did that group shoot.

J lasted a few months at his job before he was sacked, although I never saw any of the money as he never helped with any of the bills. He claimed it had been swallowed up by his debts. For all I knew, he could have been sat on a park bench getting high with winos all day instead of going to work.

There was one single event where J's slovenly ways may have been of service to me. I was doing a webcam show with a regular. We could both see each other on the screen; he was sniffing poppers and I was ordering him to bark like a dog and punish his nipples by putting tight clamps on them. "Bark louder, Puppy!" I hollered at him, and he complied.

Then I heard, "Euuugh! Oooooh! Mistress, I've cum!" I giggled and signed off.

Earlier, I'd told J to tidy up the middle bedroom on the floor below and he had gotten as far as piling bin bags full of junk, plates, bowls and cutlery onto his desk as he never finished a job. I'd often sleep upstairs in my cam room when he annoyed me or snored too loudly, but I'd happened to go in the bedroom and was disgusted with the state of it. It looked like squatters had been in there!

Anyway, I heard bags rustling and assumed the cats were rifling for a tidbit. "Stop that now!" I hollered at the top of my voice.

Being a cat mum, you need to have eyes in the back of your heard and need to let them think you are always aware of what they are doing, so I was used to shouting if I heard a noise.

I was certain it must be the cats splaying up, but a horrible feeling filled the pit of my stomach as I strained to listen more carefully. An almighty crash sounded out and I heard the clatter of bowls, plates and cutlery go flying, then the sound of many paws rushing down the stairs at top speed. Something wasn't right. The hair rose on the back of my neck and a cold chill passed through me. Somehow, I just knew that someone had broken in through the window, and then I felt a flash of fury race through me. *How dare someone come in and terrify my cats!*

I looked around the room for something to defend myself with and the best thing I could come up with was a big gold platform shoe with a chunky heel. I grabbed it and tread silently across the room to the top of the stairs, not knowing what on earth I was going to see. As I rounded the corner, an Asian lad of about twenty, dressed in a hoodie, appeared, walking upstairs as if he owned the place. For a second, we both froze and stared at one another, our eyes wide in shock. Then a bolt of furious energy charged through me, and I screamed, "Get the fuck out of my house!" He turned and fled down the stairs. Instinct took over and I followed him, running down the stairs, chasing him with my shoe and yelling at him. He ran through the lounge, into the sitting room and out of the front door. I ran out into the street, brandishing the shoe above my head, and yelled, "And don't come back, you little shit!"

I then turned to see my next-door neighbours staring open-mouthed. White Dee was on her doorstep having a chat with a neighbour and said, "What was all that about?"

"Some little thug just broke into my house!" I exclaimed.

"I don't think he'll be coming back any time soon!" she laughed.

It only occurred to me in that moment, as the adrenaline started to leave my body, that I could have got stabbed. I had just reacted without thinking and chased the guy out. Perhaps confidence *is* everything!

You might recognise the name White Dee. I was living on James Turner Street, from the show *Benefits Britain*. I also think I had a little something to do with the creation of that show. The BBC came to my house to do a documentary about the adult industry. They mentioned the area was a bit rough and asked why I was there. I didn't tell them the full story, but said I was the only person who worked on the street, everyone else was on benefits. They soon lost interest in me, but I saw them knocking on neighbours' doors … and *Benefits Britain* came about!

White Dee was a nice lady, she was just trapped and had no way of getting out of her humdrum existence, well until she appeared on TV that is.

My neighbours were pleasant enough, but the area was rough, there was no question about it. One time I had quite a well-to-do slave visit me and as I greeted him at the door, he said a gang of hoodies had thrown something at his car. I went out onto the street in my PVC (I really didn't care who saw me dressed like this in Winson Green) and called over, "Excuse me, why were you throwing things at my friend's car?"

They were only young lads of about eighteen or nineteen and one of them called back, "Sorry, Miss! We didn't realise he was with you!"

"Well, please be more careful next time, don't do that again," I called.

"No, sorry, we won't. It was only a laugh."

That's the thing – if you lived on the street, you were one of them and they looked out for you. I suppose I had earned my mark of respect the day I'd chased the intruder out with the shoe. They knew that despite the fact I was four foot ten, I wasn't someone to be messed about with.

Some of them were little rapscallions though if they thought they could get away with it. If they had been my kids, they'd have had a thick ear and been sent to bed with no supper!

After that show aired, I saw a lot of comments slating the 'spongers' on the show and it upset me. Now, I have never once claimed a penny in my life. I've never claimed benefits or jobseek-er's allowance, but that doesn't entitle me to look down on people who have. From having lived on that street, I could see that many of these people were born into a broken system. Some did not have a good education and had no means of bettering themselves or gaining employment. They had no support or encouragement of any kind, or any mentor in their lives. I often thought that if they could have attended workshops and gained some skills, it would have given them skills for life, but instead they were trapped and had no way out. It was a humbling experience and rid me of any prejudices I'd formerly had about the unemployed.

One thing I knew for sure, I didn't want to become trapped on James Turner Street. I would have to find a way to leave.

Chapter 30: Latex Trooper and the Olympic Hand Shandy

J was becoming more of a sexual deviant than ever; he had few inhibitions and boundaries on a day-to-day basis, but when he was under the influence of whatever narcotic or legal high he could get his hands on, he became a nightmare. The positive flipside to this was that I got to test run all my BDSM equipment on him before trying it on slaves; there was little he wouldn't try, and rather than allow him to pound away at me mechanically for hours giving me a hernia, I would whip out my props and gadgets. He was game for most things. I had an electro-stim kit and would wire him up with electric pads on his genitals, nipple clamps and cock rings, and it would send an electric current through these metal devices. He would tinker with crocodile clamps and create extra clamps for me to torment him with. Of course, sometimes he would meddle with things I didn't want him to meddle with. One time, he pushed a metal wire all the way through a brand-new silicon butt plug I had bought so he could be electrocuted in his backside. I complained and his response implied he was some sort of misunderstood scientific genius. Why couldn't I just let him experiment and find his calling in life? *Is your calling in life sticking all manner of household objects up your arse?* I wanted to scream.

Sometimes I would suggest something outrageous for a laugh and he would agree to it instantly. I put full make-up on him, dressed him as a girl and put a dog's choker collar made of scratchy metal spikes on him. Although I didn't realise it at the time, this was all invaluable research and practise for me in the fetish side of domination.

I was starting to be a bit naughtier with some of my work and J liked me to describe all the details of what had happened. He got off on this nearly as much as he enjoyed taking my money. It was clear he saw me as nothing more than a sexual object and would say things like, "You have a body made for sex," he even called me a "cock jockey", much to my revulsion. I couldn't stand the way he sexualised me and tried to make out I was on heat all the time when this couldn't be further from the truth. When he advanced on me, telling me things like this, I felt as if he said this in the same manner a rapist might tell his victim that they were "gagging for it". Feeling annoyed one day when he was trying to convince me I was obsessed with sex as much as him, I blurted out, "It's not all fun and games when you have to do these things to make a living. Why don't you bloody try it and see how you like it!"

In a flash, he agreed and suggested I arrange for him to interact with a guy on camera! I was flabbergasted, but somewhat intrigued. There was something extremely wrong with this context. I should have been horrified that my *boyfriend* wanted to go bobbing for hot dogs, but instead I felt partly amused and partly victorious that it would soon be him putting in some work to keep the roof over our head. I knew the perfect person to arrange this with. Latex Trooper had become a good friend by now and he often asked if I could get another guy involved in a session. Latex was one of the clients I had a bit of extra fun with because he was such a gentle guy, so sweet-natured, and we always had a good banter. He'd helped dig me out of a bit of a financial hole and I considered him a real friend. Yes, I know what you are thinking, and it is weird to reward a friend with sexy shenanigans, but I was a totally different person back then.

Anyway, I thought he would be the perfect guy to arrange a bi session with. Soon the big day arrived, we set up a camera in the corner and Latex Trooper and I waited for J to make his grand entrance. I am so pleased that we filmed this, as I am sure I would have forgotten so many of the hilarious details otherwise.

We sat waiting for J for a good hour. When he eventually entered the room with a flourish and a swish of his hair, he was wearing a sheer, black fishnet top with a cross on the front, a metal and leather ring cock cage, fishnet tights pulled high up on the waist with no undies and a pair of large sunglasses. He looked like the lovechild of Cher and Ozzy Osbourne.

The scene began with me donning the most ginormous strap-on and preparing to penetrate Trooper, who was a skinny little fellow. I had quite a belly on me at the time, so already the set-up looked quite bizarre, a chubby blonde with a huge dong next to a skinny little hunched man. Latex Trooper bent over dutifully and the massive dong seemingly disappeared into this skinny frame. Looking back at the video, there is no trace of surprise on my face. This was clearly just another day in the office.

Enter stage left – J! He was twitching, gurning, sweating profusely like a bishop in a brothel, and rocking back and forth in a merry, hazy jig. He jumped onto the bed with manic glee and without a word, stuffed his appendage into Trooper's mouth. Throughout the video, Latex Trooper sucked away with the same bland, uninterested expression throughout. This is how I knew he was enjoying himself. He really was the Keanu Reeves of porn, no expression whatsoever happened at any point.

Beforehand, I'd drank a couple of glasses of wine for Dutch courage, but still look sober in the footage; however, I did not bat a single eyelid at this bizarre spectacle before me.

There were a few fetish games involved. Using a riding crop on LT's bottom, he barely flinched, then I wrote various demeaning words across his body. It's quite bizarre watching the footage because J was the cameraman and performing in the scene, so sometimes we crawled out of shot and you can just see a foot or hear some weird dialogue that wasn't part of the scene.

At one point, I decided to fellate Latex Trooper and mid-action, J jumped off the bed and loudly called the local Chinese takeaway to order some food! In the footage, you can clearly hear him giving out the old address and giving directions. He then called me to do something, so I came out of the shot. Latex

Trooper did not seem to notice my absence and is seen consistently staring into space, while continuing to wank a now flaccid willy for about half an hour!

J then turned on an extremely loud fan. When I say loud, it sounded as if we were on an airfield and a Boeing 747 was about to take off!

Latex Trooper was lying on a pink plastic sheet which covered the mattress and by now it had crumpled up around him, obviously from the rigorous wanking and people jumping on and off the bed. The fan started to blow the plastic sheet up all around him as if a hurricane was passing through the room, but he did not adjust his position once or even blink! He carried on with that same deadpan expression in a wank marathon to end all wank sessions. He was going for gold, and nothing was going to separate his palm from that cock! He was covered in bruises, cane marks and all kinds of ruination, but was hell-bent on getting as much wrist action as he could possibly manage! Respect! The guy was a real trooper and if there were medals given for wanking, his whole chest would be weighed down with them!

At this point, J seemed to be talking off camera to an imaginary friend that no one could see or hear. (There was definitely no one else there!)

Then, in the blink of an eye and with no cue, everyone sprang into life and there was action once more! It was almost as if an unseen director was orchestrating everyone in the room. The scene fragmented briefly as I played around with Trooper's nether regions and J pranced about in the background off camera, humming loudly.

Ice pops appeared next, which were to be inserted into Trooper's butthole! I told him that I'd take the wrapper off as it might be a bit spiky on his backside. In hindsight, I thought, *Don't mind the fucking freezing ice burns, as long as it's not sodding scratchy!* Mind you, it didn't stay in his back passage for long, he soon popped it into his mouth.

Clearly in full domme mode, I attached a peg to the end of his dick to give him a ruined orgasm. He became extremely

interested in the ice pop and finally slowed the wanking down …
the poor devil must have been dehydrated after an hour-and-a-
half wankathon!

Whether he came or not is a mystery. The scene ended with
him looking quite lovingly at the ice pop and I can only guess that
J was either getting up to some deviant activity off camera or was
stuffing his face with Chinese!

You might notice that I have conveyed this passage with
humour and little emotion. That's because, from what I remember,
I was in work mode and professionally detached from the carnage
that took place. I watched the scene back recently and had tears of
laughter rolling down my cheeks. That's how I like to remember a
lot of the crazy scenes I did, with good humour. I also discovered
something that day. I quite enjoyed strolling around wearing a
strap-on and having the boys play with each other for my amusement! It beats doing it myself!!

In the past, J and I had tried some professional shoots together,
but they were always horrendous. Generally, he'd go floppy, and
we'd sit around waiting in the cold for hours. On one occasion this
happened, and the female producer told him he was useless and
sent a girl in to do the scene with me. I don't think he ever forgave
me that, even though they weren't my words. Another time, we
were on set for One Eyed Jack's Real Couples and unbeknown to
me, J had put a metal cage on his genitals, so when I slipped my
hand into his trousers, he screamed and claimed I'd injured him. I
suspected that he knew he wouldn't be able to rise to the occasion
as he was taking speed, and this was a ruse to pass the blame on
to me.

Nevertheless, shooting fetish suited me much better. I hated
having to pretend that I was having the orgasm of my life when all
I could think was, *Please stop sweating on me, and get your horrible
clumsy fingers off me!* I have ultimate respect for the performers
who can pull off scene after scene of high energy vanilla activity,
but it's not for me. I've tried it, I found it a chore. Give me a
grovelling slave on his knees and a whip in my hand any day!

Chapter 31: The Art of Kink and Men in Wigs

Whatever happens to you in life, in most cases you can turn your life around, and while some experiences may be awful at the time, they can serve as valuable lessons and you can learn from them. Quite literally in my case!

I have many subs who love nothing more than to be utterly humiliated and degraded. It is not in my nature to be instinctive about these kinds of things, but I learned methods and techniques from partners that were just abhorrent. While in real life, some of the techniques abusers use are sick and twisted, in a Femdom scenario where there is consent and safe words, these things can be quite erotic. The main difference is that the scenario is a power exchange between two consenting adults, and humiliation and degradation are employed for erotic purposes, rather than as a tool to harm another person psychologically.

Some tasks I give slaves can be degrading and some can be quite fun. I'm always careful to ask if the slave has any health problems, including mental health problems, and whether there is anything that could possibly trigger them. The art of Femdom is a fine balance and there is a narrow line between the edge of eroticism and trauma. Having given my slave their safe word and verified that they are of sound mind, I slip into my mean mistress role and deploy various tactics.

I've seen many Insta-dommes (girls who think being a domme is easy, claim to be a domme overnight and just shout and demand cash), but to truly manipulate someone and get into their mind, you wouldn't start this way. When I've entered toxic relationships before, they've always been sweetness and light, throwing on their mask and acting the role of the perfect guy. It wasn't until later that the toxic behaviour showed up. That's also how I'll begin a humiliation session, smiling sweetly, gazing into their eyes, making them feel relaxed and at ease.

I'll start with some simple tasks, such as kissing my shoes, to lull them into a false sense of security, then I'll start to up the ante when they least expect it. I'll give them a task; it can be as simple as kissing my feet, but I'll micro-manage it from start to finish, "Don't keep kissing the same place, go to the toes, no not like that, now back to the heel, support it in your hand, stroke the ankle, more enthusiasm, don't slobber!" You get the idea. If a slave's primary goal is to feel powerless, there are many ways to achieve this. You can restrain him so he cannot move, blindfold him so he cannot see, or insert a ball gag into his mouth so he cannot reply. If this is alongside pain play, I have a tapping system which they can use instead of a safe word and they can tap three times with their hand.

I don't rely heavily on ball gags myself, as sometimes I quite like a bit of cheeky banter from my slave. I can also use this as an excuse to punish them. Sessions should be fun, so perhaps instead of a ball gag, I may forbid them to speak in their normal voice and they must employ a high-pitched squeaky voice instead. I may instruct them to stand in the corner silently with their hands on their head while I scold them verbally, permit them only to crawl instead of walking, walk in heels with a sexy wiggle or wear a nappy.

Other times, I might give them a task such as cleaning, stop them almost straight away and ask them what they did wrong and make them keep guessing, and rather than get annoyed or shout, I will go silent and stare at them. It makes them feel humble quickly! I've found a lot of guys struggle to multitask, especially when in front of a PVC-clad domme, so instructing them to swap from task to task, correcting them, making contradictory statements and mocking their work keeps them on their toes and this can be exciting for a slave who wishes to feel a level of vulnerability that they wouldn't normally reach. It's a safe space where they can play out their fantasies without repercussions.

With my more extreme slaves, I don't have to worry so much about walking that tightrope between fantasy and psychological trauma. Slave A might feel that the perfect humiliation session is being told he is useless and is never to use his worthless, tiny penis again. Slave B might love having his head pushed down the toilet and being ordered to lick the bowl, and Slave C might be terrified at the prospect of any of these. It's important that you learn to know your slave and that's why I call it an art form. Some slaves may be quite happy to openly talk about their fetishes, but others clam up, that's when body language becomes your only clue as to what's in their mind.

Hypnosis can be effective too: staring into their eyes while they are in a relaxed state and planting suggestions into their mind. I've used a lot of positive hypnosis on myself over the years and found it to be useful, and the same goes for subs, but hypnosis is safe. You can only make people do things they want to do.

There are many scenarios in which you can break a slave right down, should he wish to enter such an arrangement. You can lock him in a confined space and deprive him of light. Popping on headphones with loud, jarring music will change his emotions. You can pull him out only to interrogate him and then lock him away again, leaving him in isolation for various periods of time. You can order him to eat only from a dog bowl or urinate only into a bottle. He can be given water from a glass that you hold or from your mouth; basically, the key here is to deprive him of his most human functions. For anyone trying this at home, I strongly advise you know your slaves' mental limitations extremely well and that there is ALWAYS an opt-out safe word in place.

Currently, there seems to be a huge fetish for 'forced bi', which I briefly mentioned earlier. Forced bi involves 'forcing' a man to fellate another man or partake in a sexual activity with him. Of course, they have turned up for this, so there is never any real force, but it's make-believe, built on the premise that they have to go through with it or incur the wrath of the mistress. I've done quite a lot of sessions like this over the years and it all began with that bi experience J had with Trooper. He got off on the idea that he was doing it to keep me happy, and that's how many slaves justify pushing through their boundaries and the taboo by telling themselves it's to keep their mistress happy.

Many of these guys are not homosexual, or bi, but they get off on the humiliation of engaging in a taboo activity at the hands of a mistress. If they were to do this on their own, it would be no thrill, but to be observed by a mistress is embarrassing, and ultimately thrilling for them. Orchestrating the forced bi session as the director of the show can be entertaining. I give commands, encourage, tease and laugh as I make money from my little sub-bies playing with each other, without having to lay a finger on them myself.

I think a lot of Insta-dommes are man-haters and are of the belief that all men are vermin. They shout, they rant and call slaves pigs. Some slaves might like being called a pig, but others just have a kinky fetish and would find such insults off-putting. I think sometimes Femdom can become abuse if the wrong person is at the helm of the ship, steering into the rocks. Once, I had to snatch a cane out of a domme's hand (Diamond) as she was drunk and had lost her temper and was still smashing the slave with the cane after he had said his safe word. Blood sprayed up the walls and I checked the slave to see if he was bleeding, then realised it was my middle finger on the left that was pouring with blood. It had cut quite deep, and I still have a little white scar there today. I confiscated the cane and halted the session at that point. The slave was fine, and we just watched a movie and enjoyed a few nibbles, although my finger suffered for a bit!

Another time, I was on a photoshoot and a group of us heard screams coming from inside. It turned out the 'domme' inside was drunk, high as a kite and beating her submissive boyfriend black and blue. Someone called the police, and she spent the night in the cells. It takes a lot of emotional intelligence to be a domme, and a degree of empathy. You need to know when to stop, when to communicate and ask if they are feeling OK, and when to halt playtime. There is no shame in showing compassion as a domme and it does not make you weak. It makes you a good domme. To me, being weak is when someone must throw their weight around and prove they are top dog, even to the detriment of their submissive or anyone else around them.

If you hate men, you should not be a domme. If you cannot hold back, this is the wrong profession for you. You need a degree of self-awareness because while the slave may be there to serve you, it is fantasy and should not be about someone using abuse as self-medication to somehow right the wrongs of the past.

If you can remain calm and logical, be compassionate for another individual and engage in some of the above methods I discussed, while remaining in a level of detachment and not getting too caught up in the excitement of the power you wield, you might just make a good dominatrix or master!

Chapter 32: Stay Humble

The adult and BDSM industries operate in a world of fantasy. When I wear my PVC and slip into role, I become Mistress Kaz. When my slave leaves the premises, I'll often pop on my PJs or a vest top and shorts and become regular Kaz. It's important to have that psychological divide between yourself and your alter ego. Your alter ego may be much like you, just a bit more exaggerated, but even so that divide is essential.

I have seen so many porn stars and mistresses that start to turn into their character or alter ego. When you have an online presence, you'll have your critics, but you'll also have a harem of followers who compliment you on a day-to-day basis, "You are amazing, you are a goddess, I love you, etc." As much as we all enjoy receiving a compliment, it can be just as unhealthy to bask in the glow of this heady buzz as it is to dwell on criticism. Compliments and criticism, I try to accept both with a healthy detachment as much as possible, not allowing myself to get upset over criticism, although I may think about whether the words are justified and in which case how I can seek to better myself. Likewise, with compliments, they are nice but to rely on them for self-esteem could be damaging. Real self-esteem comes from within and in my opinion is best achieved by making healthy goals and targets and doing things that are nourishing for the soul.

I've seen so many girls (and guys) buy into their own hype, and suddenly they think they are the best thing since sliced bread and become arrogant and might act as if others are below them. To me it's ridiculous that someone could feel superior because they've slipped into some PVC and are holding a stick, but somehow, they've been brainwashed by their own success. In turn, they generally become horribly boring people that are rude, abrasive and obnoxious. I have seen dommes go from being popular and well liked, to being despised, mocked and then suddenly they disappear back into obscurity. I think your own individual identity is one of the most precious things in the whole world and losing that to arrogance is a pitiful thing.

In this industry, I have seen the Good, the Bad and the Ugly. Those who practice bad and ugly behaviours are never around for long.

The subject of mental health is relevant here too. There is a misconception that working in any of the adult industries gives people mental health problems. I strongly disagree. I would suggest that many people with mental health issues are drawn to this industry as it allows them to be self-sufficient and work on their own terms. Some individuals may suffer from anxiety or insomnia and struggle to consistently stick to a nine-to-five regime. Being able to set their own hours and days off work relieves the pressure of trying to conform to a lifestyle that they're struggling to adapt to. The adult industry has a valuable place in the world, but as of yet, there is not enough done to safeguard the welfare of those within it. If the industry had a mentorship or an association where the participants could receive support, then it would certainly be a better place.

From my own point of view, when I was trapped in an abusive relationship, there wasn't anyone I could talk to for a long time and so my situation got worse. I was miles away from family, friends would often be put off coming to visit because my then-boyfriend was such an oddball, and I felt as if I had no moral support. It wasn't anyone else's fault (except for my abuser) but for many years, my only guidance and support system was the self-help books I binge-read, then squirreled away the information for a time when I felt stronger. I am so glad that I did.

Chapter 33: The Unhelpful Therapist

I've touched upon some of the mental health issues that I struggled with in the past, which now I am almost certain were a combination of PTSD and psychological abuse. At the time, however, I just thought I was messed up and that it was my fault. I would enter a room and feel nervous, and then worry that everyone would think I was weird for being shy and quiet, then the feelings of panic would amplify.

In my parents' day, they just "got on with things" and discussing feelings was never really a factor. You just had to put up or shut up, that's just the way it was. We grew up to see any kind of depression as weakness or self-pity, so I carried these feelings around like a dirty secret, afraid that they might be revealed and that I would be exposed. Nowadays, it's common for people to talk about their anxiety, bi-polar, borderline personality disorder or depression among other ailments of the mind, but back then it just wasn't done. I was career-driven and being a four-foot-ten female already put me at a disadvantage and people would take me less seriously, so the last thing I wanted to do was appear incapable and I placed ridiculous expectations on myself, not to prove myself to others, but to prove my own worth to myself.

Between 2006 and 2014, I had tried various antidepressants. They are a sticking plaster for a deeper issue and they in themselves caused more problems and side effects. When I was living in Winson Green, J and I had a row and I admitted I felt angry, irritated and miserable all the time. He twisted this round by saying that it was my mental health and that I needed counselling, although for many reasons I probably did.

My counsellor was a woman in her early thirties and

immaculately dressed. She asked what I did for a living. When I told her, I saw a micro-expression of disapproval cross her face. I could see she wasn't going to be objective about this and had already made a judgement. How could I possibly open up to her? She asked me if I was married or had a partner, and if so, what he did. I said yes, he didn't work, but sometimes helped me on the computer or gave me a lift to a shoot. She told me how wonderful it must be to have such a supportive partner. I could tell she thought he was putting himself out by choosing to help his girlfriend who worked in such a disgusting profession. Already, feelings of shame were resurfacing, and the counselling was having more of a detrimental effect upon me. Making an informed decision, I told her few details about my personal life and instead asked how I could be more assertive. What happened next was laughable. She gave me homework which consisted of going into a shop and asking for a refund. This was basic stuff. I had no problems asserting myself in this way. I struggled with relationships, but we were at cross purposes, and trying to communicate my words felt impossible as my brain froze and my words got jumbled before they reached my tongue.

Struggling with words, I managed to ask if I could have a later appointment as I often worked till 3 or 4 a.m. and getting up for a 9 a.m. appointment while on a prescription that made me sleep heavily was nigh-on impossible. She refused my request.

When my time was up, I felt as if I had taken a giant step backwards. She gave me a pamphlet and when I got home and read it, I laughed out loud. There were varying faces that looked like they had been drawn by a child, the first one sad, the next apathetic, the next happy and so on. I had to tick which emotion I was feeling that day and write why underneath. It was patronising and even though the truth was glaringly obvious, I couldn't admit to myself why I was so unhappy.

When my second appointment came about, I was ten minutes late. I'd ran all the way to the surgery and arrived puffing and panting and sucking on my inhaler. I was in a bit of a state, as being late is something that I absolutely loathe to do. The counsellor looked at me coldly and told me that she was terminating my therapy as I clearly couldn't keep time and I was being unfair to other patients. That was it. That was the support I was offered: *Don't work in a job that doesn't fit with my personal ideals, and if you fuck up once, you're out!*

I could have gotten really upset, but I could see it was probably for the best. This woman was way out of her depth and had no clue how to help someone like me. There was no support for women like me.

Instead, I began to write again. Of all the medication I have ever tried, whether prescribed or illicit, writing has always been the most therapeutic. I can pour my thoughts onto the page or even escape into a different world, and while my fingers are tapping away, I feel at ease. I wrote poetry, fiction, journals, whatever came to mind at the time. The only thing that tore me from this bubble of safety was J walking into the room, doing his best to sabotage my efforts and distract me.

So, as I sit here writing quietly on my Mac in the current day and reflecting, my kitties sleeping sweetly by my side, I feel so blessed. To have time to myself to make sense of the past, to put my thoughts into order, it feels like a luxury, a gift that cannot be interrupted or taken from me. As I write, the date is Wednesday, 15 April 2020, so while most of the public are struggling with self-isolation, I am an anomaly. Spending time alone can be extremely therapeutic and gives me the opportunity to rejuvenate and recharge my batteries. It is far worse to be with someone that makes you feel lonely or miserable than it is to spend time in your own company. So, as the rest of the world goes mad, I celebrate my freedom and my choice to exercise my own thoughts and wishes.

Chapter 34: Arrested

25 April 2009

My friend's wedding reception was set for 25 April and I was due to meet my other friend Lilly. J had been high for two days and had managed to deprive me of sleep. It had been chaos trying to get him to stop bumbling around the house and running out into the garden. As the morning came, I didn't feel at my best psychologically and I had a feeling of dread. I told myself I was just being silly and couldn't let my friend down. If only I had listened to my intuition.

Arriving at the wedding reception and drinking a glass of wine, I started to relax a little. We ate, we drank and had a good catch-up, and soon it was evening and time to leave. Anxiety reared its ugly head once more and I dreaded the train journey home. Lilly asked me to stay at hers but said she wanted to go to a club first. Another group of friends said I could go to their party. The latter were lovely people, but I knew they would be taking drugs and partying all night and I really couldn't deal with that, especially after the last couple of days with J.

Reluctant to go home, not knowing what sort of chaos I would venture into, I agreed to go to the club with Lilly. We'd been friends for about five years. She was a pretty blonde, bubbly, sensitive and gentle, and I felt that her energy would be much more reassuring to me.

We headed to the club and Lilly got chatting to the people on the door. She introduced me and said I was a porn star, trying to wing free entry. Thinking little more of it, we went inside and ordered some drinks.

We chatted, drank wine and went for a dance.

At one point, I went to the bar and asked for a glass of tap water. I had been buying alcohol and it is law to serve tap water in a public house. The bartender refused and was quite abrupt. When I pointed out it was the law, he shrugged. I said, "What if I am diabetic?" He snapped, "Then you shouldn't be drinking, should you!"

I went back to the dance floor.

Shortly afterwards, a bouncer came up to me and said that someone had reported me taking my top off and said I would have to leave. This was hard to believe as I was wearing a dress so there was no way I could have taken my top off! We followed the bouncer and walked down the stairs. At this stage, we were quite conversational and everything was hunky dory.

When I went to collect my bag with my phone, keys and money, the mood changed instantly. The staff refused to look for it and said I would have to collect it on Monday. It was Saturday and I was miles from home and had no way of getting back without my belongings. I explained all this, and the doorman stood there with a smirk on his face and told me that it was my problem. I said it wasn't really, that I was a customer and had spent money in his bar and that my safety was being compromised. I felt like I was talking to a brick wall and became quite upset.

Reaching out, I grasped the rope for support (I was wearing massive heels) and managed to trip. I admit I had been drinking, but this is not a crime and it had not been my intention to break the rope. They started shouting at me and telling me to get away from the door. I tried to reason that I only wanted my bag and would be on my way. This went on for some time and eventually realising that I would not go without my property, someone went in and fetched my bag. That's when the doorman sneered and made a comment to me. I can't remember exactly what he said, but I do remember the flash of humiliation lash through me. It was something along the lines of, "Now fuck off, you dirty whore."

At this point, I slapped him across the face in indignation and stalked off with Lilly. I heard a group of men laughing, then I felt two men grab me, knocking me almost to the floor, on my knees. Their fingers dug into my arms, leaving a sensation of stinging as they dragged me backwards. I couldn't see who had grabbed me, but I could hear laughing and jeering. It was a huge trigger, and I was transported back to that time on the school field when the school bully had grabbed me from behind and beat me up. I panicked and flailed and asked them to let me go, but they kept dragging me along the floor, round the corner towards an alleyway. I was on my knees, crying, with my hands being pulled behind my back. I could see the darkness looming ahead and was filled with terror. In a last-ditch attempt to defend myself, I struggled my arm forward and sank my teeth into the nearest hand. The hands grabbed me harder, and I heard someone yell at me to pull my dress down and to have some dignity.

One of the men shouted that I'd bitten him and to put the CCTV on. I realised then it must be doormen who had grabbed me, but I was still confused as I thought doormen were supposed to be professional bodies and not drag young women into alleyways. I was scared and just wanted to go home and couldn't understand why this had happened.

A police car pulled up and a female police officer stepped out, cuffed me and read me my rights. I was searched and made to sit handcuffed on a bench next to a drunk man that was getting lairy and trying to get into a fight with one of the overhead lockers; I tried to sidle away from him. It was chaotic, noisy and I felt claustrophobic, as if all my thoughts were crashing down on me. After a while, I was escorted to a cell and I lay there dehydrated and shell-shocked. What the hell had just happened? The police allowed me to try and phone my parents a couple of times but there was no answer. I went back to my cell and lay on the hard cot, singing gently to myself to drown out the noise of the resident nutters hollering and hurling obscenities.

Eventually, I managed to get some sleep and awoke with my mouth stuck together. I called the guard and asked for a drink, and she told me to step away from the door before delivering the drink. I explained that I was really dehydrated, and I requested another, apologising for being a pain. She must have realised by this point that I wasn't a complete nutter, as her tone changed and she came closer to the door and spoke softly.

Thankful for the water, which alleviated some of the pain in my burning throat, I thanked her. She reappeared about an hour later, offering me a choice of microwave meals. I gratefully accepted the offer; I can't remember what it was now, but I only managed a few mouthfuls as my stomach was swirling like a whirlpool.

No sooner had I started to eat, than they called me anyway and took me through to another room and told me that charges had been made against me. Common assault for slapping the doorman, ABH for biting the doorman that had tried to drag me into the alleyway, and criminal damages for tripping over and breaking the rope.

Offering to pay for the rope, I was issued with a withering look. Then they told me I was free to leave and would hear from them in due course.

I was given back my property and instantly put my long pink summer dress on that was in my bag and felt less exposed. I practically ran out of there, so pleased to feel the fresh air on my skin. I had been in there less than twelve hours but I emerged into the silence squinting, feeling like someone who had been underground in a cave for months. Clearly, I wasn't cut out for the criminal underworld.

My mobile phone was now dead, so I scoured the streets for a phone box, running this way and that, freezing and not knowing what to do. Eventually, I found a pay phone and called home. My dad answered and all my words jumbled out at once, scared of what he might say. My dad was so kind and supportive, and I was shocked at how caring he was. He said to me, "Don't worry, we all make mistakes in life. Once, when I worked on the buses, I tried to drive a bus home drunk! It's going to be OK, just get yourself home and get some sleep."

As bad as it all felt, I laughed my head off at my dad's words and I felt a little bit of normality return to me. Next, I called J and he roared with laughter. Apparently, he found it hilarious that I had been arrested for (in his words) "beating up a doorman". Perhaps he was just trying to use humour to calm me down, but I felt like he was being unsupportive.

The case itself and the process of going back and forth to Kingston Court was a lot more convoluted. This should have been a simple case for the magistrates, but a week later a lawyer phoned me and said they had added a racial charge. The first bouncer who I'd chatted with on the way down the stairs was apparently saying that I had called him "a black bastard", which was a complete fabrication. Either that or he'd confused me with another person ejected from the club. This would make sense, as on the charge sheet the bouncer described me as having a "strong Eastern European accent". I grew up in Swindon and have a West Country accent. You can't get less Eastern European than that! They said I could admit all the charges at the magistrates' court and probably get a caution, or I could go to Crown Court. I was still feeling appalled at the way I had been mistreated, but now they had thrown in a racism charge, which was untrue, so there was no way I was agreeing to that. I told them I would go to Crown Court and allow a jury to decide my fate.

Chapter 35: It's Her Party but I'll Cry if I Want To

Early May 2009 – Mum's 60th Birthday

For my mum's sixtieth birthday, my sisters had arranged a surprise party. Arriving back in Swindon, only my dad was home. It was a lovely summer's day, and he had the back door open and some Sixties music blaring out. It had been a tough two and a half weeks since the incident, but it was nice being home and seeing my dad in good spirits. "I like your T-shirt," he said, pointing at my black T-shirt with a brightly coloured rainbow skull on the front.

"Thank you, I like yours too."

He hadn't changed yet and was wearing a light blue T-shirt with a palm tree on it. Dad always wore pastel T-shirts with iconic prints or designs. He was a large chap and favoured baggy, comfortable tops. In his youth, he'd been extremely handsome, but he still had the charm when he wished to switch it on.

Dad was drinking a Bloody Mary and it was one of the few times he made me a drink, rather than telling me to make it himself.

"Kora, isn't that the best Bloody Mary you've ever had?"

I had to agree, he didn't do things by halves and in the drink was a large shot of vodka over ice, a serving of Big Tom tomato juice, some celery salt and lashings of Tabasco and Worcester sauce, finished off with a stalk of celery in the top. To this day, no one has ever made me a Bloody Mary that good, although some have tried. Mum always said it was more like a meal than a drink, it had so many ingredients in it. We had a lovely catch-up and it was the best chat we'd had in a long time. He'd really helped me when he'd been so supportive on the phone after my arrest, and he was the dad I remembered as a little kid that used to buy me Mivvi ice lollies and take me to the arcades. He may have been many things, but he was always great in a crisis and knew exactly what to say to appease your worries. It's just a shame I could never confide in him about other aspects of my life due to the nature of my work.

Everyone converged and we headed off. My sisters had arranged a surprise party for my mum and booked a venue called the Cheely Club, and all Mum's friends were there waiting. My dad and I strolled down to the pub to help set up, or to be precise, all the helpers set up while Dad delegated and told everyone what to do while he drank his pint. He was such a character, always an armchair chef or decorator. He would tell you how to do something perfectly, without ever doing it himself, and I had to laugh at his audacity.

Later, I met the girls outside as Mum thought they were meeting us to go somewhere else. Clarissa sneakily said, "Let's pop into the Cheely Club quickly first."

Mum retorted, "I don't want to go into that shithole!" My poor sister was mortified. Somehow, we convinced Mum to go to the pub, despite her protests, and as we headed in everyone jumped out, shouting, "Surprise!"

It was a great evening, chatting to neighbours and people I hadn't seen for years. We posed for photos, giggled, drank wine and it felt a million miles away from the chaos at home in that moment. I never stayed in Swindon for too long though, as Mum and Dad would end up at each other's throats.

The evening was going well, and Dad got up on the stage to do some karaoke. First, he did a rendition of Elvis Presley's "Return to Sender", then he sang "The Night Has a Thousand Eyes" by Bobby Vee. Tipsy and in high spirits, I was his biggest cheerleader at the edge of the stage. He was loving the limelight and wore a big beam on his face.

The music came to an end and Dad walked down off the stage and headed towards me grinning. Then he just fell to the floor. Screaming, I ran towards him in what I can only imagine was open-mouthed horror. The music died and a crowd formed around him. My aunty started doing chest compressions and I heard her say, "He's gone."

"No, he is not! He is my dad, he wouldn't give up like that, keep trying," I snapped, then I screamed for someone to call an ambulance, as everyone was frozen in panic. "Call an ambulance!" I screamed at the top of my lungs. "Who has a phone?"

My cousin Cherise thrust her mobile at me (I'd left mine at Mum and Dad's charging) and I took the phone, but it was a different model to mine, and I didn't know how to get to the keypad. "Please call 999," I pleaded, thrusting it back at her.

Cherise was quick to dial 999 and the ambulance took about thirteen minutes to get there, and all that time Dad wasn't breathing. When the paramedics came in, they cleared a circle. Wanting to cuddle him, I was told to step back by the paramedics. Heartbreaking. They placed the defibrillators on his chest and my lovely neighbour Wanda hugged me and told me not to look.

We were all in a state of shock as Dad was taken away in the ambulance and had no idea what to expect. Sending a prayer up to the universe, I visualised Dad getting better.

The next couple of days we were all on tenterhooks. He was put into an induced coma and had ice packed around him in ICU. We made various trips to the hospital and talked to Dad while he was wired up to the machinery, making jokes to try and ease some of the grief we were feeling. We were saying things like, "Well, you certainly managed to steal the limelight at the party!" "Trust you to become the focus at Mum's party." This would have cracked him up and he would have agreed too if he had been conscious.

Soon I had to head home to Birmingham as I had to meet with my solicitor in Kingston. I went back to Birmingham for the day, got changed, packed a case and headed into London. Just before I arrived, my sister called to say that they were going to try and wake Dad up. I desperately wanted to be there but had to be in court. When I met with the lawyer, my eyes were red, my cheeks streaked and my eyes were watery. He probably assumed it was self-pity, but my only thoughts were of my dad. I had no intention of disclosing these recent events to a stranger.

The solicitor didn't have anything useful to tell me and the meeting didn't last long. I headed straight back to Swindon. It's all a blur from this point. I remember arguing with my mother in hospital as she felt I should be holding it together better and I felt she was being cold and aloof. I couldn't stop crying and she snapped, "Are you on drugs or something?" Furious, I stormed out, waiting to be called in to see Dad. God knows how she thought I'd have time to do something like that between attending Kingston Court, trying to keep a roof over my head and rushing back and forth between Birmingham and Swindon ICU. We were all stressed out, and our nerves were frayed.

Dad didn't wake up until I went home and came back to Swindon again. When I went into ICU with my Clarissa, he was sat up and in high spirits. My heart soared to see him with a cheeky grin on his face. He was playing around with the levers on the bed he was in, so that it rose up and down, making us laugh. He'd had a tracheotomy so couldn't talk but was mouthing words and doing impressions to get us guessing the names of films and songs. Typical of Dad to be the life and soul of the party while in intensive care.

Eventually, Dad was moved to a ward. When I arrived, some relatives whom we never saw or particularly got on with were there. We later joked that perhaps they hoped they might be in the will. Dark humour was an escape from the stark reality.

Dad had been a bit of a miserable git at times, but while in hospital he was jolly and lapped up the attention from the doctors and nurses. He was quite the celebrity in there and had them all laughing. How many people come back from death and have everyone in stitches? For all his flaws, he was a special person. Dad had his tracheotomy removed and was full of wisecracks, saying that the hospital was the best hotel he'd stayed in, three square meals a day and the red wine was free!

Eventually, Dad could go home and I stayed in Swindon awhile while Mum was at work, helping him clear out his wardrobe. He was meant to be resting so he sat on the bed, and I helped him decide which clothes to keep and which to throw away. He asked me if I wanted any T-shirts and I took a selection to keep. I still have them now and they are a wonderful memory of my dad and the times we spent together.

Eventually, I had to go home to Birmingham to get back to the cats and work. I was sad to leave, never knowing if it would be the last time I'd see him.

Chapter 36: On Trial – Men in Different Wigs

10 July 2010

The events in this chapter all happened over a decade ago, so I will try to depict as accurate a picture as I can, though it may not be word perfect.

The court case ended up costing me an absolute fortune. The judicial system seems to be quite obfuscated, and they call you down for various things before the trial that I believe could have easily been discussed on the phone. Given that I lived in Birmingham, and the court case was held in Kingston, it was a trek each time. The train fares were expensive and a couple of times I had to get hotels and stay overnight in London, so missed out on a lot of work.

A legal agency called me various times and the man called Vince I spoke to just did not seem to be on my side, initially. He had a gruff voice and made me feel like trash. During our first conversation, I felt like I was under interrogation. He was abrupt and insinuated that he thought I was guilty. It seemed anyone charged with a racism offence was automatically guilty in his eyes and this felt deeply unfair. He hadn't even listened to my side of things. In time, he seemed to warm to me and in our later conversations he was extremely helpful.

The court had said I could be called upon at any time within eight weeks, and I worried that I might book in work and then have to let someone down if I was called to court. It was a struggle to make ends meet lost in limbo. A director I'd worked with then offered me a role in a zombie film which would be shot in Grand Cayman, which I didn't want to miss out on. I explained my predicament to Vince and he was able to help me block out some dates that I would be working and I was able to take part in the film. It's called *Zombie Driftwood* if you care to watch it.

I was so grateful for this act of kindness on Vince's part and the fact he was prepared to extend an olive branch to me, after his initial distrust of me.

Grand Cayman was a fantastic opportunity. They were long hard days on set and filming in the heat was tough; one of the cameramen fainted one day as he hadn't drunk enough water. I played Marianne, who is turned by a zombie and becomes *Vampella*, a saucy zombie who is always after the boys. There's a scene in the movie where you see Vampella reach down towards a man's trousers and then holds a phallic item in her hand, which is presumably a zombie penis which has rotted away.

On my day off, I headed to the beach with the make-up artist Lucy and a lady called Tansy. We swam in the blissfully warm water, drank iced cocktails and a local boatman took us out to Star City, where we gently held beautiful pink star fishes. Lucy held a manta ray and then suggested I take it. It looked peaceful, but I was taking no risks. Later, I snorkelled in the dazzling blue waters, which were perfectly clear. A blue lobster rested on the sands, as content as the ocean bed itself, its antennae floating gracefully. This really was paradise.

The cast were all lovely except for one bolshie American guy, Chad, who thought he was the bee's knees. He introduced himself by saying, "Hey, are you ready for our big love scene?"

I shrugged and responded, "I guess so, are you?"

"Of course, I'm a professional," he bragged.

During filming, he would sit there laughing at my dancing and muttering, "You are not going to be in this film."

Another time, he tried to pull a bit of dry skin off my lip without my consent. The guy seemed like he was on an ego trip, and I was thankful when our 'love scene' was pulled. The director called me to his villa and gave me words of encouragement, which surprised me as I'd not said anything, but mutterings from the crew had returned to him.

"The thing is, Kaz, you can act," he told me gently. "Chad just does that whole confused thing, which is a bit limited."

Certain he was being overgenerous with me, his kindness lifted me, nonetheless. Another actor, Morris, was also sweet to me, as he'd seen a little of what had happened. He came and found me, bringing me some delicious Jamaican brownies with a wink. Naïvely, I ate one that night and about forty-five minutes later, I realised they were hash cakes, as I started to feel stoned. I donated the rest of the brownies to someone who would be a bit more appreciative of them.

The only downside to Cayman is the massive mosquitos that love to gorge themselves on tasty human blood. A bite the size of a tennis ball rose from my arm, which burned, and I had nothing to soothe it. In desperation, I popped a banana skin in the freezer and later applied the frozen skin to my arm. The next day, the bite had gone right down. I learned that the combination of coldness and the fruit acids are just the tonic for bites – a useful tip for you!

That week, we ate Mahi Mahi, a dolphin fish (not actually dolphin like someone said to wind up the girls), and we ended with a wrap party and drinks, and an evening listening to October File, who feature in the movie.

Travelling home was a bump back down to earth, although I was thankful for the little release on my pressure valve. A new barrister was assigned to me. She was a young woman and didn't seem to have read my file, as she was asking me basic questions. Skimming through my file, she said I would have to plead criminal damage for breaking the rope even though it was an accident. The way she said it sounded like I didn't have a choice.

Collecting various character references from friends and family, my mum then wrote a letter for my defence, saying that the incident had triggered me, as I had been attacked from behind as a teenager. It seemed there were a lot of people that were supportive and happy to talk of my good character. My dad cheered me up in his own way, by mimicking various scenes in the court room from dramas and films from over the years, and he would recite long monologues in which the accusers were all found guilty of wasting court time. It was a difficult time, but he managed to have me in stitches. He always found the funny side in things, and it was his way of helping me through it.

Before my trial date was due, I was assigned yet another barrister. I knew instantly that this man was good at his job. He was methodical, organised and he had bothered to read through all the statements and had watched the CCTV from the night, which the previous lawyers hadn't seemed to have done. He spoke calmly and with confidence.

"Can I just say, I watched that CCTV and I was absolutely appalled at the way you were manhandled," he admitted. He also informed me that the bouncers shouldn't have dragged me off towards the alleyway (and off camera) as that gave me cause for panic.

He asked me how I wished to plead. I said I would plead guilty to the slap and breaking the rope, but not guilty to ABH and racism. He said that I'd have to plead guilty now to the criminal damage (rope) as I had already admitted it, but that I should have contested this earlier as it was an accident and not intentional.

On the day of court, I wore a white shirt with a black satin blazer, black trousers and tied my hair up neatly into a ponytail. I felt like my clothes were a little too big and hung off me, but they were smart at least. I seemed to wait around for hours watching intently while others went into court or waited to be called. There were people in suits, scruffy young men in ripped clothing and guys with black eyes that looked like they'd had a punch-up. I'm sure that wouldn't have boded well for them.

Eventually, my time before the jury came. I entered the room and was seated. I glanced at the jury and scanned their faces, nervous of what I would see. I'm not sure if I took anything in with regards to their expressions, just how ordinary they looked, and wondered what sort of people they were. When my job status was revealed, I wondered if some of them would pre-judge me. I noticed one kindly looking lady with white hair smiling. My barrister nudged me and said, "She is definitely on your side." I smiled back at my barrister, grateful for the encouragement.

First up on the stand was the black bouncer, who I will refer to as 'Bouncer 1'. He was the man who had led me out of the club, and I'd had a normal chat with him walking down the stairs. He was the one who had later claimed I had racially assaulted him and that I had a strong Eastern European accent. He was then cross-examined by my lawyer, who let the man dig a big hole for himself.

Firstly, he asked Bouncer 1 to point to the accused. He pointed at me.

Then the barrister glanced casually at Bouncer 1's statement and asked, "When you ejected the defendant from the club, is it possible that it was a case of mistaken identity?"

"No."

"Are you sure?"

"Yes."

He continued, "In your statement, you mention that the accused is of Eastern European descent. Is that correct?"

"Yes."

"How did you know this?"

"Because we were talking on the stairs and she had an Eastern European accent."

"And the person you spoke to was definitely Eastern European?"

"Yes."

"It strikes me as if you may not be remembering the night clearly at all, as my client is British with a local accent. Yet you seem to remember speaking to an Eastern European woman."

My barrister then asked the man how many times I had racially abused him. I could see the lawyer was trying to make him slip up here as he fired questions at him. During questioning, Bouncer 1 changed his story from saying I had used one racial insult, to that I had racially abused him all the way from inside the club to the bottom of the stairs. In front of the whole jury, he changed his story on the stand. He clearly didn't like the lawyer's line of questioning. He had a face like thunder and was practically shaking with anger and raising his voice. My lawyer asked, "Well, was it once, twice or the whole time?"

Bouncer 1 was getting wound up and had angrily snapped without thinking, "The whole time!" He seemed to have a bit of a temper and did not enjoy being questioned.

Then the barrister pointed out Bouncer 1's contradictory statements and said, "I would like to show some evidence to the jury."

The CCTV footage on the screen showed me leaving the club and waving goodbye to Bouncer 1. The man blew me a kiss and waved. The screen paused and my lawyer continued, "Well, it all seems very friendly here. You are chatting, then you blow her a kiss and wave goodbye to her. So, one of two things is happening here. Either it is all very amicable at this point, or you are blowing her a kiss to provoke her, which is it?"

Bouncer 1 was stuck for what to say and stuttered a few words and said he didn't remember.

"I have no further questions, Your Honour."

Next, Bouncer 2, the white bouncer who I had slapped, took the stand. He was a smarmy-looking guy in his forties with slicked-back hair. He looked sure of himself and smug to start with, although his demeanour changed as the questions went on. He kept referring to me as 'The Porn Star', which felt strange, because for several years now I'd pretty much only done webcam modelling and private domination sessions. It seemed his aim was to use the phrase in a derogatory fashion, to attempt to taint the jury's opinion of me.

He and his prosecution were calling it a punch rather than a slap, I noted. My lawyer fast-forwarded the CCTV footage and paused it, then asked him what he had said when he'd leaned into me and suggested that he had provoked me. Bouncer 2 flat-out denied saying anything, but the atmosphere in the room changed and it was obvious he was doing an unconvincing job of denying it. He didn't even look like he believed himself – his face was ashen.

I never put in my statement what he had said to me that night just before I slapped him. I never mentioned it in court either, because I couldn't clearly remember the words he'd used. I hadn't wanted to look an idiot on the stand by not being sure of what I'd heard, so I'd left that part out and not even mentioned it to my lawyer. My lawyer, however, was astute at reading body language, eye contact and facial expressions, and knew exactly how to get to the truth of the matter.

I could see the prosecution wasn't doing too well, but I didn't feel much relief. It was just a horrible situation that never should have happened. I wished I had just stayed home that night.

Next up was Bouncer 3. He was only a young lad, probably in his mid-twenties, clean-looking and not brusque like the other two. In a way, I felt sorry for him having to get up there. It was just an unfortunate incident that went wrong and was handled badly by the club. As he was cross-examined, it started to look as if he had been bullied by his peers into going to court. He didn't sound sure of what he was saying at all and looked as if he wanted the floor to swallow him up. The defense asked, "And is it true she asked you to let go and said you were hurting her?"

"Yes, she did."

"And did you?"

"No."

"Why not?"

"We are trained to use reasonable force to restrain people."

"I might ask, is reasonable force to pull someone's arms behind their back so that they fall to their knees, and then dragging them along on the floor?"

"No," he said, hanging his head.

"Why did you pull her away from the CCTV cameras? You go off shot for a moment here." He showed the relevant footage.

"Normally, we have more cameras."

"By an alleyway?"

"I think so."

"You think so?"

"I'm not sure."

"And was she crying?"

"Yes."

"Did she appear to be in pain?"

"Yes, I think so."

"Did she ask you multiple times to stop hurting her before she defended herself?"

"Yes."

The young lad hung his head. He had shame etched across his face.

"I have no further questions, Your Honour."

Soon, it was my turn to take the stand. Wobbly legs like jelly carried me, my head held high, hoping that justice would prevail. I glanced up at the judge and he smiled at me. He had twinkly eyes and a kind, paternal smile.

"Miss, may I ask you to just stand next to the witness box, please, to make sure you can see over," the judge requested.

The box was high up and came almost to my shoulders, but I could see over.

"And how tall are you?" he asked me.

"I'm four foot ten, Your Honour."

"You may take your seat," he nodded.

I then took the Holy Bible and swore an oath, "I swear to tell the truth, the whole truth and nothing but the truth."

Cross-examination by the prosecution began. He was a tall, skinny man that reminded me a little of the evil vizier Jafar in the Disney film *Aladdin*. He kept using the phrases "Is it that …?" and "I would suggest that …"

It was like being in a courtroom drama. It all seemed so surreal.

I was stood in the box, a sea of faces assessing me, analysing my character and deciding if I was good or evil. Unlike a courtroom drama though, the lawyers didn't argue with each other or shout "Objection!" every three seconds. I was quite disappointed about that; I think I would have liked to have heard someone yell objection when the bouncers were making it up as they went along.

There seemed to be an obvious bone of contention between the prosecution and the defence. The prosecution kept using the word "punch" and the defence used the word "slap". The judge seemed exasperated and at one point he looked at his watch and said something along the lines of, "Can we move on to what happened after this slap?" and waved his hand dismissively.

In one small statement, he had set the precedent and confirmed that it was a slap and not a punch.

The prosecuting lawyer asked me question after question, and I answered as calmly as possible for someone who has a phobia of public speaking. Welcome meetings with guests on holiday were one thing, but it's a whole different atmosphere when your life is on the line and you have the gaze of so many people in the room on you.

The prosecution turned to me, his cloak swishing behind him like a vampire, his steely gaze burning into my eyes, and shouted, "I suggest that you were not scared or in pain at all. I suggest that you had a fit of histrionics. I suggest that that is the truth. Is that correct?"

This felt like an intimidation tactic, the dramatic way he flung his cape like he was Nosferatu and eyeballed me while raising his voice. He had half-turned towards me at an angle, and visions of Golem from *The Lord of the Rings* sprung to mind as he leaned towards me with a sneer. My eyes were like saucers. Up until now, it had all been run-of-the-mill stuff and he was obviously saving his finest showmanship for the last moment.

"No," I responded, feeling shocked. I knew it was his job to paint me in the worst light possible, but I couldn't help taking it a little personally. My eyes were welling up but I refused to cry and give him the satisfaction, so I pushed the tears back, resolute.

"No further questions, Your Honour," he huffed, and turned away.

It was time for the jury to go away and deliberate. It didn't take long until a decision was reached, and the verdict was delivered.

We were all called back in front of the judge and jury, and a statement was read out.

"For the charge of racial assault, we deliver a verdict of NOT GUILTY.

"For the charge of criminal damage, we deliver a verdict of GUILTY."

"For the charge of common assault, we deliver a verdict of GUILTY.

There was a hung jury for the charge of ABH, which means that the jury could not reach a unanimous decision. If one person in the group was swayed either way, they could not deliver a verdict.

Then the judge spoke and said something like, "The prosecution has stated that they believe there is a probable cause for retrial, and I must strongly advise that they do not pursue this course of action. Enough court time has already been wasted on this matter and it is not in the court's interest to return to it."

Gratitude filled me – for my barrister for doing such a thorough job, the jury for making a professional informed decision, and for the kindly judge who clearly thought that this whole saga was a waste of court time and taxpayers' money.

The nightmare was over finally, with me being thousands of pounds worse off due to all the lost work and expenses. I didn't visit a nightclub socially for years after that, and I'm still not enamoured with them.

The weirdest thing though is when you are having those 'get to know you chats' with people and the question comes up, "Have you got a criminal record?" I answer honestly and say yes. Of course, they look at me in disbelief and ask what for, and I say, "For slapping a bouncer," and they always laugh and think I'm joking.

Chapter 37: Kaz the Thespian

Stuck in a rut, I decided attending some drama classes may do me some good and I found a group locally at the Custard Factory in Brum. Initially, I was quiet and stuck to the corners of the room, but I was soon interacting with the group, doing improv and having a great time. I got chatting with one of the ladies one evening; she was a black girl with long dreadlocks and glossy lips. She was so easy to talk to and I felt comfortable enough to tell her I was a dominatrix. "That's amazing!" she squealed. "Tell me more!!" It turns out that she was a colonoscopist and so, in a way, we both put things in men's bottoms for work. For her it was cameras, and for me it was strap-ons. OK, so the reason for doing so might have been different, but we felt like we had something in common. One was for medical reasons, and the other therapeutic. It would have been nice to have kept in touch with her; they were such a lovely group of people and I was sad to leave them all behind when I left Birmingham.

Our drama group were putting on a play, a modern-day version of *Romeo and Juliet*, and I was to play Lady Capulet, a cockney gangster. A young lad with metal frames attached to his legs was playing my husband and he was a brilliant laugh too. They were such an easy bunch of people to be around; we were there to play, have fun and just be in a state of flow. Our tutor was great too. She was an older lady in her fifties with a kindly face and a fascinating way of engaging us.

Committing to the project and after months of training and rehearsals, it was Showtiiiime!

I invited my parents down for the big night and gave J two simple jobs, "Can you buy the food on this shopping list with this money and fetch my parents from the train station at 7 p.m. please?" He agreed and I rushed off to my last rehearsal.

Finally, it was 8 p.m. and we were on stage waiting for the curtain to rise. As it rose, I felt my heart hammer in my chest and scoured the audience for familiar faces. Neither my parents nor J were anywhere to be seen.

Why aren't they here? My stomach felt as if I had metal fingers gripping it tightly, but I made my dramatic entrances and delivered my lines. Every now and then, I scanned the crowd, hoping that they would appear. About thirty minutes into the performance, my parents arrived and sat down looking disgruntled. *What had happened?*

As we reached the end, I had a fight scene with my 'husband', and perhaps this is a little prejudiced of me, but I didn't want to roll him around too hard because of his metal leg braces, uncertain if it would cause him pain. One of the final scenes ended in a brawl and none of the punches thrown looked too convincing. When we all went off stage, the audience cried, "Encore, encore," which was instigated by my dad, and we all went out and did another bow, smiling and cheering. Pushing myself to do this had been a good thing; seeing how uncomfortable I was with crowds, one of my biggest fears had been faced and I embraced it.

I greeted my parents with hugs, "What did you think?"

"Well, the fighting scenes were a bit crap," they agreed and I laughed, asking why they were late. It turned out that J was late to pick them up. They had been shivering on the platform in the rain for ages. *My poor parents!* To add further insult to injury, he hadn't gotten any of the shopping either, saying that he had run out of time. To put it into perspective, he had no job, no responsibilities as a kept man and nothing else to do that day. Suspecting he wanted my parents to feel as unwelcome as possible, I threw him a look of disgust. This suspicion was confirmed when we sent him off for takeaway and he brought back some ropey dried-up potato scallops, and some dry-looking fritters from the chip shop, not even any chips. "Everywhere was closed," was his excuse.

Birmingham is a thriving city, and you can get food there pretty much all night long, so there was no way everywhere was closed. He continued being rude and obnoxious through the visit and my parents decided to go home early. On any occasion someone was there to support me, he did everything he could to drive them away. It was yet another nail in the coffin of our 'relationship'.

Chapter 38: False Friends

Diamond often disappeared in and out of my life and popped up when she needed money, as I would do webcam with her and split our earnings or organise double domme sessions. It did cross my mind that our relationship was a little one-sided, but I reasoned that she was my friend and just a bit disorganised and chaotic. Plus, I always felt a bit sorry for her. She usually broke or ripped my things when she visited, and I just accepted the fact she was a bit careless. At the time, I believed she really cared for me, but I know now this was not the case at all and I was simply a tool to be used.

One night she came over and I was telling her how much I hated where I lived, and she and her husband suggested a house share in Wales with them. We thought it could work well as we could shoot content together and share travel costs. When they went home, she said she would call me in the week to discuss this further. I didn't hear from her again from months. In hindsight, this was a blessing in disguise. When I heard from her next, she said she'd left her husband and now he was living in a mental institution as he couldn't cope, poor fella.

Heading down to Wales, I met Diamond for a bondage shoot together with a local photographer we knew well. It was easy stuff; basically, the photographer used a rope technique called Shibari and tied some pretty, intricate knots and harnesses round us as we posed for photos. We had a great shoot and a real laugh, but as soon as the photographer left, her new boyfriend turned up and stayed over in the room of our little B&B, which felt a bit overcrowded. The next day, I was mortified as he said, "Diamond and I will head down for breakfast first, then you go down and they won't know I'm not meant to be here." I still had sleep in my eyes and was desperate for a coffee, but he'd swept all the tea and coffee into his rucksack, along with the soap and everything else that wasn't bolted down. He hadn't even asked if I'd wanted a drink before he snaffled all the beverages. I was just glad that the room wasn't in my name. I tried not to judge but I couldn't help wondering if she had made the best choice with this new fella. I didn't really click with him but thought if Diamond likes him, then that's all that matters.

A few weeks later, she invited me and J to join them for a social in Wales. She was moving to Spain soon and that would be the last chance we would get to see each other for a while. As we sat in her lounge that evening, J opened his big, fat gob to release a stream of verbal diarrhoea. He bragged loudly that I made lots of money just doing webcam and how easy it was. Webcam is not easy; you must engage your viewers, keep the energy high and talk for extended periods of time. It involves lots of late nights and you must be ready at the drop of a hat to cam with someone. Yes, it can be great fun, but I didn't like the way he made it sound like money for old rope.

Diamond's boyfriend's name evades me, but the photographer coined him 'the Slug', so that will suffice to keep things simple. The Slug's ears pricked up and I could tell the thought of easy cash was appealing. He kept whispering in Diamond's ear and laughing. He struck me as a bit snidey and untrustworthy. They then organised a deal with J, who would teach them how to do all the tech. It was agreed that he would run Diamond's profile for her and take 5% for uploading videos and helping her with tech support. All this work chat was dull and I tried to steer the conversation away, but they weren't having it, so we ended up talking shop for most of the weekend, with J monopolising the conversation and talking of his expertise.

A week later, Diamond and the Slug turned up at my house at the last minute to webcam and brought a massive wicker basket, claiming their bedding was inside. I thought it was a little strange as she had never brought bedding before in the six years I had known her, or even a packet of crisps for that matter.

"Please don't arrive before 4 p.m. as I have some eBay parcels to sort," I told them. I was selling fetish wear and poppers on eBay at the time. They turned up at 2 p.m. and she kept interrupting me, asking me to get her various things, and wouldn't let me sit down for a moment to sort the parcels. I made them some food and then started sorting the webcam room out. Later, she wanted more food, and I said I would make dinner in a moment, I just had to put the washing on, and was gobsmacked when she came into the kitchen and snapped, "Where's my dinner?"

Seemingly, she had changed overnight. She'd gone from someone who was a bit chaotic and scatty but generally fun, to someone who was mean and self-centred. She spent the whole evening demanding, "I need some false eyelashes, I haven't got any stockings, give me a pair, get me a dress, I want some crisps, pour me more alcohol."

She even helped herself to my belongings, opening drawers without asking. Aghast, I wondered where my friend had gone. Who was this person she had become? She behaved dreadfully and I couldn't wait for them to leave. My house was trashed by the end of it. Diamond had peed in various glasses on webcam and then just went home and left the stinking mess on the side for me to clean up. I had the shock of my life when I tidied up. I didn't have much in the way of worldly possessions at that time, or furniture. We didn't even have a TV. What I did own though they had taken. They'd taken my SLR Canon camera, several dresses, my Logitech webcam, my make-up and various other bits and pieces. It mounted up to several hundred pounds' worth of goods. The biggest sting though was that she was supposed to be my friend. She was one of the few people I had allowed into my life and in the past, I had counselled her, given her money, fed her, even paid for her and her ex-husband's flights to Turkey, and she repaid me by treating me like a skivvy and stealing from me. My heart shattered into pieces.

They didn't pay J for the work he did for them either, and of course it became all about that and how J had been wronged. He said he was glad she'd shown her true colours and was out of our lives. Of course he was, he had me all to himself again.

Chapter 39: The Doctor, the Lawyer and the Shoe Collection

Over the past several years, I have not only become aware of my strengths, but I have also become aware of my weaknesses and how to manage them. After doing some extensive reading and inner work, I realised one of my weaknesses was the fear of rejection. Through much of my life, I have pushed people away before they had chance to reject me, which of course is counterproductive. My sister once said to me, "You don't let people in," and other people have said that I "built up walls or barriers".

At the time, I reasoned that I was protecting myself and preferred to get to know people slowly, but I wasn't aware of how I pushed people away in carrying this protective layer about me. It was an old survival habit that had been necessary when I was a child, but no longer served me and was in fact now detrimental to any chance of having healthy relationships. It's something I've been working on. If I don't hear back from someone, I apply logic and don't take it personally. I've allowed that aloof exterior to melt away a little and replaced it with the genuine interest that was always underneath.

If I went for an interview and didn't get the role, I would always reason that either the job wasn't right for me, or I wasn't right for it. Now, I apply this reasoning to all kinds of relationships in life, instead of believing I'm not good enough and going on the defence by shutting down. For someone who was bullied severely at school every day and has been in abusive relationships, it's not an easy feat, but it's such a rewarding process and now I find I am able to open up more without triggering feelings of shame and abandonment. I will never be the most confident person in a large group, but some of that is my personality. That is who I am. Observing others interests me, watching what makes people tick and learning more about them. My gut instinct I rely on heavily too; it always knows what's best and most of the time now I can tell if it's my gut instinct or an irrational worry.

Being a dominatrix has been so good for my confidence. In a way, it is like speed dating without the romantic connotations. You usually have five to ten minutes at the start of the meeting to find out as much as possible about the other person, so I've learned to read body language and visual cues a great deal. Sometimes during or after the session, the slave might ask you some questions. In the beginning, I would close right down and be as vague as possible, convinced I had to maintain the fantasy, but this is not the case. While I am careful about divulging information which is too personal to strangers, with my regulars I now chat away freely and we have built a much better rapport. Being more expressive and open has allowed me to build better working relationships, and it has had a knock-on effect on the rest of my life. I will quite happily invite a friend for a drink or to stay for some tea. If they say yes, it's a bonus, and if they say no, I understand that they are tired or just not in the mood that day. Rarely do I suffer from irrational thoughts or think, *They must not like me.* If someone doesn't like me, I think, *So what? That's me, you can't please everyone.*

It's clear now how this fear dynamic has been a toxic pattern throughout my life, and by no longer falling into its trap, I'm happier, like a ton of bricks have been lifted from my shoulders.

Being a dominatrix is still a taboo. Some people think it's great and can understand how empowering it can be to build a career out of dominating men. Others think it's a bit seedy and will say things like "What's a girl like you doing this for?" or "You are too pretty to do this" or even, "But you have a degree. Didn't you want to do something else?"

Fairly recently, I was at someone's house (we'll call him Ryan) with my slave and a couple of others. Everyone was drinking quite a bit and it was a chilled atmosphere. Then a female lawyer turned up, started talking to my sub and he told her he was my slave. First, she said to me, "What are you doing with your life? You are better than this! When you want to get out of it, come to me. You shouldn't be doing this work!" I'd known her less than twenty minutes and this tirade went on for some time.

Ryan then asked me to go upstairs to look at his shoe collection. He has a fetish for high heels and had some beautiful stilettos which he tried on. It was obvious he was proud of his collection and was enjoying being able to show them to someone.

Then he asked me to put him on a collar and leash and take him downstairs. I was feeling mischievous and listened to that little devil on my shoulder. I popped a leash on him and told him he was under strict instruction to take orders from me. Ryan followed me down the stairs then dropped to his hands and knees. When the lawyer saw him, her jaw dropped. "Get up, Ryan. Stop that!" she hollered, anger in her voice.

"I only answer to Mistress Kaz now," Ryan spoke almost hypnotically.

"Stop that, stop it now!" she shouted at him. When he failed to obey her order, she flounced out and demanded my sub LB walk her out. What I had missed is that in my absence, she had grilled my sub over his fetishes, which are cross-dressing and strap-on play, and had told him that he was perverted! Like a true gentleman, LB walked the lawyer out of the building as she had requested, but we both thought it was extremely rude to rain down judgement on people you had only just met.

Ryan seemed absolutely thrilled that someone had listened to him and not judged his fetish, so all in all I considered it a successful evening. Just to be clear, Ryan wasn't paying me for this. LB and I had bumped into him and one of his female friends in a bar and got chatting. We'd only nipped out for a bite to eat! We'd all got on well, so Ryan had extended his hospitality to us, and I was enjoying helping him express himself.

Luckily, I do not hear such negativity from my slaves; luckily for them I should say, they know better than to question their mistress's decisions! They understand why a woman would be drawn to such a career, and how it can be a mind-broadening experience.

I see my role as helping slaves on their journey, especially the newcomers. They are eager to understand their submissive sides and explore in a safe environment. When one of my slaves, Stephie, first came to me, she was so shy and struggled to verbalise what she was seeking. We experimented with applying some make-up and she dressed in her feminine clothes. Her shyness I could relate to; I've felt it myself in the past and I wanted to draw her out of her shell. We began to see each other regularly and one day we passed the make-up store Mac. She made a glib comment about always wanting to have a makeover and I dragged her in there.

The make-up artist who approached us was trans and knew exactly how to put Stephie at ease, and she was a real wizard with the make-up brush. As Stephie studied herself in the mirror, I could see how good she felt. She was comfortable with this and had faced one of her fears of being judged. As time went on, Stephie was able to make bold changes in her life, developed her feminine side and accepted that she was bisexual. She made some staggering transitions in her lifestyle and began blossoming into a much happier person.

Being part of that journey was rewarding for me. Sometimes my job is about kink, but other times I am able to act as an ear, to listen to people, to encourage them to accept themselves and to understand the feelings of shame that they might have and the root cause. In a way, I have been through a similar journey of self-acceptance and want to help others find their way. It's a wonderful feeling when my little fledglings find their wings.

Some mistresses hold their slaves on a tight leash, metaphorically, and they sometimes hold them tight in case their fledglings fly the nest. The thing is, if you hold a butterfly too tightly, you will crush it, so you must let it fly. One day that butterfly may come back to you, and if not, there will be more butterflies. If you give out good energy, to the right people, then ultimately good energy will follow you.

Various slaves have visited me who have been brought up in deeply religious families. They are eager to explore kink but suffer from feelings of shame due to their upbringing. I try to help them see that exploring their sexuality or their desires in a consensual and safe environment has no impact on their worth as a person. Enjoying a spanking, for example, doesn't mean that they are a bad Muslim, Christian or Jew. For some, it helps to separate the two and see that in everyday life, they are a good person who practices good, ethical behaviour, and when they want to blow off a little steam and de-stress, they like to take a spanking and put on a frock and Ned turns into Nora.

I'm not going to disparage religion as the mother of all evils, as I think for many people religion is important. Everyone needs something to believe in, to give them help, to guide them to help them to be better, and if worshipping an unseen God helps them live a good life, then who am I to judge? However, I do think the way religion has been manipulated over the years by leaders as a method of control and coercion is deeply wrong, so I try to encourage them to see how these ideologies might have been corrupted to control the populace. Often the slaves have had their own doubts anyway, as they wouldn't have arrived on my doorstep otherwise. The problem is that if you tell someone, "If you sin, you are a bad person," they might start believing it and they will end up making more mistakes and following reckless paths. As much as people need to believe in something, they also need to be *believed in*. A person who has encouragement, guidance and support is far more likely to make better judgements than someone who is told they are bad all the time.

Our upbringing is far more important than we might expect. The conditions, environment and messages that are repeated to us in these early years have a massive impact on our development, and it can take a lot of positive reinforcement to reprogramme the mind into healthy patterns. After all, I should know.

Chapter 40: Enchanted by DMT

2011

When you work in the adult industry, people treat you differently. You become used to being called a slut and stalked and abused on social media. When someone suggests you have lowered yourself or says things like, "I bet your parents are so proud," for a while you might play up to other people's judgements of you, and for a while I did. Somewhere along the line, J and I had entered into an open relationship. It's difficult to pinpoint at which point this happened, but the first few times we experimented with three-somes was back in 2005 at the beginning of our relationship. It simply evolved from there. Eventually, this transitioned into both of us being happy with the other engaging in playtime with other parties. Looking back, I don't think either of us truly loved the other person, although I thought I did at the time. With what I know about psychology now, it seems I was trauma-bonded to J and perhaps we were a little co-dependent and both unsure how to part and move on.

Sometimes J would ask me to try and get my female friends to play with him, and he would start bringing out the alcohol and whatever else he had. This was difficult. As a female, I had to protect other women and didn't want them to get jiggy just because they were drunk. J most likely saw it as me cock-blocking him.

One time, some friends we used to swing with had some DMT. DMT is a naturally occurring chemical in the body and exists in certain foods in small amounts. If you smoke it, however, it can give you one hell of a trip, for just a few moments. So, after listening to my friends raving about the spiritual experiences they'd had, I was keen to see if I would be able to see beyond the veil and experience something mind-blowing. My mind was blown in the most exquisite manner. I took a little puff and my friend said, "No, puff harder, then hold it." So, I did, as much as I wanted to release the hot air from my lungs. What happened next was so serene. Closing my eyes, I saw a dark room where several shimmering light beings entered. They were composed of different colours of light – yellow, red, blue.

Most of them possessed a glorious, joyous energy which seemed to penetrate my body and soul. One of them possessed a darker energy, but I was able to create a barrier between them and myself with my mind. The good light beings then summarised my life, like a life review, and gave me feedback. They told me that I was here on the planet to do good, and I had done my best, even when circumstances had been difficult. They pointed out that I had made mistakes and made some poor choices along the way, but that these were a learning curve and instead of dwelling on these, I must take lessons from them and help them shape my future. They suggested that at birth my soul had been given a blueprint, and that I might go astray at times and lose sight of my purpose, but that as long as I remained positive, I would eventually return to the path my blueprint intended for me.

I didn't hear these words aloud; it was as if the beings were feeding these concepts into my mind with kinetic thought. Even more important than the words spoken was the feelings these loving entities filled me with. Feelings of warmth, acceptance and encouragement. When the chemical wore off and they drifted away, I didn't want them to go and heard a thought, *Everything you need is already within you.*

It was a sublime experience, and even though moments later I was sober as a judge, the warm feelings stayed with me. Perhaps it was all nonsense and the product of a brain clouded by the DMT; however, it was extremely therapeutic. Throughout the weeks that followed, I felt reassured that in the grand scheme of things there is good in the universe and that you can tap into it by doing good things and remaining positive. Of course, even if it was my own mind making up this illusion, the DMT helped me to find this part of myself and work it into my psyche. I do believe drugs like this could be used by medical practitioners in depressed patients to help them break negative patterns and ways of thinking, and perhaps we are not too far away from that now. Drugs like ketamine and various other psychoactive drugs are being used by doctors to treat patients who do not respond to generic drugs.

J had a different experience to me. He had no epiphany, no eureka moment. Instead, he was compelled to try and hump my friend Viola's leg and begged to orally pleasure her. At first, she was amused, then her amusement turned to annoyance, and we had to all tell him to sit his butt down and behave. This leads me to suspect that the experience was indeed built on our own internal thoughts and that DMT simply allows you to access your subconsciousness. The hidden core of your mind comes to the forefront, and in J that core was all about humping.

I would love to believe that light beings exist, but one must be practical. I will neither believe nor not believe, I will keep an open mind to all possibilities, and multiple theories all at once. In a way it's a bit like Schrödinger's theory (is the cat in the box dead or alive?) that something may be in two states at once until they are observed by consciousness (in his theory, electrons, particles, matter). I believe that there may be dimensions that we cannot see because we are made of dense matter. Perhaps the beings I saw under the influence of DMT were made of light matter.

Many scientists now believe in the multiverse theory. This theory suggests that there are many universes out there, and in addition to this some scientists believe that for every thought we have or action we make, we create an alternative parallel universe where we live a different life, taking alternative paths. Some philosophers and spiritualists even believe that our souls are split into fragments and each experiences a different lifetime to accrue spiritual knowledge. When we die, all those soul fragments unite to form a complete understanding of what it means to be human. Even if it might be a load of old codswallop, isn't it a wonderful way to stretch the mind and broaden one's thinking? I find it fascinating.

Chapter 41: An Unusual Birthing Partner

One good thing had come from living in *Benefit Britain*'s Winson Green. I was returning home one evening and J said, "Did you hear that mewl?" Instantly, I searched for the source of the noise. It was a bitterly cold night, and I could see the steam rising from my mouth as I breathed. If there was a kitten, I couldn't allow it to stay out in these conditions. Calling softly, a tiny furry head poked out from behind the bush. A little Calico kitten made its way towards me and soon she was in the house, happily wolfing down meat, and later curled up on my lap, much to my other cats' disgust.

Having a little kitten around again was good for me and I would sit there roaring with laughter as she tumbled round the floor playing with a toy mouse, exploring and pouncing on things. She was a real mischief and if you told her not to do something, she would do it anyway, unlike my other cats who were well behaved. She was always pushing glasses of water onto the floor and would sit looking smug as it smashed below. She was such a character you could never be annoyed with her for long. It was infuriating when she did things like push my camera over and break it, and I had to spend money I didn't have to replace it, but then she would sidle round me and jump onto my lap purring. How could you be cross with such a sweet girl!

Naming her Seven after the Cyborg in *Star Trek: Voyager* seemed apt, which would confuse people as they thought she was the seventh cat. I already had Tinkerbell, Crackers, Piskie, Tabstick and Furkin, which made Seven the sixth member of the Caterarchy.

KAZ B

There was another cat that used to come in who belonged to a neighbour and he was coined "Fat Arse" because he was a massive cat – poor thing! Crackers would often befriend the neighbourhood cats and try to bring them home, but we had to put a stop to this with Fat Arse as he tried to dominate the other cats.

Fat Arse would sneak through the cat flap then hide on the windowsill behind the curtains. I would only become alerted to his presence when I heard a hissing if I got close to the curtain. I thought it was funny, until I caught him hissing and trying to bat my smaller cats, so that was it then, Fat Arse was no longer welcome.

We had no idea how old Seven was and she must have been small for her age as when we took her to the vet's to get her spayed, the vet said she was already pregnant, but they could induce an abortion. That wasn't an option I considered and I stated that Seven should go ahead with her pregnancy, but that the kittens should be re-homed once they were strong enough.

During her pregnancy, Seven became so cuddly. She was always purring and stopped being as mischievous. She was a mother to be and had to set an example now!

As she approached her ninth week of pregnancy, Seven started to have spasms and she became even clingier. One evening, I just had a feeling that she was due to give birth and I insisted on putting an old mattress on the floor of the lounge and spending the night downstairs. J mocked me and said he was going up to the comfortable warm bedroom, but my gut instinct told me I needed to be downstairs with her. I put a box down with an old blanket for Seven near to where I would be sleeping, turned the light out and snuggled up on the old mattress. It wasn't long before Seven began to make odd noises. In the light that filtered through from the downstairs bathroom, I could see her stomach moving around as if there was an alien inside. She climbed onto the mattress next to me, lying as close as she could, and then proceeded to give birth.

I was stunned, watching this miracle of life in front of me. The

278

first kitten came out in a little sack, and I was amazed watching as she licked away at the sack until the baby cat's head was free and it started to breathe independently for the first time. I didn't dare call J; Seven needed as little disruption as possible at this time and I felt honoured to be included in her special moment. She cleaned the kitten up, cleaning away all traces of the sack, and nuzzled it into her teat, where it clawed around for a while before instinctually latching on and feeding. Then came another kitten and the process was repeated, and another.

By the time the sixth kitten came out, I could see Seven was exhausted. She was doing her best to be such a good mum, but she was only young herself and it was a lot of kittens. Finally, the eighth kitten came out, she licked half-heartedly at the sack, then laid back exhausted. I knew this wouldn't do; the kitten would die unless I intervened. Stroking Seven's weary head, I told her she was a good girl, then I fetched a clean cloth and some cotton buds. It's important not to touch the kittens, as the mother will not recognise their scent, but I couldn't just let it suffocate in the sack, and so I picked it up with the cloth and copied what I had watched Seven do, but using a cotton bud and not my tongue!

I cleaned the sack away from its face, and I saw it take its first breath, a big gasp of air, and then he started mewling. Cleaning the poor boy up, I put him next to Seven's belly. She picked him straight up and went into the kitchen towards the cat flap. Her intentions were obvious. This was the runt of the litter and she intended to dispose of him. Luckily, she was slow on her feet after pregnancy, and I made it to the cat flap before her and locked it shut. She allowed me to retrieve the kitten from her and she made her way back to the mattress. I couldn't let her abandon this poor mite. In the wild, this is commonplace, and cats will abandon any weak kittens so they can care for the others better. This wasn't necessary though; she had me and she was keeping that kitten! Holding the kitten on the cloth, I rubbed him against Seven's fur and against every single one of the other kittens to get their scent on him, so that she might accept him as part of the pack. Eventually, she gave him a lick and I helped him latch on to one of her teats. After that, Seven just seemed to accept my judgement. The way she looked at me was as if to say, "OK, Mum, if you think he can make it, we'll keep him!"

I barely slept the rest of the night, in fear she might pick him up again and leave him in a corner, but I need not have worried, for soon she was nuzzling him in along with the rest.

In awe of this amazing experience, I couldn't believe how J didn't seem to be that interested when I excitedly ran through the previous night's events. Still, I was far too excited by the new arrivals to really care, and every day I would watch as they progressed. They were so tiny that at first, I would stroke them only with a cotton bud as I didn't want to be too rough with them. Over the following weeks, they started being able to walk around on their own, tumbling at first then finding their feet. As they got bigger, they would try to climb out of the box and Seven would patiently pick them all up and pop them back in. I would help her do this, certain that she would know best when they were to be allowed out of the box. The other cats took a strong interest in the kittens and would watch them. Crackers looked at them lovingly and would stand guard sometimes, but Tinkerbell was not impressed at all and would throw them hilarious looks of disgust.

In time, the kittens grew, and the place was chaotic with bundles of fluff wrestling each other playfully. The runt, who was later named Titch, was doing well and turning into a handsome kitten. He was becoming strong and playful; it was a delight to have played a small part in that. Thank God I hadn't gone to bed that night; Seven would have abandoned him outside and I would have never known he had existed.

With Crackers standing guard, Seven would go off hunting, her maternal instinct kicking in. She came back with all sorts of things for the kittens when they were weaned onto solids; these things were generally 'confiscated' and thrown in the bin, and I definitely had to draw the line when she came home with a roast potato! Where she got that from, I'll never know, but the thought of her nicking a potato off someone's Sunday dinner was hilarious! The problem is, you never know if someone has poisoned it, and I was strict in ensuring they only ate food supplied from our home.

We decided that it would be best to re-home the kitties at twelve weeks, when they had their best immunity from the mother's milk and were starting to become a little more independent. We put an ad in the paper and had various people come around to see the kittens.

One day, we did a thorough tidy up and a lovely, chatty black lady came round to choose a kitten for her kids. I was mortified when she pointed at the shelf and said, "Oh, I have one of those, they are really good, aren't they?" She was pointing at a blow-up ball with a dildo on it that I instructed my subs to use. It was just a little too high up to be in my eyeline unless I stood on tiptoes! God knows how it got there, but I decided we would have a more thorough tidy up!

One by one, the kittens left, even Titch, who went to live with J's mum along with his tortoiseshell sister Tabitha. They were great company for her, as she said it eased her depression at times.

Eventually, there was one kitten left. Seven didn't seem phased by their departure but the kitten got distressed every time one of his brothers or sisters left and would hunt around for them and cry. We decided he had already been through enough losing his play mates, and so we decided to keep him and named him Seiko. We hadn't named the kittens at this point, because once you name them, you become really attached. It was already difficult letting them go. Seiko became a confident kitten but did develop some abandonment issues; if he came into the house and couldn't see you, he'd cry, and I'd have to call him to reassure him he wasn't alone. He would bound over and then be happy that we hadn't all left him, poor boy. Seiko was our seventh cat and turned into a real hunter. The house was far too small for seven cats but giving them up wasn't an option. We would have to move to somewhere better-equipped for my fluffy fur face gang.

Chapter 42: Latex Trooper Moves In

Living in Winson Green was becoming too much and I was stuck in a rut in more ways than one. A couple of times slaves turned up and much to my disgust tried to pay me in drugs, so I knew that I needed to relocate to a better area soon. Plus, as I mentioned, we had seven cats now and they needed their space too, as squabbles would sometimes break out between them.

I got chatting with Latex Trooper one evening and he told me he felt like he needed to be more independent and move out of his parents' house. I told him that we were thinking about moving and that maybe we could do a house share. He thought about it and said he thought it would work well. We viewed various houses and I fell in love with a place called Fox Hallows. It had three bedrooms, a large kitchen where no doubt J would spend his time, a dining room, lounge, two bathrooms and a garage. It also had a huge garden, which would be great for the cats, and I could see myself growing herbs and vegetables. It was a real lovely area too, miles away from Birmingham.

We accepted the house and soon moved in. The only problem was when it came to the moving day, Tinkerbell was nowhere to be seen! We locked the cat flap so she could only enter and not exit the house, and put cat food and water down, certain that we would be able to collect her the next day.

Moving into the new place, we unpacked and settled in. J and I had the downstairs bedroom, the front bedroom upstairs was to be my playroom and Latex Trooper would have the back room upstairs. *It will start to feel homely once we get it sorted*, I thought.

The next day, we went back to Birmingham to find Tinks but there had been a disaster. The cat flap in the back door had been torn off its hinges. Hazarding a guess, Fat Arse had come in, got trapped due to his size, then forced his way out of the door. I roamed the streets calling Tinks and knocked on doors, but no one had seen her.

Urging J for us to go back, he refused. It felt like he just didn't care about Tinkerbell and kept saying, "She's probably found somewhere else to live."

Tinks was on my mind constantly and I imagined her wandering the streets, wondering why she had been left, and this had me in tears. I will never understand to this day why he wouldn't take me back to find her. Perhaps it was so he could be in control again, or perhaps he just viewed it as an inconvenience.

I put missing cat adverts online, but sadly never saw my beautiful Tinks after that.

***

Sometimes in life, I have been a little too optimistic and I have always thought that a change of scenery might change other factors around me. I have since learned I can only change myself and not others. There is a powerful lesson in that that stops you from making bad choices. For a time, I had a bit of an angel complex, believing that if I showed someone enough love and supported them, that they would change for the better. Mistakenly, I believed that it was my purpose to try and change people for the better and gave them chance after chance. It's also referred to as 'magic thinking', which means if you believe in something enough it will happen. The truth is that you can only change what is inside of you, not what is inside of other people. However, I refuse to let the past define me, and I will always try to see the best in every situation and take something from it. If you don't, you let your abuser win.

For a while, I was almost content in my new abode. For the first couple of months, J behaved a little better and Latex Trooper was great company. Troopsie and I would watch movies on the big screen and play games like *Rayman Raving Rapids* on the Playstation. We'd rush to the TV set to watch *True Blood* and *Breaking Bad* and would have lengthy chats about the characters and possible plot twists. It was nice to have a friend to talk to that understood the industry and I started to almost feel like a normal girl for a little while. My desire for normal things became stronger.

Investing in a plastic greenhouse, I planted strawberries, tomatoes and herbs, and would tend to them every morning as I watched the cats stalk and jump through the grass. It turned out I was good at it and ended up with thirty tomato plants, many of which I donated to family and neighbours.

Webcam featured a lot during this time, and J would sometimes jump on or sometimes he would encourage Latex Trooper to cam with me instead. It seemed a happy dynamic, for a short time.

J soon started to slip into his old ways and began creating piles of mess. His hoarding of broken items got worse, and he would hide things in the garage, clothes that needed washing or had been washed, toys, whatever he was tinkering with at the time.

Abusers are not awful all the time, they work in cycles and use something called 'intermittent reinforcement' to condition you. This is a reward punishment system, similar to the domme/ sub dynamic with the colossal difference that there is consent between dommes and subs and a safe word, so that they can halt play at any given moment. Unfortunately, there was no safe word for me. Sometimes, he would love bomb me – this is where the abuser says you are their 'soulmate' or 'best friend', that they have never met anyone like you before and you are meant to be. They will try to imitate normal behaviour for a while but there is only so long they can keep this up for before they grow bored and start craving mischief and drama.

The first few months in Fox Hallows were relatively calm, but J lapsed once again and chaos, conflict and drama became part of daily life once more. His behaviour became extremely erratic; he would do things like take the beds apart and not put them back together for a week. There would be nowhere to sleep and I'd be begging him to put the bed back together. Other times he would lay screws and nails over the floor and as soon as I picked them up and put them in a pot, he would tip them over the floor again. He went through a phase of wearing a mining torch on his head and creeping round the garage in the dark and taking all kinds of things apart – furniture and mechanical items.

On other occasions he would take sex toys and try to construct something new from them, which left them shattered and useless. He would try to infer that he was a genius professor and knew what he was doing, but to a sober mind he just looked like someone who was suffering great delusions.

Cleaning the kitchen was an endless drain, I'd come in to find empty packets everywhere, breadcrumbs on every surface and a stack of washing up. He thrived in chaos and squalor, but I found it left me drained and nauseous. He would also make dreadful noises while sitting on the loo to call attention to himself. Sometimes they were sexual in nature and made me feel queasy. He even did this when Latex Trooper and I were chatting nearby once and we looked at each other as if to say, "What the actual fuck?"

I believe these inappropriate displays of behaviour were designed to make people feel uncomfortable and to show them he had no shame and didn't give a damn.

J soon fell out with Trooper, who was a tidy and orderly person. He was not only frustrated with the mess and seeing the way that J treated me, but also the way J spoke to him. It was fast becoming an unhealthy dynamic. When Latex Trooper was at work, J would slag him off and moan about him. He would hide my things in the garage and blame it on our flatmate. In time, Latex Trooper became withdrawn. He would come in, go to his bedroom and slam the door. I tried to talk to him and sometimes he would let me in, we'd have a chat and I'd give him a hug, and other times he would want to be left alone. The whole situation wasn't healthy for him either.

One time, Latex Trooper went away for the week and J was on model behaviour. He was tidier, ran me baths and made picnics in the garden to convince me that the past was behind us, and that Latex Trooper was the problem now, and perhaps for a short time I believed it. Abusers do not tend to go for unintelligent people or people that they feel are below them. Quite the contrary, they target people who are highly empathic, and in doing so strive to make their victim believe that they are below their abuser, and that is what he did. My empathy was my enemy. He would dish out emotional blackmail and talk of how much he suffered with depression, and I would feel sorry for him and try to help. This is how the cycle of abuse operates:

I hadn't yet educated myself fully about abusive partners and wasn't familiar with this model. I only knew that sometimes he seemed to be trying and that other times he would be a nightmare. Had I been aware of this, perhaps it would have been different. Sometimes I'd predict when an incident was due to take place now though, and I would feel tense and anxious, willing everything to be OK. Something would happen, I would be upset and then he would minimise what had taken place, making excuses, saying it had been trivial, or would attempt to rewrite history and deny my version of events completely. Sometimes I wondered if I was going mad.

People always say to victims of abuse, "Why didn't you just leave him?" but it's not as easy as that. Your abuser conditions you from day one, before you even realise that the relationship is toxic. They work hard to entwine your lives so that you may believe that you need them, or you may be scared to leave, or you may just be so broken down and bled dry of energy that you can't think straight and don't know how to exit the relationship. It's similar to becoming a cult member. Intelligent people have fallen victim to cults and by the time they realise what is happening, they are too scared to leave.

When your body is repeatedly flooded with stress hormones,

adrenaline, cortisol and norepinephrine, your body goes into fight or flight mode, or you may freeze like a mouse. I'd done all three – at times I fought back verbally; I tried reasoning, only to be denied and gaslighted or stonewalled; I tried fleeing away to my family for short periods and sometimes I froze, which entailed me lying on the bed for a couple of days, staring at the ceiling and wondering what to do. At times, you want to appease your abuser anything for an easy life when your energy levels are compromised. This only works for a short time, but the more you allow them to push your boundaries, the more they will take advantage of you. There is only one way to deal with an abuser and that is to get them out of your life. I was trying to take those tentative steps to do this, but often it would be a case of one step forward and two steps back. There were times when I felt suicidal, but I would never have gone through with that. There were a few things that ensured it wasn't an option:

1) My family. I would never, ever want to leave them feeling in pain and I knew they would blame themselves. I couldn't do that to them.

2) My cats. I never saw them as 'our' cats. They were my babies and I fed and looked after them, paying for their food and treatments, and I knew J wasn't responsible enough to look after that many cats. There was no way I could abandon them.

3) The film *It's a Wonderful Life*, starring James Stewart. This film had such an impact on me as a youngster and I returned to it many times, especially when I was feeling sad, and it would lift me, thinking of the moment the angel made George Bailey (Stewart) no longer exist and Bedford Falls, the place where he lived, changed dramatically. His wife was now a sad and lonely widow, the housing he created for his community no longer existed, his little brother

was dead in this version of life as there was no George to save him. Everyone he loved had been affected negatively because George no longer existed. If you have never seen this film, I strongly recommend you watch it.

We all have an impact on others in this world. We have consoled people, acted as the listening ear without judgement and been a friendly face when they have felt low. Who knows, perhaps at some point you – the reader – and I have saved someone from a worse fate just by being there for them, and there isn't anything more worthwhile in life than that.

However awful those times were, it has enabled me to see how someone might be feeling and understand that they need some support or guidance. Years ago, I thought people who committed suicide were selfish, but I now understand that they were incredibly lost, and that if they'd had the right life lessons, or a friendly hand, things might have turned out differently. It's all sliding doors, cause and effect, and it's easy for even the most confident person to lose control of their lives in an instant. We should practice more compassion and less judgement for those that are struggling – the homeless, the destitute, sex workers and even ourselves.

This chapter may be regarded as being a little dark, but I don't see it that way. I see it as an emotive and analytical journey into the human psyche. It's an exploration of how we find our way through dark times and learn from them and become whole again.

There were things in life to be thankful for, such as my beautiful cats, who gave me unconditional love, Tabstick especially. She would gaze into my eyes, love radiating from them, then curl on my head or shoulder, which felt like a guardian angel protecting me, nurturing me. They say that the eyes are the window to the soul, and I can see an old soul in Tabstick's eyes, peaceful, loving and pure.

Lengthy chats with my parents on the phone were much more commonplace now. Their reactions to J were generally annoyance or bemusement as to how someone could be "such an idiot".

Whenever I was on the phone, he would keep coming into the bedroom. "Do you want a drink?" "I'm going to the shop." "I'm going in a minute, are you sure you don't want anything?" They would say something like, "Is he going to go to that bloody shop or does he want to just talk about it."

They didn't believe a word J said, but sometimes I still stuck up for him as I thought he was telling the truth. A lot of abusers and narcissists are pathological liars, and they will say anything to gain control, to gain the upper hand or to hide their behaviour. A normal person can struggle to believe that others are capable of this level of deceit, it just sounds far-fetched, madness, and I wasn't yet prepared to believe that he was capable of this level of wicked, twisted behaviour. If I so much as questioned one of his 'stories', he would become annoyed or bereft, and say, "How could you ever think such a thing of me? After all I've done for you, how could you suggest such a thing? I'm so hurt!" In this, he was weaving another deceit, and covering it with pseudo-emotions, but it was hard for me to comprehend that another person could carry out such a terrible action and then cover it with a lie, and so I believed him. As they say, "The lady doth protest too much", and he did.

His lying was pathological; he would lie about anything and everything. At times it would be to maintain control or belittle me, or other times it would be for no reason at all.

One afternoon, he said he'd found some new sci-fi authors on Amazon, and they were starting to self-publish using the platform. "Perhaps I could get something published on there," I thought aloud.

"Oh no, not just anyone can publish on there! They specifically only accept hard sci-fi anyway," he scoffed, his brow twitching and lip curling to one side in a sneer. He didn't approve of me writing and the idea of me having any success was poison to him, and it was only when I saw my family that I saw a different perspective.

My parents' little jokes at J's expense when he wasn't present made me laugh, and as they say, laughter is the best medicine! I was around eighteen months away from becoming enlightened at this point and craning to see the light at the end of the tunnel.

It was a crazy existence we led, and I also remember Latex Trooper joking once about what a madhouse we lived in. He said, "If someone came and looked through the window, they would think we were nuts! They would see you bouncing around on webcam talking to slaves on camera and ordering them to do crazy things, then they'd look through my window and see me on cam, wearing a gimp mask and wanking, then they would see J off his head in the kitchen doing mental things!"

He was right and I am sure it was the closest thing to an asylum I will ever experience.

My dad was astute and picked up a lot without me saying anything. To an extent, I still covered for some of J's behaviour, but Dad was sharply observant. He and Mum were planning a holiday and invited me along, and he was keen to add that J wouldn't be welcome. I said I didn't have the funds, but Mum said she would lend me the money and I could pay it back in instalments, which was kind of her. Also, I think the presence of a third party gave them a bit of a break from each other. Dad had a brilliant way of pronouncing Corfu – in his broad Wiltshire accent it came out as "Korphew", which always made me chuckle inwardly.

September 2013, we arrived at our luxurious hotel in Corfu to discover that it was infested with wasps. Apparently, the grapes from the vineyards ferment at that time of year. The wasps descend on them, become inebriated, then fly around like drunk nuisances, launching into things. At the time, it was an irritation as the wasps wouldn't let you relax; they seemed hell-bent on making their drunken antics known to all, though I reasoned the wasps were a more minor irritation compared to J, so I was determined to appreciate the holiday. They were ever so persistent though, and one day on the beach the wasps kept trying to land on me and Mum, so we made a Bedouin tent out of sarongs. Mum finally ended up taking a bat to the beach and whacked an over-eager wasp with it as it tried to land on her face. It went spiralling through the air and landed in a man's lap! We looked at each other in shock then quickly lay down on our sun loungers with our sarongs over our heads, pretending to be asleep and giggling like naughty schoolchildren.

At night, we'd sit on the balcony or in the bar having a drink. Sometimes it was tricky as they would both want to dominant the conversation, so it was tough trying to give them both the same amount of attention. I'm sure most women in their thirties would struggle on a holiday with their parents, but I enjoyed it. My dad would do Stan Laurel impressions and Mum would roll her eyes, but she'd often laugh as well. I think that's what people do when they've been together that long.

One day, there was a terrible storm, the beach was covered in driftwood and seaweed, and a chill came into the air. Staying in the apartment and watching a film with Dad felt preferable, but Mum insisted I go swimming with her. It was bloody freezing! Feeling a bit sorry for myself when we got back to the apartment, Dad suggested I watch the film *Genevieve* on his spare phone. It was a wonderful old movie about a car race down to Brighton and soon I was snuggled up, entranced as the story unfolded. He had known exactly how to cheer me up and I fell asleep feeling happy and content.

We were sat on the loungers one day, my dad under an umbrella due to his fair skin, when a couple in their late fifties we'd been chatting with came over. My Kindle was held over my face, so I heard the voice before I noticed them. The lady said, "Oh, what are you reading? Have you read *Fifty Shades of Grey*? It's brilliant!"

Startled, I was quite taken aback for a moment. All my life I had been careful not to reveal my profession to strangers and there was this older woman discussing the merits of BDSM! *Perhaps the world is beginning to progress,* I thought.

When the holiday came to an end, that familiar sad feeling arose in me. If I had known that it would be our last holiday together, I would have been bereft, but I didn't so I enjoyed every moment and have many fond memories.

During this year, I met with Aiden for the last time. I was travelling down to see my family and he met me at the station in Swindon. It felt awkward as he wasn't talkative and didn't look at me when he spoke. We'd chatted in such a carefree manner when I'd last seen him. Perhaps he was detached because I was still with J, or maybe he just didn't want to be there. Ill at ease, I ended up getting more than squiffy and embarrassing myself by being overly affectionate. We ended up in a hotel together and this time the sex wasn't good. I was too drunk, there was no emotional connection, and I could tell he had his own baggage he was dealing with. Inviting him to my sister's party the following night, I was half relieved and half disappointed when he made his excuses. Staying for just one drink and going to my parents' house was what I should have done the previous night.

My sister's party was a good laugh. It ended up with all of us girls in the hot tub, chatting nonsense to each other while we were served wine. The funny thing is, however, as bad as a hangover is, you never tend to remember those, you just remember the good times and the laughs. Perhaps that's part of the human condition and why we insist on punishing ourselves in this manner, because the good outweighs the bad.

Soon, Christmas was nearly upon us. I've always loved this time of year – the fairy lights, the festive spirit, that sense of excitement in the air. I loved the Christmas carols, the old movies and everything about it.

Christmas Day was at my big sister's house in Wiltshire. J consumed copious amounts of Red Bull on the drive, stopping at every service station on the way for snacks, and we arrived late, with everyone else waiting to eat.

He asked my sister where the toilet was and she said there was one down by the dining room, and one upstairs. J dashed immediately into the downstairs loo, which was unfortunately opened out onto the dining room. After a while, my brother-in-law's mum Nelly said, "What's that smell?"

We all turned our noses up as the stench from the downstairs loo hit us. J obviously had a belly problem. My dad being the wind-up merchant that he is sat there with a mischievous glint in his eye and said, "What's that horrible smell, Nelly? Can you smell it?"

Nelly then stood by the loo door, wafting her hands around dramatically and going, "Eugh, what a horrible smell!" This of course drew everyone's attention, and they instantly became aware of what was happening.

When J eventually emerged from the bathroom, there was a great deal of mocking that took place as J explained he had the runs. My sister was furious he had chosen the bathroom right next to where the dinner was being served and my dad stirred the pot all the more, saying, "Why didn't you go upstairs?"

I think part of my dad enjoyed ribbing J, partly for devilment, but partly for the way he'd treated me. My family didn't know the full story, but they had witnessed a lot. A great hullaballoo arose, with air fresheners being sprayed to drown out the assault on our nostrils, and everyone moaning at J. He looked like he couldn't care less.

In the photo I took of everyone in the room at the time, you can see the smirk of amusement on my dad's face. I treasure that photo; it reminds me of my dad's fun side and how he could turn an unpleasant event into hilarity.

The incident went down in family history as 'Toilet Gate' and J never lived it down. I remember being sat at the kitchen table with my dad one day in Wiltshire, and Dad chuckling, "I feel a bit sorry for J in a way. Whatever he does now in life and in years to come, he will always be remembered as the bloke who stunk the toilet out!"

Chapter 43: God Awful Humming and a Sugar Daddy

2013

Latex Trooper spent about a year with us before it all became too much for him and he decided to move out. Sad to see him go, we promised to stay in touch, which we have to an extent. He's a decent guy and has a good heart, and regardless of whatever momentary disagreements we had, I think a lot of him as a person.

After Latex Trooper left, J assumed himself the alpha male of the house, but I considered our cat Crackers more of an alpha male. He didn't have to strut around like he owned the place, he had a quiet confidence and all the other cats respected him.

J was smug about Latex Trooper leaving and happy that he'd gotten his own way again and driven another friend of mine away with his rudeness and bizarre ways.

He had become overly cocky and now did less than ever, allowing rubbish to pile up and not allowing me to enter the kitchen. I'd be up in the playroom working and would look out the window to see him sat cross-legged on the grass smoking and there he would stay for most of the day, quite happy to sit around while I worked to provide.

His drug habit returned with a vengeance, or perhaps I just hadn't noticed it as much while Latex Trooper was there. One night, he told me he'd uploaded a couple of videos so he felt he deserved some drugs and could he buy some. I said no and he left the room. Five minutes later, he entered the room and told me he'd ordered them anyway as he felt he deserved to have a share of my money as he had worked so hard on uploading my video clips. This is what I now know is called 'narcissist entitlement'. They feel entitled to things they haven't worked for and feel that the world owes them a living.

He'd also taken to humming tunelessly; every now and again he would half sing and half mutter words that I could just make out, such as, "Bitch," and I knew he was trying to antagonise me. He would sing awful words and when I challenged him, he would act innocent and deny everything. It got to the point where he only needed to start humming and a feeling of dread would come over me, a bit like Pavlovian conditioning. It is loathsome to think of the power he had over me and how he was able to affect my emotions with a droning hum. I think this was the beginning of me accepting that there was something extremely wrong with him.

He started the drug binges again and would stay up for several nights, leaving screws and computer parts all over the floor. Then he would sleep for a couple of days. One time, he took some fishnet tights out of the bin I'd thrown away and inserted a butt plug into his back entrance. I caught him running round the back garden like that, dressed in fishnets pulled up to his chest without a stitch on underneath, and the cord to the vibrating butt plug swinging back and forth between his legs. He did not care, he delighted in being able to do whatever he wanted, playing music unsociably loud and taking what he wanted.

Another time he was running round butt-naked, and I kept asking him when he was going to lock the house up. Eventually, I headed to bed, Tabstick settled on my head, and I managed to fall asleep, listening to her purring sounds. Waking in a panic at 5 a.m., I wandered into the kitchen. All the doors were open – the patio, the dining room doors and the back door. J was flat out, naked on the trampoline, bar for a pair of fishnet tights! Furious, I insisted we could have been burgled. He told me I was overre-acting and that it was a safe neighbourhood. *Not with you in it*, I thought. He had become even more of a sexual deviant and if I brought a female friend to the house, he was bugging me to try and get her to have sex with him. I said if she was interested it would happen anyway, and you can't persuade someone to sleep with you. In a way, I wished someone would have slept with him to keep him quiet, but I wouldn't have wished that on any female!

***

In the year 2013, I started seeing a sugar daddy called Max. There were no romantic connotations, it was a friendship. He enjoyed my company, and I enjoyed going out for nice meals and enjoying normal conversations. Max paid for my time and so of course J was happy with this arrangement. Plus, it gave him a free house to engage in his pornography addiction.

The first time I went away with Max, we went to Dublin while he was working over there. He was working during the day, and in the evening we'd go for a nice meal and a glass of wine and chat. Dressing up, I'd do some modelling for him, and we would share the content. It was a mutually convenient friendship. He was going through a bad break-up then and I was a shoulder to cry on. He was usually in love with one girl or another and I'd give him advice which he never took, bless him! He was so funny; he'd always be besotted with some young lady and wore his heart on his sleeve. I would tell him to play it cool, and then he would tell the girl everything that was going on in his mind almost immediately. It did make me chuckle, but I hoped he would find happiness.

Shortly afterwards, I started hanging around with a porn star called Briony. Briony had just split from her partner and was going through a tough time. I'm not sure how it started but she began coming round to my place to webcam with me. She was a right giggle and suffered no nonsense. She'd say to J, "Go get us some drinks," and he would as he always wanted people to believe he was the doting boyfriend. Then she'd say, "Right, get out of our hair now, we have women's work to do!" I could tell he hated her as she often stood up for me and corrected J when he was being an arse. She was extremely assertive, perhaps a little over-domineering at times, and he feared her.

I brought Briony into the Max dynamic shortly afterwards and the three of us would go out for meals or stay in a hotel, and Briony and I would webcam, with Max filming us girls on webcam together. She was pushier than I, and she suggested Max take us on holiday. He loved the idea but said he would take us separately as then he would get two holidays. She wasn't happy with this at all and said he was selfish, but I reasoned it was his money and up to him how he spent it.

Briony chose to go to the Maldives with Max for their holiday. From what I heard, it didn't go well. She would call me and say he had upset her, or not been gentlemanly or opened doors for her or taken her to the beach. Seeing both sides of the argument, I tried to be the diplomat, which failed spectacularly. By the time they got home, they weren't on speaking terms.

Max said I could choose anywhere I liked for our holiday, and I chose L.A. as I'd always wanted to visit the Sunset Strip in Hollywood and see the sights.

On the day we were due to fly, I was at my sister's house in Bristol with my mum, dad, sister and brother-in-law. They were concerned that I was flying off to foreign soils with someone who was a stranger to them. When Max turned up in his car with his balding head, glasses, nervous posture and smile, my family's shoulders sagged in relief. They could see that he was a harmless guy that just wanted some company.

We flew into Miami, watching a few movies, and arrived late. We were starving when we arrived at the hotel. Max got me a Hershey bar out of the vending machine, which didn't really fill the gap but we were exhausted. The hotel we were staying in wasn't what I had hoped for. I hadn't wanted to take the mickey when choosing a hotel so had opted for a low-priced one and it was quite tatty and in the middle of nowhere, but I figured I had gone there to see L.A., not to worry about how luxurious the surroundings were. At least it was clean.

I made the mistake of mentioning the Hershey bar incident to Briony on the phone and she called up Max and gave him a right old roasting. To give her her due though, we did eat decent meals after that! One night we ate sushi, another night we visited a Teppanyaki bar and explored L.A.

At the Sunset Strip in Hollywood, I was delighted to slip my hands into the concrete handprints of the legend Doris Day, and discovered her hands were much bigger than mine! There were a lot of out-of-work actors on the strip and they were quite forceful in trying to charm you and sell you their wares – CDs, magic acts, donations and so on. We got chatting to a guy that was dressed up as Wolverine from *X-Men*. He was friendly and not pushy like many of the others, so Max ended up inviting him to come and have a drink in the bar with us. He was quite helpful and told us where to go and what to avoid.

Getting around without a car was not as easy as over here. You had to either hail a cab or take a tram which took forever to get anywhere. After lots of travelling to look at beaches and walk around, I decided we needed a little excitement and I suggested we go to a strip club. On arrival, we necked various margaritas and so when a lap dancer sidled up to me and suggested I have a lap dance, I turned to Max and grinned, "I want a lap dance." Max passed over the notes and the lap dancer grinded on my lap, flashed her cleavage in my face and rocked her sultry hips. I was curious to know what it felt like for a man. We ended up chatting instead once the novelty was over and Max had had several of his own lap dances.

The thrill was the fact that it wasn't usually the sort of place women go, unless they work there. Having special access to a man's world and being welcomed was novel and Max and I downed margaritas as I encouraged him to go and speak to the dancers. Away from all my troubles at home and feeling wild, I think there might have even been a snog between me and one of the Mexican dancers at one point, it's all a little blurry. This was as far away from my mundane reality as you could get!

Towards the end of the week, Max had a little panic about money and his bank account was temporarily stopped because he hadn't made them aware he was going abroad, so for a while he was anxious and morose. Overall, it was a great experience and I got to see the Hollywood Hills, the yellow American cabs, and to soak up a completely different experience.

Returning home, things were hunky dory until one night. Max had gone round to his ex-wife's house, and she had gotten him drunk with vodka. As he lay there passed out, she went through his phone and got my and Briony's numbers out. She started calling us and wanted to meet up. I wasn't comfortable with it and said no, but Briony started suggesting he send the three of us to a spa. I could see the funny side but could also see how horribly wrong this could go! Then his ex asked if we would invite him round, tie him up and then bring her in so he could be punished. I explained that that wasn't what domination was about and that revenge was not going to bring her any peace in the long term. By this point, Briony was furious that this woman kept contacting her, and I wasn't exactly over the moon about it either. Whatever mess Max was in, I knew I didn't want to be involved in it and I cut contact. Briony did the same.

Max spent months trying to get back into our good books, then one cold winter's eve this reached a conclusion. Briony and I had booked a hotel room where we dominated slaves, livestreamed on webcam and took photos of one another for our online profiles. That night we were dominating an Asian sub called Harry, who loved to be humiliated, and we'd also got through quite a bit of Prosecco! Harry had taken some coke and was off his face, which resulted in him having a rather limp penis, so we were laughing our heads off. He would lick our feet, then crawl off to do a line, then lick our feet and say to us, "Can you get me some cock?"

Max phoned Briony soon afterwards; she had been taunting him about where we were staying and all the fun he was missing out on. She said to him, "If you really want to make it up to us, buy us some wine, come round and do as we say."

When he knocked on the door, Max's head was bowed, and he could look neither of us in the eye. Briony told him to get on his knees and grovel, and he did, practically begging us for forgiveness. I felt slightly uncomfortable, but I could also sense that Max was strangely enjoying the attention.

"That's not all," she said coldly, a mischievous glint in her eye. "If you really want our forgiveness, you will suck Harry's cock." Harry looked ecstatic about this and mumbled from the corner, "Yeah, make him suck my cock!"

To my amazement, Max agreed and crawled over to Harry, and began to do as Briony had requested. I was merry from Prosecco and giggling my head off as Briony lectured him on his recent behaviour. As she admonished him, I threw in some odd comments such as, "You better do a good job."

Eventually, Briony had decided that Max had endured enough punishment and said he could stop. Harry kept calling from the corner, "Make him suck my dick again," but no one was listening to him, and Harry was ignored and sent on his way.

Max took us out for a pub meal, where we chatted away over a bottle of wine and talked as naturally as if we had just been to the zoo! That's how quickly things change in this world. One minute you are telling a guy to suck off another man, and in the next moment you are sharing a bottle of wine with him! It was just another day in the office! To give Max his due, our friendship must have meant a great deal to him to have gone through with that. Back then, he did have some parts of his personality that needed some work, and he has worked hard to correct some of those things and has emerged a much more caring person. Perhaps Briony and I had a bit of a role in that, Briony with her 'punishments' and me with my brutal truths and advice.

At one stage in the past, he was a little too dependent on us and so I encouraged him to seek other companions, which did him the world of good. Bri wasn't overly pleased with this as she saw him as 'our' Max. He was still good to us though; he'd take us both shopping and buy us nice things, but he'd often say, "Don't tell so and so I did this for you." I would say, "I don't discuss our arrangement with anyone, Max."

Max was still on probation for having upset us previously and trying to prove his loyalty, so one night he came to a hotel we had booked, and we tied him up on the sofa and made him watch as Bri and I had a play around, then we sent him on his way. It was a form of female cuckolding and I'm sure it was a source of both frustration and enjoyment for him!

It was often a good laugh meeting up as a trio but often the dynamic was a little strained. Sometimes Bri thought she wasn't getting enough attention, or didn't like something Max said, but generally we had fun.

While we have moved on from this arrangement, we are still good friends to this day and Max and I will often call each other to run business ideas past the other or advise each other about different websites. We also have a project in the pipeline – watch this space!

Chapter 44: A Hellish Sitcom and a Crocodile Roll

Despite living in Birmingham and my family living in Wiltshire, I had seen a lot more of them over the last couple of years. While J still had a hold of me, it was weakening, and I rebelled against his tyranny.

Trips down to Bristol and Swindon to see my parents and sisters were commonplace, and sometimes we would meet in London for shopping. Finally realising how bad my situation was with J, they started to visit me more. My dad and I would meet up in Reading and head for the record stores. HMV was still open then and he would show me all his favourite DVDs. We'd pop into a café for a cup of tea and a cooked breakfast, or a sandwich, and our favourite haunt was the old pub next to Reading train station where we sat outside on the bench, him with a beer or a Bloody Mary and me with a glass of wine. We'd chat about films, books and authors, and Dad would tell jokes and anecdotes. We never ran out of anything to talk about, though Dad did most of the talking and I was his audience.

We visited the Solid Silver 60s in Weston Super Mare and performing were various singers from the Sixties such as The Moody Blues, Chuck Berry and Chris Montez.

After the show, Dad wandered over to Chris Montez, who was signing autographs, and struck up a chat. He was a lovely gentleman and happy to engage in conversation.

Being by the seaside always filled me with excitement, having a blast of nostalgia and listening to the music I'd grown up with, and seeing my parents tolerating each other's company for once.

Most people there were in their sixties and seventies and I found it odd how they sat there so quietly and just listened to the music without reacting. I was jigging around in time with the music, which amused my dad. He hadn't expected to see me get so excited over Sixties music.

After the concert, we enjoyed some fish and chips. The smell of vinegar lingered in the air, conjuring up memories of past holidays, and was eventually swept away by the breeze, which brought the smell of the ocean with it.

The joy in life had started to return. It wasn't an overnight process, it was a slow progression, but little by little I started to gain strength. Seeing more of my family and friends was a big factor.

J's erratic behaviour had become intolerable. By this point, he had become addicted to GHB (a toxic cleaning product that can make you fall asleep) and had become a danger to himself and others.

I reached out to his mum Dianne and said I couldn't see the relationship continuing if he couldn't change, and even then, I had my doubts! She said she would come and stay for a week and see what was going on.

On the first night of Dianne's visit, I cooked us a meal and we sat in the lounge to eat. J obviously wasn't even able to leave the drugs alone for his mother's visit, as it was obvious from his behaviour that he had been at the Geebs (GHB) again. He was twitchy, pulling peculiar faces, and sat there swaying with his dinner on his lap while Dianne and I conversed. Then his head flopped forward, his face resting in his dinner. It was all like something out of a hellish sitcom. I was sat there thinking, *This is the moment, she will realise what he is like.* Then she completely took the wind out of my sails and said, "Oh dear. I do think J is rather tired."

I couldn't believe it, *How deluded is she?*

The next day, he got high and went for a bath. We could hear sounds akin to a crocodile death roll as it submerged under the water with its prey.

"Perhaps you should go check him," she said.

"Maybe you should," I replied with deliberation.

Would she finally open her eyes to what was going on? It was me who ended up going into the bathroom to see a drugged-up J and the whole of the bathroom carpet saturated with water.

Trying to make his mum feel welcome wasn't easy while J seemed distracted and didn't seem to really care that she was there.

Diane thought it might be best if we had some time with just me and her to talk, so I took her to lunch and poured my heart out, avoiding the full extent of his drug problem, but I said he refused to work, spent my money and made my life difficult. She told me that it was abuse, and I hadn't realised until that point that it was abuse, because he didn't hit me. Upon reflection, J didn't need to hit me, he knew how to control me with tantrums, covert behaviour, causing chaos, manipulation and gaslighting me. He knew that if he hit me, I would leave instantly.

Years before, we had been midway through sex when something hit my head. I didn't see what as my eyes had been closed, but I went berserk and said how dare he hit me, and it was over. He insisted I had leaned back into the light switch, and it took him an hour to calm me down. He would have known from that point that violence would be a deal-breaker and employed emotionally abusive tactics instead to control me.

As his mother uttered those words, it finally dawned on me, and if I am honest with myself, I finally broke up with him in my mind there and then, even if not physically just yet.

I paid for Dianne's lunch and then we headed to Tesco, and she picked up a packet of fish and said, "Might we have salmon for dinner?" I ended up paying for everything again and thought, *Like mother, like son.*

Looking back, I'm not sure why I had been so surprised at this. The previous year she'd sent me a Christmas wish list of presents their family would like. She did this knowing full well that her son didn't work or contribute in any way.

***

I had been thinking for a long time about moving to Bristol and this seemed to be a good time to tell Dianne, explaining that after everything that had happened over the past eight years with J, I needed the support of my family and wanted to move to Bristol. Also, with my dad's health not being so good, I wanted to spend more time with him.

She said, "What about J though? You would be taking him further away from us. Why not move closer to us so J can be nearer his family."

I couldn't believe what she was saying. She wanted me to fund another house move nearer to them for J's benefit, for the guy who I now realised had been abusing me for eight years. Why couldn't *she* move him nearer to them? She was his mother after all.

For the rest of the visit, I was civil and a good host, but it had been an absolute waste of time.

Chapter 45: Christmas is Cancelled

In September, my mum called and said her brother had invited her to Spain, but she didn't want to leave Dad on his own. Not missing a beat, I offered, "He can come to me."

Dad wasn't best pleased Mum was going without him but came around to the idea of visiting me. It was a mixed bag. We enjoyed some walks round the local town, looking at music memorabilia in the charity shop, and he could be great company at times. In the supermarket, a lady started chatting in the queue. She had twins and a spine condition that made her life difficult. Dad gave her words of encouragement and as she left, he said, "Be big," which was a quote from a Laurel and Hardy movie. Her face was glowing when she left, he had lifted her spirits.

He could be lovely at times, but hard work at others. He was supposed to watch his alcohol intake and so I didn't buy alcohol, which he was quite grumpy about. He got annoyed when I had to go off to work and again when I was late back to him with our fish and chips as my shoot had overrun. It started to occur to me that Dad wasn't quite as well as he let on and didn't like being left alone anymore. Still, I enjoyed having him there and he said, "Kora, I'm going to sort your life out for you."

One evening, we sat with some wine and watched the 1953 MGM movie, *Lili*. It is about a travelling fair with a puppet show and the young girl Lili is in love with a man who plays the puppets. Dad sang along and out of the blue gave me a massive cuddle and said, "I love my wonderful daughter." J smirked and found it hilarious, but I was genuinely touched, as he wasn't a particularly cuddly person.

"Love you too, Dad."

At the end of the week, J drove Dad back to the station, but Dad called me up furious because he was confused about the platforms and had struggled to find his way. It was puzzling, as he'd always been capable.

Mum phoned me up later and revealed Dad had been raging and saying, "Your daughters think it's disgusting you went to see your brother and not your daughter."

No one had said any such thing. Why did everything have to be a fight? I reassured Mum and suggested Dad wasn't himself.

The weeks passed by, and Christmas was nearly upon us again. Where had the year gone? I put a tree up, but unlike the rest of the street we didn't have any window lights or displays. J hated Christmas and never wanted to join in with any of the festivities; he even hated the classic carols I played – Bing Crosby, Sinatra and Judy Garland, all singing about the wonders of Christmas. For me it's a special time, I love it, the air just feels magical, like anything is possible. J always sucked the joy out of any occasion though. This seems to be a consistency about narcissists, and they hate any event that doesn't focus on them. The thought of visiting my sisters this Christmas kept me going, I couldn't bear the thought of spending it on our own.

The days hurried by, and a cold spell of weather arrived. It was Christmas Eve and Jack Frost wrapped his icy fingers around the lands and everywhere glistened, white and frosty as if someone had iced the city like a big Christmas cake. Icicles hung from the window, which was amazing to see. My joy quickly diminished, however, when J said he would not be driving with ice on the road.

"But we have to go to my family!" I protested.

"I'm not driving with ice on the road," he said in a tone which implied I was a moron for suggesting that he should.

"It's really important that we go this year. My dad's not been well, and you never know, it could be his last Christmas."

"I'm not driving and that's final," he spat, and stormed off out of the room.

My heart dropped. There would be normality this Christmas

and my family wouldn't get their presents on time now, which made me feel terrible. I pictured Dad doing impressions of film stars and listening to his iPod, Mum bustling around in the kitchen with Clarissa. It was not to be.

Because we hadn't planned to stay home for Christmas, we had no food in the house, so there would be no Christmas dinner, wine or turkey, just whatever I could summon up from the kitchen, so we'd probably end up having pasta or fish fingers. We didn't even have any crisps or snacks in the house.

When Latex Trooper left, he'd taken his TV, so we didn't even have a television to watch. J had always had this strange aversion to television and would create a fuss if I talked about getting one, so it looked as if we were set to have a gloomy Christmas.

My family were furious with J for being so selfish, but there was little they could do about the horrible situation. J made out that I was the selfish one for expecting him to drive and I had begun to doubt myself, until I spoke to my family and friends, who said that he was controlling me again and making sure he did what he wanted to.

It was a morose Christmas Eve alone in that big house in Walsall. J tried to placate me by offering me my Christmas presents early. He didn't normally buy Christmas presents and this was the first year he'd gifted me anything, but then I'd given him £100 to get me some presents.

I got him a dressing gown, slippers and clothes, but it was Christmas every day for him because he'd never had to work for anything. He got me some second-hand video games from CEX and some little bits and pieces. Then he gave me my Christmas card, which struck me as odd as he didn't do cards. I opened it and inside the card on the left side there was taped a little bag of special K.

He probably realised I was fuming about not going to my family and knew I would figure out that the video games didn't cost £100, so he'd phoned up a dealer and put that tempting little white baggy into a card for me. Looking at that bag with icy white crystalline powder resembling icing sugar, I welcomed the warm, cosy feeling it would bring me.

Doing a little bump lifted me out of my sombre mood and I wanted to play my games immediately, so J set up the games on the computer and left me to play, wandering in and out now and again to placate me so I wouldn't moan about being on my own.

In my little K bubble, the games were exciting and shiny. There was a dance game I played first, in which you followed the moves of the shiny, vibrant figures on screen. Under the influence, my body felt light and flexible, and I followed the dance patterns easily. Everything in life seemed to have greater meaning; when the narrators of the game spoke, I felt as if they were not just talking about the game, that their message was relevant to the rest of life, that there was deep meaning in everything, that all I had to do was listen and I'd know what to do.

A small bump of K can make you feel electric. It's as if the rest of the world melts away and your inner world becomes the focus. Everything you see and read suddenly becomes so important, and you feel like you mustn't forget it. It's not real though, it's a delusion. It's like sticking a plaster over a wound. Once the plaster comes off, the wound will still be there if you haven't healed. Scientists are starting to use Ketamine for depression now, but that is under medical conditions, monitored and alongside therapy. I would never advocate the use of drugs; they can cause a great deal of harm. For the sake of the story though, I'll share my insights.

There are various stages in a K trip depending on how much you take. There is the ego-centric part where you feel as if your destiny is to do things; there is the sliding, the feeling that you are sliding up and down through other dimensions and lands, on a journey of great importance; and there is the stage where the ego dissolves. That can be extremely confusing, but quite fascinating to witness. To experience the world without ego can give you fresh insights.

In those states of awareness, I felt a connection with the

universe, a greater state of empathy for mankind and all the creatures of the planet. Probably the strangest sensation I had ever experienced was feeling that I was a record spinning around and around, but that was years ago, before I had learned to explore the depths and recesses of my psyche.

Eventually, I became tired of dancing and playing games, and decided to do a bigger bump, then jumped on the couch with a blanket. The snow and icicles had been on my mind, so when I laid back and closed my eyes, I felt as if I was in a snowy landscape. It was bright and sunny, the slopes twinkling with ice. In my mind's eye, I was wearing a big, cosy jumper and fluffy earmuffs, my hair perfectly styled. Sliding around on the slopes, watching the passing scenes, kids building snowmen, people cheering as I slid by waving, and people frolicking and having fun in the snow. Bells were ringing, Christmas songs played, and everyone was full of glee. The picture was so clear, it was like watching a movie. My heart felt warm, full and satisfied, and I felt connected to all the people in my life and in the trip. That's the thing with K, you can feel strong connections to people and animals that are not even there. I guess that was the pull for me. If I felt empty, it filled me up inside.

K can be a bit like alcohol in that too much can accentuate what you are already feeling, so if you are feeling sad inside, those feelings will manifest in ways which are unpleasant and the trip you experience can be quite bizarre and dysphoric. So later, I found myself feeling worse than before and obsessing about not being able to go to my family for dinner.

At some point, I was so fed up with my own circular thoughts that I started googling facts about aliens and ended up reading some wacky stories from nutcases who think the Queen's a lizard. In a way, those were a comfort. I reasoned that I may be slightly mental, but at least I didn't think that the Royal Family belonged in a Kenneth Grahame book or ate flies for breakfast and lunch. I suppose I thought that if there were people crazier than me, then perhaps I was doing OK, which did little to diminish my guilt for taking the K. While a little bit of powder on a Saturday night might not have felt like an issue in the past, it was Christmas Eve and I felt like I should be doing normal things, going to bed and feeling excited about Christmas. Not laid on my own on the sofa, sniffing powder and enjoying fantasies of fake people around me that only existed in my imagination. Something needed to change.

Christmas Day came and went, nothing to celebrate and nothing to look forward to. The years were passing by and I was wasting them. I had to do something.

Chapter 46: Leaving the Narcissist

On New Year's Eve, J and I went to Ravers and Storm in Leicestershire. That was the last time I went to a nightclub (apart from networking in later years). J seemed quite twitchy, and we didn't stay that long. I think he was more interested in trying to find wackier drugs than caring about the music. I'd hoped a night out might improve things, but I still wasn't able to forgive him for the Christmas Day fiasco. New Year came and went with little to celebrate.

Briony popped up on my radar again and she came over. A Facebook friend who acted in gangster films invited me down to one of Dave Courtney's parties. Dave had a lot of notoriety, yet still I didn't think it was wise to go alone and so I invited Briony. We dressed up to the nines and as we were due to leave, I said I had a bit of a headache. "Take this," J said, "and your antidepressant, and maybe one of your old ones to offset this one just in case." I protested a little and he asserted that he knew what was best for me.

"He's always pushing tablets on you. You shouldn't let him control you like that," Briony warned me.

It was the first time I'd seen it that way. I'd always assumed in the past that he was trying to take care of me, but bit by bit my eyes were opening.

Briony and I took the train down to Brighton and met up with some cockney geezers, Larry and his pal Stew. We arrived at the party, which was in full swing, and everyone we met on the way in greeted us with friendliness and warmth, which indicated to me that the party was going well. Larry took Bri into the loo and they came back a minute later, Bri rubbing her nose. She was laughing and saying, "He has a massive bag of coke!"

He called me into the bathroom next and chugging on my glass of wine, I followed suit. The marble bathroom was impressive; I gazed around as Larry chopped up a line of white powder on the edge of the marble bath. I took the proffered note, leaned forward and delicately sniffed up the white powder, feeling the sensation hit me in the chest. My body started to tingle, and I lifted my face and asked, "Is my nose OK?" to Larry.

"Fine," he said, then he swooped in and kissed me. He wasn't anything to write home about, but a kiss under the influence of marching powder was a seductive and sensual thing at the time, and so I left that bathroom with a warm glow in my tummy and grabbed Bri, "Come on, Chicky, let's go get another glass of wine!"

We all ended up pretty trollied but had some deep conversations. Bri told some of the others about J's behaviour and their reaction to it had a powerful impact on me. There was a dawning realisation – J had gaslighted me for so many years that I would make excuses for his behaviour or blame myself for not being understanding enough. My eyes were opening wider by the moment.

By the time I got home, I knew I was going to finish with J and asked Bri to come with me. I was surprised to see he'd cut his long greasy hair off, put on a clean shirt and tidied the lounge. "Too little, too late," Bri said to him. It became clear that she'd had words with him before we had left for the party.

We went through to the kitchen and, trembling, I revealed I wanted to end things. J went deathly silent. The atmosphere felt so uncomfortable with him just staring into space, and I wondered if he was going to do something crazy for a moment.

"Well, aren't you going to say something?" snapped Bri, who clearly wasn't enjoying the awkward silence and wasn't going to let J intimidate us.

"Yes, I'm just, errrr, processing," J replied in a calm voice.

He didn't sound like he could care less and just seemed to be figuring out his next move. It was such a strange reaction to someone telling you they wanted to break up with you. There was literally no emotion in his face.

I told him he would need to leave but I would give him a week to get his things together. I assumed he would go back to one of his parents.

In the meantime, I went to Bri's for a few days; she said I could bunk in with her and that she would be happy if I bought some food and helped keep the kids entertained. The first few days couldn't have gone better. I chatted with her kids and took them off her hands for a bit to give her a break. They were lovely kids. We'd all eat dinner together in the evening, which was nice as I'd had no such routine previously. Then when they were tucked up asleep, we would close the lounge door, pop on the webcam and make some money. It felt nice to have a normal routine and it was a strong reminder that life with J was abnormal.

Then it all went a bit wrong. Some guy Bri had met at the party turned up, Wooders, a skinny bloke with strange blue eyes that seemed to stare right through you. He said he'd left his wife for Bri. They'd only had a snog as far as I knew and now he was on her doorstep wanting somewhere to live, so I was relegated from Bri's bedroom to the sofa while Wooders shared her bed.

Trying to make myself useful round the house, I entertained her youngest while she was busy, but I started to feel unwelcome. My only possessions with me were a small bag of clothes, but if I got it out to get something she would complain about the mess. After a week had passed and J had made no effort to leave my house, I decided I'd have to take a stand. In fact, it was my sister Clarissa that pushed this. She has often been the voice of encouragement in life when I've needed to break away from toxic individuals. My mum and Melanie have too, but Clarissa and I spoke regularly, and I was able to confide in her a great deal more. She reminded me I was letting it go on way too long and that I was paying hundreds in rent and bills so he could live a cushy lifestyle, while I slept on a mate's sofa, playing gooseberry and glorified babysitter.

I contacted J to ask him how his plans were progressing, and I was astounded by what came out of his mouth next, "I don't want to go, why don't you go?"

"Because, J, in case you hadn't noticed, I'm the idiot paying the rent and bills! You don't work, how are you going to keep the property on?"

"I'll go on benefits and get housing assistance."

I laughed out loud at this point.

"Legal aid isn't going to cover a three-bed house in the nice part of Walsall," I pointed out.

Over the next couple of days, J almost drove me to insanity with his madness. He'd flip between saying he didn't want to leave the property, to suggesting that he could go on benefits and be my lodger! I don't think he was particularly upset about the break-up, but his pride was injured, and he was determined to make my life as difficult as possible. His mother became involved then and started telling me that I was being unfair and should give J as much time as he needed. She suggested that I had been thinking of moving with him to Bristol and implied it was unfair of me to change my mind and not want a relationship with him! All I could see was a mother who didn't want the hassle of having to deal with her son. Reluctantly, I called his father – a born-again Christian – and told him that the situation needed to be resolved and that J needed his family's support. Reluctantly, he agreed to collect him.

Once J had left, I went home to the cats, who were delighted to get their mum back. Slipping on a pair of marigolds, I cleaned the house and made it as homely as I could, scrubbing until it glistened. Weaning myself off my antidepressants was my next task, as well as throwing out any strange-looking chemicals J had left around. There was even a pot of engine oil next to the gas ring, which could have been disastrous.

It was March or April of 2013, and it was time to make a fresh start.

J insisted he wanted us to stay friends and would ring me at regular intervals to complain about having to leave, that his religious dad was too strict, that he didn't like living there, that he didn't think it was fair, etc. Allowing him to moan until he ran out of steam, I interjected little apart from to say there was nothing that could be done about it. He still suggested he move back in as a lodger, and I still dismissed it as a ridiculous notion.

Chapter 47: Coping on My Own

Spring 2013

I'd popped down to Swindon to see my mum and dad, Clarissa and brother-in-law Mack. Their gorgeous dogs were there and the two fur faces greeted me with excitement. The house was bustling, and it was a beautiful summer's day.

Mum was doing my sister's hair and putting some highlights in it, and we were all catching up on recent events. My sister was taking the mickey out of J, I can't even remember what we were laughing so hard about now, but I was in hysterics and practically falling off my chair. My dad had a little smirk on his face and a glint in his eye. He was bemused and happy I'd left the toxic relationship. He asked me to come upstairs and showed me his new bits and pieces he'd bought, mostly Beatles memorabilia.

Dad gave me two presents. One was a clown on a swing he named Dusty and the other was a little musical box with a clown and it played "Send In the clowns". I loved turning the key and hearing the tinkling notes play. Dad was so upbeat and happy that day. It was to be the last time I saw him, and a lot would happen in the meantime.

Over the coming weeks, time seemed to speed up. Bri came over and I started to see a side to her that I wasn't comfortable with. She was being loud and confrontational, and when I pulled her up on it, she said I was being oversensitive.

"What's wrong with you. You aren't yourself," she started.

"Nothing, chick, I'm fine."

"No, you are not. You are getting upset over everything I say. I think you might be pregnant, and your stomach is bloated right out. I think you should do a pregnancy test!"

Obviously, I wasn't pregnant and felt she was being awkward, but I did the test to appease her in the end, which looking back was ridiculous. Instead of telling her to worry about her own problems, I took the test which showed a negative result, and I'm sure I saw disappointment flash in her eyes.

We planned to go out that night and while we were getting ready, Bri managed to sink nearly a bottle of wine. She was acting strange and a little manic, but I put it down to the stroke she had suffered in the past.

My dad called and chatted a while, and Briony seemed displeased I had been on the phone for some time, but I can pinpoint the exact time her mood really seemed to flip. At the time, I was weight training and lifting a lot of heavy weights. I did a few sets before I had my shower, and she decided to have a go. I'd been training for months so suggested putting the weight down for her a little bit. She did not like my comment at all. In her eyes, I may as well have called her weak, even though it was a completely harmless comment. When she went to lift the weights, she found she couldn't and she was irritated that someone smaller than her could lift more. It didn't seem to matter that I'd been gradually building up the weights for months, she just expected to be stronger. I headed off for a shower and to get away from the tense atmosphere that was building, in the hope she'd calm down a bit.

Later, we headed to a local pub near my house and ordered some wine at the bar. Bri downed it and then immediately whipped out her phone and started talking selfies. Over time, they became increasingly suggestive, with her heaving her breasts as far out of her top as possible. Guys began to lean in and make comments, and she snapped at them. There was an atmosphere developing and it felt as if things could suddenly turn unpleasant.

"Errr, maybe that's not a good idea to do that in here," I suggested.

That was it. I had raised a red flag to a bull. She stormed out of the pub and I followed, not wanting her to walk on her own in the dark. She took out her phone and called (or pretended to call, I'm not sure which) Woody, and loudly shouted down the phone that she would do what she wanted and wouldn't be told what to do. Her reaction was totally out of proportion to what I'd said. She was still ranting and raving when we reached my house and said she was going to drive home. At first, I tried to reason with her and suggest that I book her a taxi and that it wasn't worth risking the drive after a drink.

"I won't be told what to do. I'll fucking drive if I want to."

"I'm not telling you what to do," I said, "but there are usually police cars around this area."

"Don't fucking tell me what to do! I don't give a fuck if there's police!"

She became increasingly hostile, and I trembled inside but tried to keep a calm and rational tone, though it was having no effect. She just wanted someone to be angry at. It seemed the situation would escalate to violence unless I stood down, and I did not want it to come to that. While I might have been able to lift a few extra kilos, she was a good eight inches or so bigger than me, and besides, physical violence is something I avoid, so I backed down. As much as it pained me to do so, I had to let her get into her car and drive off. About an hour later, I received a text message from her with a barrage of abuse.

There was no procrastination this time, no rumination. I decided to cut off the friendship.

A long time later, we met once more but it ended with drama, which is a shame as I liked her a lot, but I just needed to have serenity in my life and realised the friendship wasn't healthy. I hope she is doing well in life and wish her the very best. I'll always be thankful that she was the catalyst in me leaving J.

It was a strange month ahead. I'd lost touch with many of my friends and the more local ones had been driven away by my ex. My family were around eighty miles away too. Still, being on my own was a price I was willing to pay for a peaceful life. The weeks flew by and soon the novelty of my new-found freedom wore off. Aside from work, when someone came to the house, I barely saw another living human, which was not healthy. I signed up to a couple of dating sites not really knowing what I was looking for. I was traumatised by my previous relationship and terrified of letting anyone get too close to me.

I adopted a veneer of fun, happy-go-lucky aloofness. It was my shield, and no one could hurt me if I didn't allow them to get underneath it. I went out on a few dates, but if anyone expressed interest in me beyond the physical, I withdrew. If they were full on sexually but uninterested in conversation, I tossed them aside. I was a walking contradiction. Being a female, from a young age you are subjected to ideologies about relationships. Society tells us that you need to be in a relationship to be happy. It bombards us with celebrity couples, articles about how to get a man and dream weddings. If I could go back in time, the thing I would tell my younger self, or any youngster, is this: "Society wants to condition you, and the media will make you believe you need to be in a relationship and behave a certain way. You don't need to conform to this nonsense! You can be happy being single, so never feel pressured to stay in a shitty relationship because you feel guilty or because you think leaving it makes you feel like a failure. It's not failure when you leave something that doesn't work. It means you are strong enough to deal with difficult decisions, even when it seems a formidable task. Also, always walk away immediately from anyone who doesn't show you respect."

Chapter 48: For Dad

This is the hardest piece of writing I've ever had to write, so please bear with me, dear reader, if this chapter is somewhat muddled. It was Sunday evening when Dad called, and we chatted about going on holiday. He said he wanted to go to Vegas, and we talked about how we'd have to go by cruise ship as he was unable to get flight insurance with his health not being so good in recent years.

I'd just found out my landlord was selling the house and told my dad, and was surprised when he said, "Well, you can always come back home."

"Thank you, maybe I will," came my startled response.

At one point, he said he thought he had wind because he was suffering stomach pains. "Go to the bloody doctor!" I chided.

Dad didn't like doctors and would always do his utmost to convince them that he was in optimum health. He had previously cheated death and called himself 'The Miracle Man'.

"I'm healthier than you!" he'd tell the doctors, and because he was so convincing, it was a huge shock when he went into hospital three days later and never woke up again. He was put in an induced coma and the doctors said he was suffering from septicaemia.

Bedside vigils became a routine once more. The doctors said if he came out of his coma naturally, it was likely he'd have brain damage and a colostomy bag. Dad wouldn't have wanted to live like that. This time I didn't pray. Even if some greater entity was listening and could pull my dad away from the clutches of the Grim Reaper, I wouldn't have wished him a life like that. He'd always had an excellent mind and had been the Wiltshire champion in various chess tournaments. He would never have wanted to be dependent on anyone else to carry out routine tasks like eating and dressing.

Alone on the sofa late at night, I got the call. Dad's kidneys were shutting down, his fingers and toes were turning black … they were going to turn off the machine as his defib kept kicking in, restarting his heart, and he was suffering. It was more detail than I could handle, and I knew he was lost to us. It was the right decision for him, and I tried to think of his spirit soaring into the air and being free, but all I could think was, "I'll never see him again." It was just three days before his sixty-eighth birthday. It felt like someone had ripped the bottom of my stomach out, a bottomless pit, a heavy, formidable place. The world had turned grey, as if shrouded demons huddled around me with menacing faces.

It was a dark time, and the only moments of relief were the moments of laughter shared with my sisters when reminiscing.

Somehow, we managed to get through the coming weeks. There was a family feud because Dad had wanted to be buried and my sisters and I wanted his wishes to be honoured, but not everyone in the family agreed. We couldn't bear to think of him being cremated against his wishes, and so we campaigned for his burial. Eventually, it was agreed, and he got his final wish. First, though, I wanted to see him in the chapel of rest. My dad had been the only person out of his seven brothers and sisters to see his father in the chapel of rest and had always told me he thought that was sad.

My family and the funeral home suggested it might not be the best idea and told me to mentally prepare myself. They inferred it may not be the dad I'd known before; he had deteriorated as the days had gone on. People also asked, "Is that how you want to remember your dad?" I replied that I had many memories of my dad and wasn't limited to the final memory. It was something I had to do and I would not have been able to live with myself if I hadn't gone to see him, my mind was made up.

The big day arrived and my mother came too. We bought

bright yellow flowers to lay on his chest – he loved anything bright and cheery, and it was a fitting parting gift.

I'd built myself up for the very worst after everyone had warned me to prepare myself for a shock. I almost expected a monstrous corpse with hollow, sunken eyes in a withered skull, with clawed hands. Seeing my dad lying there in his Beatle suit and John Lennon glasses was a relief. He had a slightly waxy pallor to his face, and there was a little bloating from fluid retention, but it was not the stuff of horror movies. It was just my dad's body and he was free of his shell now. I fully respect both of my sisters' reasons for not going, it wouldn't have been the right decision for them, especially my sister who was with him at the very end. For me, it was the right decision, and it brings me comfort to know I was one of the last to see him. Perhaps he looked down at that moment from his celestial body and said, "I knew you'd come, thanks for popping in. Well, see you at the funeral then."

We had a humanitarian funeral and my sisters and I had written eulogies that were full of humour and stories, such as when Dad accidentally ate dog treats thinking they were chocolates. We all wore bright colours and treated it as a celebration of his life. At one point, the speaker got Dad's name wrong and made a few other errors, and there were titters of laughter from my sisters and I and some of the crowd. Dad would have loved it.

Mum chose to play "Nights in White Satin" at the end as one of the songs as that had been one of *their* songs, and then we chose to have the James Bond theme tune played as the coffin went out. It was a real fitting end. It wasn't the Viking burial he'd often gone on about, with a boat drifting out to sea and fiery arrows launched into the boat, but for modern times it was a bloody good send-off and so many people came to pay their respects.

Ellie, one of my best friends from my childhood days, came up to me afterwards and said, "As far as funerals go, that was the best one I've ever been to!" I laughed through my tears and thanked her for coming and for putting a smile on my face. Only a good friend knows they can make a joke like that, and that you won't be offended. What followed that day was a descent into alcohol by me and Dad's friends and family, who all sought solace at the end of a bottle. *Numb the pain.* We shared stories, laughed, cried, and refilled our glasses. If life had played a soundtrack to those moments, it would have been Nat King Cole's version of "Smile" playing:

Smile though your heart is aching
Smile even though it's breaking
When there are clouds in the sky
You'll get by

For Dad, The Miracle Man

As I gazed upon you one last time
I held your precious hand in mine
I prayed so hard that you'd hang on
I didn't know you'd soon be gone

That late night call, tore me apart
Shattered pieces of my heart
It can't be true, it must be wrong!
But grim reality did not take long

I heard your voice
I heard your music
I really thought that I would lose it
I wandered along a broken path
Lost at sea without a raft
I never thought I'd find myself
Grief attacks you with such stealth
It took so many years to heal
Even now, it doesn't seem real

As years go by you don't lose hope
But find a million ways to cope
One thing that helped, the greatest truth
Was knowing that I'm part of you
Nothing can take that truth away
Not even the longest, darkest day

I always hear your music play
I know you're with me every day
Even though you did depart
I carry you with me, in my heart

Chapter 49: A Date, a Medium and Closure

The days passed by and somehow, we managed. What other choice was there? I felt the urgent need to visit a psychic medium. Strange things had started to happen around the house, coincidences; I'd turn on the radio and one of Dad's favourite songs would be on. We'd see some of his obscure sayings written on things and I felt like he was trying to communicate with us. It wasn't just me; my mum and sisters were seeing signs from him daily. Mum and I decided to visit a medium and while some people suggested it was too soon, something was telling me that this was the best time. We found a lady called Shirley who was a psychic medium and booked an appointment with her.

First my mum's dad came through. He'd always been a devout atheist and had always said, "When you are gone, you are gone." Shirley described my grandad to a tee and used those exact words. She said it was a big shock for him when he passed over and discovered he was wrong and that he had been waiting a long time to speak to my mum. He had tried in the past, but none of the psychics had been strong enough.

My dad came through next. Shirley's voice changed and became more like my dad's, she even adopted language he would use. She said my dad had said "Let this gent go first" (meaning my grandad), which is exactly what he would have said. She said that unlike my grandad, my dad had been a firm believer in the afterlife and always knew he'd come back. This was also true. Then, she completely stunned us when she said he'd loved the colourful funeral and upbeat songs, and that he'd thought it funny when they'd gotten his name wrong. She painted such an accurate picture that my mouth just hung open. If part of me was a sceptic before, I was now a firm believer in the afterlife.

She told us, "I have a young man here who died tragically and took his own life. He wants to let you know it was an accident and he didn't mean to die." That was my cousin, who died of inhaling gas in a glass when he was fourteen and I was a little girl. I had almost forgotten dear Warren, among thoughts of my dad, but perhaps he hadn't forgotten us.

Later, I watched the movie *Lili* again and realised how poignant the words to one of the songs in the film, "Hi-Lili, Hi-Lo", were:

A song of love is a sad song
Hi-li Hi-lili Hi-lo
A song of love is a song of woe
Don't ask me how I know
A song of love is a sad song
For I have loved and it's so
Hi-lili Hi-lili Hi-lo Hi-lo

Sometimes I would be struck by a worry, or wonder what to do in life, and sometimes the right record would come on just when I needed to hear it. Coincidence perhaps, but reassuring, nonetheless.

We were comforted by our trip to the medium but still heavily grieving. As a result of this, I made some poor judgements over the next few years. I went on some dates with a guy, Norman, who had a problem with alcohol and anger management. At the end of the evening after one date, we popped into McDonald's to get some fries. Some guy touched my butt and in the next moment Norman was on the ground wrestling with this guy and punching him. I was so embarrassed at him causing a scene that I left, and he followed me down the street a few moments later. That guy could have gotten into a punch-up with a lamp post if he thought it had looked at him funny.

A few dates occurred with a guy who seemed nice and normal, until after our third date, then every time he messaged me, he would talk obsessively about his kink and threesomes. While I would have no problem with a guy I dated having a (harmless) kink, I don't want them to date me just because they think I'm available to fulfil their fetishes – so that was the end of that one.

It wasn't the end of my mistakes and unfortunately, I tend to give people way more chances than they deserve, but when I'm done, I'm done, and there is no going back. It's as if the fog lifts away, my vision clears, and I can see that individual for who they are, finally!

The future looks positive now and I know what I value and what I don't, so nowadays I can quickly see through someone who is insincere. Looking back over the years, I feel like I have danced with the devil to the point of exhaustion, then I stood, expelled the devil and carried on dancing. There have been many failures, but I always get up again. There's no bitterness about everything that's happened, and I feel that I have been given an extremely powerful gift – the gift of insight to humanity and our many foibles, an intuition.

Being with men who are weak-minded has helped me to see I'm strong and capable. In the past, I suffered with self-esteem issues, but seeing how much these men relied on me has finally convinced me that they saw a strength in me they needed. Choosing to see the glass as half full in life and seeing the funny or positive side in things takes work but it's worth the effort.

At times, I do get flashbacks from the past, but I can see the bigger picture and the lessons I've learned, emerging with a stronger faith in myself.

In the past, I felt I had to be in a relationship to be happy because women are conditioned by society from a young age to believe that men complete them; I now know this to be utter codswallop! If you have found love and you are ecstatically head over heels, then that's brilliant, but we don't all need to do the same things to be happy. In fact, I have been happier during the periods where I am single than when I've been in relationships. Being in love when I was a teenager was brilliant, full of excitement and the joy of life, but it's been downhill ever since and I'm in no hurry to force anything because I'm settled now and I have my routine, plus my job which many guys would struggle with or feel inadequate with me having an Only Fans account and whipping men for a living.

I've published a couple of erotic romance novels; one of them, *Dreaming in the Dark*, won Best Fetish Novel at the UK Fetish Awards, and I have nearly completed a screenplay and am focused on my career. Most of the men I've met seem unable to define you outside of your main job though. Luckily, I have some special friends that understand me and are not bothered by my chosen profession – Amber, MLA, Dakota, Steph, JB, LB and many more.

I am certainly not lacking for anything.

Every night, I curl up at bedtime with my cats, and while snuggling up with a guy on occasion would be nice, I wouldn't be able to have a man try and upset this harmonic balance. He'd have to be extremely understanding to be compatible and realise that he could be an addition to my life and not the focus. The longer I am single, the more I enjoy my independence, and I've finally got time to do things for myself.

I was given the body of a four-foot-ten female. Perhaps I chose this avatar, who knows. Over the years, I was verbally, mentally and physically beaten down, but I got up every time and I showed the universe that I would not be beaten. If you break a bone, it grows back stronger. That's what happened to me; every time someone tore me apart, ripped me to shreds, I went away, I regrouped, and in time I rebuilt myself. I shed my old skin and became something new.

I am a Scorpio. I believe I'm here to help those who need me, but along the way I forgot who I was and got caught up in trying to save the unsavable and giving my energy to the entitled. The thing is, you can't fill from an empty cup and for so long my cup was emptied by the undeserving. Now my cup will overflow, and I will be cautious who drinks from it. There is a reason I became unbreakable and that something inside me made me keep going even when I wanted to curl up and sleep forever. I think that reason is so I can help others that are going through similar things and that's what has compelled me to keep writing this book and blogging about narcissistic abuse. Jen Hopkins and I have now started a channel to help people who have kinks and are struggling with feelings of shame and unworthiness. We have also started to address issues of domestic violence publicly, a cause we are both passionate about.

Writing this book, there have been fond memories, and at times tears streamed down my face remembering those who aren't here anymore, and while there may have been huge gaps in between me returning to it, return to it I did.

If my book can give one person strength and help you to realise how special you are and make you see that you deserve so much better than what is happening in your life, then it is worth every single moment I have poured into its creation. No one has the right to make you feel inferior, to hurt you, to erode your sense of self-worth. You need to know that every single one of you deserves to find happiness, whether you are rich, poor, whatever your class status is or any other detail that society measures us by. If you are a good person, you deserve to be happy and to be treated fairly. So, if you are in a relationship where you are not valued, or perhaps you are mistreated or abused, you must find a safe way out. It may take days, it may take weeks, months or years, but plan for that day and don't reveal your plans until you are safely away. Imagine that day when you are leaving and humming the theme to *The Great Escape* to yourself, isn't that thought blissful?

Abusers are also good at making you think you NEED them when in fact it is the other way around. They will try to use guilt, shame and emotional blackmail. They may twist everything around, project, deflect, minimise, sleep-deprive you and beat you down until you believe that you need their 'love'. The truth is, abusers never love you, they only ever have a 'need' of you. I know, it's a painful pill to swallow, it got caught in my throat a few times on the way down. So, know this, you do NOT need them, and you never have done. Have faith in yourself. No one has ever regretted escaping an abuser and going no contact. Just make sure you are safe and that they do not know how to contact you. Then only look forward, never look back.

When I was a little girl, I feared monsters and thought they were hiding under the bed waiting to catch my ankle, or in the closet ready to burst out! As an adult, it turned out those monsters were much better hidden than that, because they looked just like ordinary people but with dark, angry hearts. They are like black holes that near-on suck the life out of you. There is no worse monster than one who masquerades as a friend.

Many say that life is not a song, but it is if you make it, if you fill your world with music, flowers, books, feel-good movies, people or animals that you love. The inspiration is there for the taking if you open your eyes and see it. My song for this moment of realisation would be "Waiting for a Star to Fall" by Boy Meets Girl as I stroll off into the sunset with my kitties, or I write my journal, a poignant smile on my face as the camera zooms out the window.

This wasn't the end of my bad decisions, but perhaps that's a story for another day.

Whatever happens in life we can draw on our inner strength, so paint on a smile and let's face the music and dance and remember, it's never too late to start over. Be big.

Acknowledgements

Special thanks to those who believed in me, my family and friends. It's been a journey.

Thanks to Gadfly Publishing for publishing my autobiography.

If you enjoyed this book, you can visit Kaz B's Amazon page: https://www.amazon.co.uk/By-Kaz-B/e/ B07D177PJY%3Fref=dbs

Visit her Instagram page: https://www.instagram.com/authorkazb/

Watch her interviews on Shaun Attwood's YouTube channel: Dominatrix, Slaves, Tricks & Kinks Part 1: Kaz B | Podcast 240: https://www.youtube.com/watch?v=jOHauqnb1k0

Dominatrix, Slaves, Tricks & Kinks Part 2: Kaz B | Podcast 269: https://www.youtube.com/watch?v=QyJz6sWL4BE

Other Books by Gadfly Press

By Johnnyboy Steele:
Scotland's Johnnyboy: The Bird That Never Flew

By Ian 'Blink' MacDonald:
Scotland's Wildest Bank Robber:
Guns, Bombs and Mayhem in Glasgow's Gangland

By Michael Sheridan:
The Murder of Sophie:
How I Hunted and Haunted the West Cork Killer

By Steve Wraith:
The Krays' Final Years:
My Time with London's Most Iconic Gangsters

By Natalie Welsh:
Escape from Venezuela's Deadliest Prison

By Shaun Attwood:
English Shaun Trilogy
Party Time
Hard Time
Prison Time

By Johnnyboy Steele:

Scotland's Johnnyboy: The Bird That Never Flew

"A cross between *Shawshank Redemption* and *Escape from Alcatraz*!" – Shaun Attwood, YouTuber and Author

All his life, 'Johnnyboy' Steele has been running. Firstly, from an abusive father, then from the rigours of an approved school and a young offenders jail, and, finally, from the harshness of adult prison. This book details how the Steele brothers staged the most daring breakout that Glasgow's Barlinnie prison had ever seen and recounts what happened when their younger brother, Joseph, was falsely accused of the greatest mass murder in Scottish legal history.

If Johnnyboy had wings, he would have flown to help his family, but he would have to wait for freedom to use his expertise to publicise young Joe's miscarriage of justice.

This is a compelling, often shocking and uncompromisingly honest account of how the human spirit can survive against almost crushing odds. It is a story of family love, friendship and, ultimately, a desire for justice.

By Ian 'Blink' Macdonald:

Scotland's Wildest Bank Robber: Guns, Bombs and Mayhem in Glasgow's Gangland

As a young man in Glasgow's underworld, Ian 'Blink' MacDonald earned a reputation for fighting and stabbing his enemies. After refusing to work for Arthur "The Godfather" Thompson, he attempted to steal £6 million in a high-risk armed bank robbery. While serving 16 years, Blink met the torture-gang boss Eddie Richardson, the serial killer Archie Hall, notorious lifer Charles Bronson and members of the Krays.

After his release, his drug-fuelled violent lifestyle created conflict with the police and rival gangsters. Rearrested several times, he was the target of a gruesome assassination attempt. During filming for Danny Dyer's Deadliest Men, a bomb was discovered under Blink's car and the terrified camera crew members fled from Scotland.

In *Scotland's Wildest Bank Robber*, Blink provides an eye-opening account of how he survived gangland warfare, prisons, stabbings and bombs.

By Michael Sheridan:

The Murder of Sophie: How I Hunted and Haunted the West Cork Killer

Just before Christmas, 1996, a beautiful French woman – the wife of a movie mogul – was brutally murdered outside of her holiday home in a remote region of West Cork, Ireland. The crime was reported by a local journalist, Ian Bailey, who was at the forefront of the case until he became the prime murder suspect. Arrested twice, he was released without charge.

This was the start of a saga lasting decades with twists and turns and a battle for justice in two countries, which culminated in the 2019 conviction of Bailey – in his absence – by the French Criminal court in Paris. But it was up to the Irish courts to decide whether he would be extradited to serve a 25-year prison sentence.

With the unrivalled co-operation of major investigation sources and the backing of the victim's family, the author unravels the shocking facts of a unique murder case.

By Steve Wraith:

The Krays' Final Years: My Time with London's Most Iconic Gangsters

Britain's most notorious twins – Ron and Reg Kray – ascended the underworld to become the most feared and legendary gangsters in London. Their escalating mayhem culminated in murder, for which they received life sentences in 1969.

While incarcerated, they received letters from a schoolboy from Tyneside, Steve Wraith, who was mesmerised by their story. Eventually, Steve visited them in prison and a friendship formed. The Twins hired Steve as an unofficial advisor, which brought him into contact with other members of their crime family. At Ron's funeral, Steve was Charlie Kray's right-hand man.

Steve documents Ron's time in Broadmoor – a high-security psychiatric hospital – where he was battling insanity and heavily medicated. Steve details visiting Reg, who served almost 30 years in a variety of prisons, where the gangster was treated with the utmost respect by the staff and the inmates.

By Natalie Welsh:

Escape from Venezuela's Deadliest Prison

After getting arrested at a Venezuelan airport with a suitcase of cocaine, Natalie was clueless about the danger she was facing. Sentenced to 10 years, she arrived at a prison with armed men on the roof, whom she mistakenly believed were the guards, only to find out they were homicidal gang members. Immediately, she was plunged into a world of unimaginable horror and escalating violence, where murder, rape and all-out gang warfare were carried out with the complicity of corrupt guards. Male prisoners often entered the women's housing area, bringing gunfire with them and leaving corpses behind. After 4.5 years, Natalie risked everything to escape and flee through Colombia, with the help of a guard who had fallen deeply in love with her.

By Shaun Attwood:

Pablo Escobar: Beyond Narcos

War on Drugs Series Book 1

The mind-blowing true story of Pablo Escobar and the Medellín Cartel, beyond their portrayal on Netflix.

Colombian drug lord Pablo Escobar was a devoted family man and a psychopathic killer; a terrible enemy, yet a wonderful friend. While donating millions to the poor, he bombed and tortured his enemies – some had their eyeballs removed with hot spoons. Through ruthless cunning and America's insatiable appetite for cocaine, he became a multi-billionaire, who lived in a $100-million house with its own zoo.

Pablo Escobar: Beyond Narcos demolishes the standard good versus evil telling of his story. The authorities were not hunting Pablo down to stop his cocaine business. They were taking it over.

American Made: Who Killed Barry Seal? Pablo Escobar or George HW Bush

War on Drugs Series Book 2

Set in a world where crime and government coexist, *American Made* is the jaw-dropping true story of CIA pilot Barry Seal that the Hollywood movie starring Tom Cruise is afraid to tell.

Barry Seal flew cocaine and weapons worth billions of dollars into and out of America in the 1980s. After he became a government informant, Pablo Escobar's Medellin Cartel offered a million for him alive and half a million dead. But his real trouble began after he threatened to expose the dirty dealings of George HW Bush.

American Made rips the roof off Bush and Clinton's complicity in cocaine trafficking in Mena, Arkansas.

"A conspiracy of the grandest magnitude." Congressman Bill Alexander on the Mena affair.

The Cali Cartel: Beyond Narcos

War on Drugs Series Book 3

An electrifying account of the Cali Cartel, beyond its portrayal on Netflix.

From the ashes of Pablo Escobar's empire rose an even bigger and more malevolent cartel. A new breed of sophisticated mobsters became the kings of cocaine. Their leader was Gilberto Rodríguez Orejuela – known as the Chess Player, due to his foresight and calculated cunning.

Gilberto and his terrifying brother, Miguel, ran a multi-billion-dollar drug empire like a corporation. They employed a politically astute brand of thuggery and spent $10 million to put a president in power. Although the godfathers from Cali preferred bribery over violence, their many loyal torturers and hitmen were never idle.

Clinton, Bush and CIA Conspiracies: From the Boys on the Tracks to Jeffrey Epstein

War on Drugs Series Book 4

In the 1980s, George HW Bush imported cocaine to finance an illegal war in Nicaragua. Governor Bill Clinton's Arkansas state police provided security for the drug drops. For assisting the CIA, the Clinton Crime Family was awarded the White House. The #clintonbodycount continues to this day, with the deceased including Jeffrey Epstein.

This book features harrowing true stories that reveal the insanity of the drug war. A mother receives the worst news about her son. A journalist gets a tip that endangers his life. An unemployed man becomes California's biggest crack dealer. A DEA agent in Mexico is sacrificed for going after the big players.

The lives of Linda Ives, Gary Webb, Freeway Rick Ross and Kiki Camarena are shattered by brutal experiences. Not all of them will survive.

Pablo Escobar's Story (4-book series)

"Finally, the definitive book about Escobar, original and up-to-date." – UNILAD

"The most comprehensive account ever written." – True Geordie

Pablo Escobar was a mama's boy, who cherished his family and sang in the shower, yet he bombed a passenger plane and formed a death squad that used genital electrocution.

Most Escobar biographies only provide a few pieces of the puzzle, but this action-packed 1000-page book reveals everything about the king of cocaine.

Mostly translated from Spanish, Part 1 contains stories untold in the English-speaking world, including:

The tragic death of his youngest brother, Fernando.

The fate of his pregnant mistress.

The shocking details of his affair with a TV celebrity.

The presidential candidate who encouraged him to eliminate their rivals.

The Mafia Philosopher

"A fast-paced true-crime memoir with all of the action of Goodfellas." – UNILAD

"Sopranos v Sons of Anarchy with an Alaskan-snow backdrop." – True Geordie Podcast

Breaking bones, burying bodies and planting bombs became second nature to Two Tonys, while working for the Bonanno Crime Family, whose exploits inspired The Godfather.

After a dispute with an outlaw motorcycle club, Two Tonys left a trail of corpses from Arizona to Alaska. On the run, he was pursued by bikers and a neo-Nazi gang, blood-thirsty for revenge, while a homicide detective launched a nationwide manhunt.

As the mist from his smoking gun fades, readers are left with an unexpected portrait of a stoic philosopher with a wealth of charm, a glorious turn of phrase and a fanatical devotion to his daughter.

Party Time

An action-packed roller-coaster account of a life spiralling out of control, featuring wild women, gangsters and a mountain of drugs.

Shaun Attwood arrived in Phoenix, Arizona, a penniless business graduate from a small industrial town in England. Within a decade, he became a stock-market millionaire. But he was leading a double life.

After taking his first ecstasy pill at a rave in Manchester as a shy student, Shaun became intoxicated by the party lifestyle that would change his fortune. Years later, in the Arizona desert, he became submerged in a criminal underworld, throwing parties for thousands of ravers and running an ecstasy ring in competition with the Mafia mass murderer, Sammy 'The Bull' Gravano.

As greed and excess tore through his life, Shaun had eye-watering encounters with Mafia hitmen and crystal-meth addicts, enjoyed extravagant debauchery with superstar DJs and glitter girls, and ingested enough drugs to kill a herd of elephants. This is his story.

Hard Time

"Makes the Shawshank Redemption look like a holiday camp."
– NOTW

After a SWAT team smashed down stock-market millionaire Shaun Attwood's door, he found himself inside Arizona's deadliest jail and locked into a brutal struggle for survival.

Shaun's hope of living the American Dream turned into a nightmare of violence and chaos, when he had a run-in with Sammy "the Bull" Gravano, an Italian Mafia mass murderer.

In jail, Shaun was forced to endure cockroaches crawling in his ears at night, dead rats in the food and the sound of skulls getting cracked against toilets. He meticulously documented the conditions and smuggled out his message.

Join Shaun on a harrowing voyage into the darkest recesses of human existence.

Hard Time provides a revealing glimpse into the tragedy, brutality, dark comedy and eccentricity of prison life.

Featured worldwide on Nat Geo Channel's Locked-Up/ Banged-Up Abroad Raving Arizona.

Prison Time

Sentenced to 9½ years in Arizona's state prison for distributing ecstasy, Shaun finds himself living among gang members, sexual predators and drug-crazed psychopaths. After being attacked by a Californian biker, in for stabbing a girlfriend, Shaun writes about the prisoners who befriend, protect and inspire him. They include T-Bone, a massive African American ex-Marine, who risks his life saving vulnerable inmates from rape, and Two Tonys, an old-school Mafia murderer, who left the corpses of his rivals from Arizona to Alaska. They teach Shaun how to turn incarceration to his advantage, and to learn from his mistakes.

Shaun is no stranger to love and lust in the heterosexual world, but the tables are turned on him inside. Sexual advances come at him from all directions, some cleverly disguised, others more sinister – making Shaun question his sexual identity.

Resigned to living alongside violent, mentally ill and drug-addicted inmates, Shaun immerses himself in psychology and philosophy, to try to make sense of his past behaviour, and begins applying what he learns, as he adapts to prison life. Encouraged by Two Tonys to explore fiction as well, Shaun reads over 1000 books which, with support from a brilliant psychotherapist, Dr Owen, speed along his personal development. As his ability to deflect daily threats improves, Shaun begins to look forward to his release with optimism and a new love waiting for him. Yet the words of Aristotle from one of Shaun's books will prove prophetic: "We cannot learn without pain."

Un-Making a Murderer:
The Framing of Steven Avery and Brendan Dassey

Innocent people do go to jail. Sometimes mistakes are made. But even more terrifying is when the authorities conspire to frame them. That's what happened to Steven Avery and Brendan Dassey, who were convicted of murder and are serving life sentences.

Un-Making a Murderer is an explosive book, which uncovers the illegal, devious and covert tactics used by Wisconsin officials, including:

– Concealing Other Suspects

– Paying Expert Witnesses to Lie

– Planting Evidence

– Jury Tampering

The art of framing innocent people has been in practice for centuries and will continue until the perpetrators are held accountable. Turning conventional assumptions and beliefs in the justice system upside down, *Un-Making a Murderer* takes you on that journey.

Hard Time by Shaun Attwood
Chapter 1

Sleep deprived and scanning for danger, I enter a dark cell on the second floor of the maximum-security Madison Street jail in Phoenix, Arizona, where guards and gang members are murdering prisoners. Behind me, the metal door slams heavily. Light slants into the cell through oblong gaps in the door, illuminating a prisoner cocooned in a white sheet, snoring lightly on the top bunk about two thirds of the way up the back wall. Relieved there is no immediate threat, I place my mattress on the grimy floor. Desperate to rest, I notice movement on the cement-block walls. *Am I hallucinating?* I blink several times. The walls appear to ripple. Stepping closer, I see the walls are alive with insects. I flinch. So many are swarming, I wonder if they're a colony of ants on the move. To get a better look, I put my eyes right up to them. They are mostly the size of almonds and have antennae. American cockroaches. I've seen them in the holding cells downstairs in smaller numbers, but nothing like this. A chill spread over my body. I back away.

Something alive falls from the ceiling and bounces off the base of my neck. I jump. With my night vision improving, I spot cockroaches weaving in and out of the base of the fluorescent strip light. Every so often one drops onto the concrete and resumes crawling. Examining the bottom bunk, I realise why my cellmate is sleeping at a higher elevation: cockroaches are pouring from gaps in the decrepit wall at the level of my bunk. The area is thick with them. Placing my mattress on the bottom bunk scatters them. I walk towards the toilet, crunching a few under my shower sandals. I urinate and grab the toilet roll. A cockroach darts from the centre of the roll onto my hand, tickling my fingers. My arm jerks as if it has a mind of its own, losing the cockroach and the toilet roll. Using a towel, I wipe the bulk of them off the bottom bunk, stopping only to shake the odd one off my hand. I unroll my mattress. They begin to regroup and inhabit my mattress. My adrenaline is pumping so much, I lose my fatigue.

Nauseated, I sit on a tiny metal stool bolted to the wall. *How will I sleep? How's my cellmate sleeping through the infestation and my arrival?* Copying his technique, I cocoon myself in a sheet and lie down, crushing more cockroaches. The only way they can access me now is through the breathing hole I've left in the sheet by the lower half of my face. Inhaling their strange musty odour, I close my eyes. I can't sleep. I feel them crawling on the sheet around my feet. *Am I imagining things?* Frightened of them infiltrating my breathing hole, I keep opening my eyes. Cramps cause me to rotate onto my other side. Facing the wall, I'm repulsed by so many of them just inches away. I return to my original side.

The sheet traps the heat of the Sonoran Desert to my body, soaking me in sweat. Sweat tickles my body, tricking my mind into thinking the cockroaches are infiltrating and crawling on me. The trapped heat aggravates my bleeding skin infections and bedsores. I want to scratch myself, but I know better. The outer layers of my skin have turned soggy from sweating constantly in this concrete oven. Squirming on the bunk fails to stop the relentless itchiness of my skin. Eventually, I scratch myself. Clumps of moist skin detach under my nails. Every now and then I become so uncomfortable, I must open my cocoon to waft the heat out, which allows the cockroaches in. It takes hours to drift to sleep. I only manage a few hours. I awake stuck to the soaked sheet, disgusted by the cockroach carcasses compressed against the mattress.

The cockroaches plague my new home until dawn appears at the dots in the metal grid over a begrimed strip of four-inch-thick bullet-proof glass at the top of the back wall – the cell's only source of outdoor light. They disappear into the cracks in the walls, like vampire mist retreating from sunlight. But not all of them. There were so many on the night shift that even their vastly reduced number is too many to dispose of. And they act like they know it. They roam around my feet with attitude, as if to make it clear that I'm trespassing on their turf.

My next set of challenges will arise not from the insect world, but from my neighbours. I'm the new arrival, subject to scrutiny about my charges just like when I'd run into the Aryan Brotherhood prison gang on my first day at the medium-security Towers jail a year ago. I wish my cellmate would wake up, brief me on the mood of the locals and introduce me to the head of the white gang. No such luck. Chow is announced over a speaker system in a crackly robotic voice, but he doesn't stir.

I emerge into the day room for breakfast. Prisoners in black-and-white bee-striped uniforms gather under the metal-grid stairs and tip dead cockroaches into a trash bin from plastic peanut-butter containers they'd set as traps during the night. All eyes are on me in the chow line. Watching who sits where, I hold my head up, put on a solid stare and pretend to be as at home in this environment as the cockroaches. It's all an act. I'm lonely and afraid. I loathe having to explain myself to the head of the white race, who I assume is the toughest murderer. I've been in jail long enough to know that taking my breakfast to my cell will imply that I have something to hide.

The gang punishes criminals with certain charges. The most serious are sex offenders, who are KOS: Kill On Sight. Other charges are punishable by SOS – Smash On Sight – such as drive-by shootings because women and kids sometimes get killed. It's called convict justice. Gang members are constantly looking for people to beat up because that's how they earn their reputations and tattoos. The most serious acts of violence earn the highest-ranking tattoos. To be a full gang member requires murder. I've observed the body language and techniques inmates trying to integrate employ. An inmate with a spring in his step and an air of confidence is likely to be accepted. A person who avoids eye contact and fails to introduce himself to the gang is likely to be preyed on. Some of the failed attempts I saw ended up with heads getting cracked against toilets, a sound I've grown familiar with. I've seen prisoners being extracted on stretchers who looked dead – one had yellow fluid leaking from his head. The constant violence gives me nightmares, but the reality is that I put myself in here, so I force myself to accept it as a part of my punishment.

It's time to apply my knowledge. With a self-assured stride, I take my breakfast bag to the table of white inmates covered in neo-Nazi tattoos, allowing them to question me.

"Mind if I sit with you guys?" I ask, glad exhaustion has deepened my voice.

"These seats are taken. But you can stand at the corner of the table."

The man who answered is probably the head of the gang. I size him up. Cropped brown hair. A dangerous glint in Nordic-blue eyes. Tiny pupils that suggest he's on heroin. Weightlifter-type veins bulging from a sturdy neck. Political ink on arms crisscrossed with scars. About the same age as me, thirty-three.

"Thanks. I'm Shaun from England." I volunteer my origin to show I'm different from them but not in a way that might get me smashed.

"I'm Bullet, the head of the whites." He offers me his fist to bump. "Where you roll in from, wood?"

Addressing me as wood is a good sign. It's what white gang members on a friendly basis call each other.

"Towers jail. They increased my bond and re-classified me to maximum security."

"What's your bond at?"

"I've got two $750,000 bonds," I say in a monotone. This is no place to brag about bonds.

"How many people you kill, brother?" His eyes drill into mine, checking whether my body language supports my story. My body language so far is spot on.

"None. I threw rave parties. They got us talking about drugs on wiretaps." Discussing drugs on the phone does not warrant a $1.5 million bond. I know and beat him to his next question. "Here's my charges." I show him my charge sheet, which includes conspiracy and leading a crime syndicate – both from running an Ecstasy ring.

Bullet snatches the paper and scrutinises it. Attempting to pre-empt his verdict, the other whites study his face. On edge, I wait for him to respond. Whatever he says next will determine whether I'll be accepted or victimised.

"Are you some kind of jailhouse attorney?" Bullet asks. "I want someone to read through my case paperwork." During our few minutes of conversation, Bullet has seen through my act and concluded that I'm educated – a possible resource to him.

I appreciate that he'll accept me if I take the time to read his case. "I'm no jailhouse attorney, but I'll look through it and help you however I can."

"Good. I'll stop by your cell later on, wood."

After breakfast, I seal as many of the cracks in the walls as I can with toothpaste. The cell smells minty, but the cockroaches still find their way in. Their day shift appears to be collecting information on the brown paper bags under my bunk, containing a few items of food that I purchased from the commissary; bags that I tied off with rubber bands in the hope of keeping the cockroaches out. Relentlessly, the cockroaches explore the bags for entry points, pausing over and probing the most worn and vulnerable regions. *Will the nightly swarm eat right through the paper?* I read all morning, wondering whether my cellmate has died in his cocoon, his occasional breathing sounds reassuring me.

Bullet stops by late afternoon and drops his case paperwork off. He's been charged with Class 3 felonies and less, not serious crimes, but is facing a double-digit sentence because of his prior convictions and Security Threat Group status in the prison system. The proposed sentencing range seems disproportionate. I'll advise him to reject the plea bargain – on the assumption he already knows to do so, but is just seeking the comfort of a second opinion, like many un-sentenced inmates. When he returns for his paperwork, our conversation disturbs my cellmate – the cocoon shuffles – so we go upstairs to his cell. I tell Bullet what I think. He is excitable, a different man from earlier, his pupils almost non-existent.

"This case ain't shit. But my prosecutor knows I done other shit, all kinds of heavy shit, but can't prove it. I'd do anything to get that sorry bitch off my fucking ass. She's asking for something bad to happen to her. Man, if I ever get bonded out, I'm gonna chop that bitch into pieces. Kill her slowly though. Like to work her over with a blowtorch."

Such talk can get us both charged with conspiring to murder a prosecutor, so I try to steer him elsewhere. "It's crazy how they can catch you doing one thing, yet try to sentence you for all of the things they think you've ever done."

"Done plenty. Shot some dude in the stomach once. Rolled him up in a blanket and threw him in a dumpster."

Discussing past murders is as unsettling as future ones. "So, what's all your tattoos mean, Bullet? Like that eagle on your chest?"

"Why you wanna know?" Bullet's eyes probe mine.

My eyes hold their ground. "Just curious."

"It's a war bird. The AB patch."

"AB patch?"

"What the Aryan Brotherhood gives you when you've put enough work in."

"How long does it take to earn a patch?"

"Depends how quickly you put your work in. You have to earn your lightning bolts first."

"Why you got red and black lightning bolts?"

"You get SS bolts for beating someone down or for being an enforcer for the family. Red lightning bolts for killing someone.

I was sent down as a youngster. They gave me steel and told me who to handle and I handled it. You don't ask questions. You just get blood on your steel. Dudes who get these tats without putting work in are told to cover them up or leave the yard."

"What if they refuse?"

"They're held down and we carve the ink off them."

Imagining them carving a chunk of flesh to remove a tattoo, I cringe. He's really enjoying telling me this now. His volatile nature is clear and frightening. *He's accepted me too much. He's trying to impress me before making demands.*

At night, I'm unable to sleep. Cocooned in heat, surrounded by cockroaches, I hear the swamp-cooler vent – a metal grid at the top of a wall – hissing out tepid air. Giving up on sleep, I put my earphones on and tune into National Public Radio. Listening to a Vivaldi violin concerto, I close my eyes and press my tailbone down to straighten my back as if I'm doing a yogic relaxation. The playful allegro thrills me, lifting my spirits, but the wistful adagio provokes sad emotions and tears. I open my eyes and gaze into the gloom. Due to lack of sleep, I start hallucinating and hearing voices over the music whispering threats. I'm at breaking point. Although I have accepted that I committed crimes and deserve to be punished, no one should have to live like this. I'm furious at myself for making the series of reckless decisions that put me in here and for losing absolutely everything. As violins crescendo in my ears, I remember what my life used to be like.

Prison Time by Shaun Attwood
Chapter 1

"I've got a padlock in a sock. I can smash your brains in while you're asleep. I can kill you whenever I want." My new cellmate sizes me up with no trace of human feeling in his eyes. Muscular and pot-bellied, he's caked in prison ink, including six snakes on his skull, slithering side by side. The top of his right ear is missing in a semi-circle.

The waves of fear are overwhelming. After being in transportation all day, I can feel my bladder hurting. "I'm not looking to cause any trouble. I'm the quietest cellmate you'll ever have. All I do is read and write."

Scowling, he shakes his head. "Why've they put a fish in with me?" He swaggers close enough for me to smell his cigarette breath. "Us convicts don't get along with fresh fish."

"Should I ask to move then?" I say, hoping he'll agree if he hates new prisoners so much.

"No! They'll think I threatened you!"

In the eight by twelve feet slab of space, I swerve around him and place my property box on the top bunk.

He pushes me aside and grabs the box. "You just put that on my artwork! I ought to fucking smash you, fish!"

"Sorry, I didn't see it."

"You need to be more aware of your fucking surroundings! What you in for anyway, fish?"

I explain my charges, Ecstasy dealing and how I spent twenty-six months fighting my case.

"How come the cops were so hard-core after you?" he asks, squinting.

"It was a big case, a multi-million-dollar investigation. They raided over a hundred people and didn't find any drugs. They were pretty pissed off. I'd stopped dealing by the time they caught up with me, but I'd done plenty over the years, so I accept my punishment."

"Throwing raves," he says, staring at the ceiling as if remembering something. "Were you partying with underage girls?" he asks, his voice slow, coaxing.

Being called a sex offender is the worst insult in prison. Into my third year of incarceration, I'm conditioned to react. "What you trying to say?" I yell angrily, brow clenched.

"Were you fucking underage girls?" Flexing his body, he shakes both fists as if about to punch me.

"Hey, I'm no child molester, and I'd prefer you didn't say shit like that!"

"My buddy next door is doing twenty-five to life for murdering a child molester. How do I know Ecstasy dealing ain't your cover story?" He inhales loudly, nostrils flaring.

"You want to see my fucking paperwork?"

A stocky prisoner walks in. Short hair. Dark eyes. Powerful neck. On one arm: a tattoo of a man in handcuffs above the word OMERTA – the Mafia code of silence towards law enforcement. "What the fuck's going on in here, Bud?" asks Junior Bull – the son of "Sammy the Bull" Gravano, the Mafia mass murderer who was my biggest competitor in the Ecstasy market.

Relieved to see a familiar face, I say, "How're you doing?"

Shaking my hand, he says in a New York Italian accent, "I'm doing alright. I read that shit in the newspaper about you starting a blog in Sheriff Joe Arpaio's jail."

"The blog's been bringing media heat on the conditions."

"You know him?" Bud asks.

"Yeah, from Towers jail. He's a good dude. He's in for dealing Ecstasy like me."

"It's a good job you said that 'cause I was about to smash his ass," Bud says.

"It's a good job Wild Man ain't here 'cause you'd a got your ass thrown off the balcony," Junior Bull says.

I laugh. The presence of my best friend, Wild Man, was partly the reason I never took a beating at the county jail, but with Wild Man in a different prison, I feel vulnerable. When Bud casts a death stare on me, my smile fades.

"What the fuck you guys on about?" Bud asks.

"Let's go talk downstairs." Junior Bull leads Bud out.

I rush to a stainless-steel sink/toilet bolted to a cement-block wall by the front of the cell, unbutton my orange jumpsuit and crane my neck to watch the upper-tier walkway in case Bud returns. I bask in relief as my bladder deflates. After flushing, I take stock of my new home, grateful for the slight improvement in the conditions versus what I'd grown accustomed to in Sheriff Joe Arpaio's jail. No cockroaches. No blood stains. A working swamp cooler. Something I've never seen in a cell before: shelves. The steel table bolted to the wall is slightly larger, too. *But how will I concentrate on writing with Bud around?* There's a mixture of smells in the room. Cleaning chemicals. Aftershave. Tobacco. A vinegar-like odour. The slit of a window at the back overlooks gravel in a no-man's-land before the next building with gleaming curls of razor wire around its roof.

From the doorway upstairs, I'm facing two storeys of cells overlooking a day room with shower cubicles at the end of both tiers. At two white plastic circular tables, prisoners are playing dominoes, cards, chess and Scrabble, some concentrating, others yelling obscenities, contributing to a brain-scraping din that I hope to block out by purchasing a Walkman. In a raised box-shaped Plexiglas control tower, two guards are monitoring the prisoners.

Bud returns. My pulse jumps. Not wanting to feel like I'm stuck in a kennel with a rabid dog, I grab a notepad and pen and head for the day room.

Focussed on my body language, not wanting to signal any weakness, I'm striding along the upper tier, head and chest elevated, when two hands appear from a doorway and grab me. I drop the pad. The pen clinks against grid-metal and tumbles to the day room as I'm pulled into a cell reeking of backside sweat and masturbation, a cheese-tinted funk.

"I'm Booga. Let's fuck," says a squat man in urine-stained boxers, with WHITE TRASH tattooed on his torso below a mobile home, and an arm sleeved with the Virgin Mary.

Shocked, I brace to flee or fight to preserve my anal virginity. I can't believe my eyes when he drops his boxers and waggles his penis.

Dancing to music playing through a speaker he has rigged up, Booga smiles in a sexy way. "Come on," he says in a husky voice. "Drop your pants. Let's fuck." He pulls pornography faces. I question his sanity. He moves closer. "If I let you fart in my mouth, can I fart in yours?"

"You can fuck off," I say, springing towards the doorway.

He grabs me. We scuffle. Every time I make progress towards the doorway, he clings to my clothes, dragging me back in. When I feel his penis rub against my leg, my adrenalin kicks in so forcefully I experience a burst of strength and wriggle free. I bolt out as fast as my shower sandals will allow and snatch my pad. Looking over my shoulder, I see him stood calmly in the doorway, smiling. He points at me. "You have to walk past my door every day. We're gonna get together. I'll lick your ass and you can fart in my mouth." Booga blows a kiss and disappears.

I rush downstairs. With my back to a wall, I pause to steady my thoughts and breathing. In survival mode, I think, *What's going to come at me next?* In the hope of reducing my tension, I borrow a pen to do what helps me stay sane: writing. With the details fresh in my mind, I document my journey to the prison for my blog readers, keeping an eye out in case anyone else wants to test the new prisoner. The more I write, the more I fill with a sense of purpose. Jon's Jail Journal is a connection to the outside world that I cherish.

Someone yells, "One time!" The din lowers. A door rumbles open. A guard does a security walk, his every move scrutinised by dozens of scornful eyes staring from cells. When he exits, the din resumes, and the prisoners return to injecting drugs to escape from reality, including the length of their sentences. This continues all day with "Two times!" signifying two approaching guards, and "Three times!" three and so on. Every now and then an announcement by a guard over the speakers briefly lowers the din.

Before lockdown, I join the line for a shower, holding bars of soap in a towel that I aim to swing at the head of the next person to try me. With boisterous inmates a few feet away, yelling at the men in the showers to "Stop jerking off," and "Hurry the fuck up," I get in a cubicle that reeks of bleach and mildew. With every nerve strained, I undress and rinse fast.

At night, despite the desert heat, I cocoon myself in a blanket from head to toe and turn towards the wall, making my face more difficult to strike. I leave a hole for air, but the warm cement block inches from my mouth returns each exhalation to my face as if it's breathing on me, creating a feeling of suffocation. For hours, my heart drums so hard against the thin mattress I feel as if I'm moving even though I'm still. I try to sleep, but my eyes keep springing open and my head turning towards the cell as I try to penetrate the darkness, searching for Bud swinging a padlock in a sock at my head.

Printed in Great Britain
by Amazon